AF070985

LONDON
City of the Dead

LONDON
City of the Dead

DAVID BRANDON & ALAN BROOKE

Cover image courtesy of Simon Marsden

First published 2008
Reprinted 2022

The History Press
97 St George's Place,
Cheltenham, Gloucestershire, GL50 3QB
www.thehistorypress.co.uk

© David Brandon & Alan Brooke, 2008

The right of David Brandon & Alan Brooke to be identified as the
Authors of this work has been asserted in accordance with the
Copyrights, Designs and Patents Act 1988.

All rights reserved. No part of this book may be reprinted
or reproduced or utilised in any form or by any electronic,
mechanical or other means, now known or hereafter invented,
including photocopying and recording, or in any information
storage or retrieval system, without the permission in writing
from the Publishers.

British Library Cataloguing in Publication Data.
A catalogue record for this book is available from the British Library.

ISBN 978 0 7509 4633 9

Typesetting and origination by The History Press Ltd.
Printed by TJ Books Limited, Padstow, Cornwall

Contents

	Introduction	7
1.	'A Good Send-Off'	9
2.	Resurrectionists and Bodysnatchers	27
3.	Controversies	47
4.	Bizarre Deaths	63
5.	Churchyards and Other Burial Places	81
6.	Death and the Afterlife in the Arts	103
7.	Irrational Aspects	117
8.	Death and Disaster	133
9.	Pestilence and Public Health	147
10.	Commemoration and Memory	167
11.	Curious Memorials and Monuments	187
12.	People and their Pains	211
13.	Chronicling Death	233
	Bibliography	243
	Index	251

Introduction

London has always been lethal. Death – anticipated or brutally sudden – has plucked the old, the young, the vulnerable, the innocent, the villainous, the foolhardy, the brave and the timorous from those around them and has done so with a callous and insouciant lack of discrimination.

Through much of the period under review, mortality in London was markedly higher than in any other part of the country. London could be a dangerous place. Life was short and early death was common. Death was a part of life and Londoners found ways of coping with its pervasive presence just as they managed to handle the other demanding challenges that came their way.

Has any city had more written about it than London? It seems that all the obvious and also every arcane or obscure aspect of its past have received the attention of writers over the centuries. Many of them have clearly been imbued with an absolute, uncritical love and awe of London. Others have been captivated, even spellbound, by the lure of the metropolis, but this attraction has sometimes been a mixed one, laced with concerns about London's sheer enormity and the bewilderingly complex nature of its past. How can it be possible to comprehend even a small percentage of this? Yet others have found London at one and the same time fascinating and repulsive. For them it is like a great maelstrom: turbulent, confusing, threatening and on occasion destructive yet for all that, it is a constant source of attraction and excitement worthy of research and recording.

Because death has been such a feature of London's past, it has inevitably been written about extensively and from a wide variety of approaches and angles. Books and articles galore have dealt with the effect of major epidemic diseases; with London's murders and accidental deaths; its calamities and disasters; its judicial executions; the demise of particular Londoners, especially where these deaths have been unusual; with the development of measures to tackle avoidable death; with its statues and memorials; its rituals of commemoration; its places of interment, its cemeteries and ghosts; the evolution of mourning, death and burial practices; perceptions of the afterlife and controversies concerning death.

Why, then, another book dealing with death in London? This book is intended to be an informed, informative and hopefully entertaining general introduction to the subject of death in London. It is aimed at the general reader of history. It does not pretend to be all-inclusive; more specialised and detailed works on the subject are referred to in the bibliography and we have drawn on them extensively. The issue of death throws a fascinating light on so many aspects of the human condition and the development of culture and society. This book's main thrust is to consider the 'everydayness' of death in the life of London's citizens and how that has been reflected in the culture they have created. It is this approach that the authors believe offers something that has not been specifically done before. The book's time frame runs from the medieval period to the end of the First World War.

I
'A Good Send-Off'

Funerals, Feasts and Fashions

The pressing need to find more places to bury the dead in London became increasingly apparent as the population expanded from the sixteenth century. At the beginning of the century the population of London was approximately 70,000 with the majority living in the City, although there were significant numbers in Westminster and Southwark. By the late seventeenth century, this trend was reversed with about three-quarters of the population living outside the City. Between the sixteenth and the eighteenth centuries, London witnessed a significant transformation: it changed from being a compact settlement to a sprawling metropolis. Fields and meadows, waste and woodland, particularly to the west of the City, were consumed by this urban expansion. As London grew, it experienced rising rates of mortality and these prompted differing responses to the problem of how they should be tackled. The administrative means and the necessary scientific knowledge to do so effectively did not exist at this time.

Although there was a continuity of some pre-sixteenth-century rituals in relation to death, there were also changes which, by the mid-nineteenth century, amounted to the emergence of a 'mourning industry'. The Victorian period became associated with a highly visible culture of mourning although much of the groundwork for this had begun in the eighteenth century. The proliferation of popular publications such as newspapers, magazines and books of etiquette, provided an outlet as well as an influence for the growing industry of death. Commercialisation, of which advertising was an important part, allowed the purveyors of mourning – undertakers, businessmen, retailers, manufacturers of coffins and coffin furniture – to promote their goods and services.

Medieval burials generally followed a standard Christian procedure but would vary according to social rank. Burials in this period included interment without a shroud; with a shroud (which was more common); in a shallow grave, wooden coffin, lead-lined coffin or stone sarcophagus; mausoleum burials; laying in an east–west alignment and embalming. For the majority however the standard practice was burial in a shroud without a coffin. The distinction between a 'good death' (a natural death, one which had been prepared for) as opposed to a 'bad death' (unnatural such as suicide, accident or murder), was of absolute importance. Hence, the expectation was that one should be ready for death and be able to fulfil all the appropriate religious rituals and practices.

The deathbed epitomised a good death. As death became imminent, doors and windows would be opened in order that the soul could be released. A priest would usually arrive to administer the last rites and the dying person would be asked to declare his or her faith and to make confession. Having been absolved, anointed and commended in prayer, and once death had taken place, the body was washed, the eyelids closed (as this is the first part of the body where *rigor mortis* sets in), orifices plugged, body straightened then wound in a clean linen cloth or garment. In the period between death and burial, the body would be 'watched over', a ritual that dates back to at least the fourteenth century. Elements of this practice – the wake and the viewing of the body – have continued down to the present. After Mass the body was taken to the grave and sanctified by a priest. Family and friends would normally accompany the funeral procession bearing candles or torches. Those who were wealthy or held a prominent position were generally interred inside the church with a memorial. Most people would be buried outside the church in the graveyard or a burial site and could expect little more than a shallow mound marked with a wooden cross. In times of mass death such as during plague epidemics, disposal became more urgent and corpses were buried in large pits such as the Black Death cemetery in East Smithfield.

The elite classes predictably had more elaborate burials. For such dignitaries, until the late thirteenth century, the body might be embalmed ready for their funeral display. The process of embalming had been known since ancient times. During the medieval period, embalming involved cutting the body open from the throat to the groin, evisceration (removing organs and intestines), immersing the body in alcohol and inserting spices, preservative herbs and salt. The body would then be wrapped in tarred or waxed sheets. This process was used on a number of kings such as Canute, William the Conqueror and Edward I.

The people of medieval London were reasonably free to choose their place of burial. However, after the sixteenth century increasing pressure on space meant that previous burial sites were removed to make way for new ones. Another method was the formation of vaults or repositories for the bones or bodies of the dead. These charnel houses were often found in church crypts. In addition to the 107 pre-Reformation parish churches in London, there were also religious houses that accommodated burials such as the Cistercian abbey of St Mary Graces near the Tower and the Augustinian priory and hospital of St Mary Spital on the north side of Folgate Street.

The Museum of London Archaeological Service has cast much light on the history of burials in London. Excavations at St Mary Graces near the Tower between 1986 and 1988 found large parts of a medieval burial ground with some 420 burials from the fourteenth century. In the parish cemetery of London Blackfriars in Carter Lane, burials from the thirteenth to the sixteenth century revealed wooden coffins, one lead coffin and grave linings.

At the monastic Cemetery of Bermondsey Abbey burial sites have been found dating from 1099 until the dissolution in 1538. Excavations of the site of the medieval graveyard of St Lawrence Jewry near the Guildhall, which dates from the eleventh century, showed that copper alloy bells were found in a number of graves. At the Augustinian Priory of St Mary Merton 738 burials were found, some of which consisted of stone-lined graves and also monolithic stone coffins with a lining of grey ash and charcoal. Some of the graves contained artefacts such as chalices, copper buckles, leather straps, and in one case, a pendant lamp. Burials at St Benet Sherehog (lost in the Great Fire) in Sise Lane (now off Queen Victoria Street), were consistent with other graves revealing skeletons lying with their heads to the west end of the graves.

Post-Reformation burials, such as those at Chelsea Old Church (destroyed in the Second World War), and St Brides Cemetery on Farringdon Street, show that the dead were interred mainly in wooden coffins, some with lead lining and coffin plates. An excavation at the Cross Bones Cemetery in Southwark, which served a poor parish and eventually became a pauper's graveyard in 1769, found remains of clothes and shrouds.

Another pauper site used up until the seventeenth century was found at St Thomas' Hospital in Southwark where more than 200 interments were found. These bodies had been buried without coffins and large numbers of shroud pins were present.

By the early sixteenth century a widely accepted set of rites and practices had become associated with burial. The Church, which had largely taken responsibility for burying the dead, specified what was essential regarding the service and ceremonial. Burial orders issued in the 1550s made the length of the burial service much shorter. In addition to the provisions made by the church, a number of secular rituals continued and, as we will see later, expanded. These included the conduct around the deathbed; the watching of the corpse; the procession to church; bell-ringing and the distribution of alms. Eating and drinking after the burial varied in scale depending on the status of the deceased person.

The Church took the responsibility for burying the dead through the work of joiners, gravediggers and clergy. In pre-Reformation England, the Knights Hospitallers buried executed felons while officers of the College of Arms (founded 1484) controlled the management of funeral ceremonies for the elite classes during the sixteenth and seventeenth centuries. However, the College of Arms lost this trade with the emergence of undertakers at the end of the seventeenth century. One of the earliest known of London undertakers was William Boyce in 1675 whose trade card advertised him as a 'coffinsmaker at the White Hart and Coffin ... Ould Bayley near Newgate.' Sir Anthony Wagner (1908–1995), who was one of the leading authors on heraldry and genealogy as well as an officer of arms at the College of Arms, claims that the first modern undertaker was William Russell, a member of the Painter Stainer's Company and a painter of hatchments for heraldic funerals who took up coffin-making later. His trade card was illustrated with a skull and crossbones. Although modern funeral undertaking arose in the last two decades of the seventeenth century, it began to flourish in the eighteenth century. *Read's Weekly Journal* in June 1739 reported that Azariah Reynolds was 'the oldest undertaker for funerals in town' when he died at his house in Hackney at the age of ninety.

With the growth of the undertaking business came advertisements, trade cards and a whole culture of mourning. During the eighteenth century when the undertaker became well established, he continued a centuries-old tradition of supplying all the requirements of a burial – equipment, clothes, carriages, food, drink, flowers and invitations. In 1747 the *London Tradesman* wrote:

> An undertaker's business is to furnish the funeral solemnly with as much pomp and feigned sorrow as the heirs and successors of the deceased choose to purchase.

With this growth in the number of undertakers and the commercial enterprise that accompanied the trade, accusations of greed were inevitable. Edwin Chadwick (1800–1890), secretary to the New Poor Law Commission from 1834 to 1842 and commissioner for the Board of Health from 1848 to 1852, made harsh criticism of undertakers who dealt with funerals of the working and middle classes. Commenting on the large number of undertakers in London in his *A Supplementary Report on the Results of a Special Inquiry into the Practice of Interment in Towns* (1843), he argued that a small number of masters actually monopolised the trade thus giving rise to a corrupt system of exorbitant costs. He noted that the 'greatest severity on the poorest classes, acts as a most severe infliction on the middle classes of society ... and involves so many other evils'.

What pushed up the expense of funerals was all the accompanying pomp of horses with plumes, silks, hearse and the coachmen and mourners. The latter rightly invited much scorn. Professional mourners included staff-bearers and 'mutes'. Mutes wearing white or black sashes, top hats, gloves and carrying staffs draped in cloth, were a common sight in the capital. Looking suitably solemn on the day of a funeral they positioned themselves near the church door or the home of the deceased. Charles Dickens portrayed the image of the mutes and the accompanying funeral pomp in *Martin Chuzzelwit* (1844):

> [on] the day of the funeral ... two mutes were at the house and door, looking as mournful as could be expected of men with such a thriving job; the whole of Mr Mould's establishment were on duty ... feathers waved, horses snorted, silk and velvets fluttered; in a word, as Mr Mould emphatically said, 'everything that money could do was done.'

The mutes would then accompany the funeral procession and, as Chadwick recorded in his Report, they would often stop 'in parties in public houses on their return from burials' thereby making a 'mockery of solemnity'.

By the mid-nineteenth century, there were 750 undertakers in London. William Tayler, a footman who worked in the employ of a wealthy widow at No. 6 Great Cumberland Street (now Great Cumberland Place) opposite Marble Arch, started to keep a diary in 1837. In February he recorded an outbreak of influenza in London. It was so great, Tayler noted, that 'every day the streets are regularly crowded with funerals and mourning coaches ... all the undertakers are making their fortunes.'

Despite the extravagance of some high-profile funerals such as Nelson's and Wellington's in the nineteenth century and the perception of the Victorian age as one associated with the outpouring of mourning and all its trappings, there were many among the middle and upper classes who requested low-key funerals. Chadwick identified a strong case for the reform of funeral ceremonies when he acknowledged the claim by undertakers that the well-to-do classes were requesting in their wills to have a plain and simple funeral. Two notable London funerals within the space of two weeks in 1845 proved to be relatively private: The Marquis of Westminster expressed his opposition to a public funeral in his will, and the following week the Earl of Mornington requested a private funeral with only close family in attendance.

No matter how private or plain these funerals were, neither compared with the stark poverty and the stigma of a parish funeral. An example of this is given in a letter of October 26 1849 in Henry Mayhew's *London Labour and the London Poor, 1849–50* in which a poor woman conveyed her experience:

> A friend gave me half a sovereign to bury my child. The parish provided me with a coffin, and it cost me about 3s ... I would give the undertaker three shillings to let a man come with a pall to throw over the coffin, so that it should not be seen exactly that it was a parish funeral. Even the people in the house don't know ... I had to give 1s 6d for a pair of shoes before I could follow my child to the grave ... I think there's some people at the docks a great deal worse off than us.

The great stigma in death, as in life, was to be recognised as a pauper. They were denied the send-off that befitted the respectability of a working-class funeral.

Mourning dress also became an important accessory to death, although black mourning clothes had been adopted from the late fourteenth century and mourning cloaks and hats continued to be popular with chief mourners until the late seventeenth century. Additional accessories gradually emerged for men such as black gloves, belts, waistcoats, hats, shoes, stockings and buttons. Women wore dresses made from black silk and white linen and black and white caps beneath veils or hoods. The wearing of a black armband, particularly among men during the eighteenth century, became an established symbol after the death of someone close.

In addition to the personal grief suffered by the loss of a loved one, death also had a deep impact on the financial vulnerability of widows. For working-class women in particular the loss of a husband or partner represented a huge deprivation in security and protection and many had to resort to parish support. There are many sad stories recalling how generations of widows finished their days in the workhouse. The Friendly Almshouses, formerly the Friendly Female Society in the borough of Lambeth, made few concessions to sensitivity when it advertised itself as a place for the 'relief of poor infirm aged widows ... who have seen better days.' Others had to rely on the support of their family, a Friendly Society or simply had to try and make ends meet. Not surprisingly, many looked to the church or spiritual means for comfort and solace.

Class distinctions in death had been apparent from early times and were determined by what people could afford. Such distinctions applied on the Necropolis one-way train between London and Brookwood from its opening in 1854. First-, second- or third-class coffin tickets were available with separate carriages for Anglican and Nonconformist corpses, the latter divided between 'Roman Catholics, Jews, Parsees and other Dissenters'. David Bartlett, an American writing in *London by Day and by Night* (1852) commented on the 'unpleasant subject' of 'London burials'. Noting the grand tombs and memorials to the rich and powerful he asked: 'where are the poor buried'? This question led him to discuss the issue of Enon Chapel in Clement's Lane (opened 1823) off the Strand, which became a subject before a Committee of the House of Commons. A corrupt Baptist minister, Mr Howse, had promised that for a fee of fifteen shillings he could provide burials. In the vault, which was 60 feet long, 29 feet wide and 6 feet deep, he packed in some 12,000 corpses over a twenty-year period. One way of getting rid of these human remains was to mix them with loads of mingled dirt and then to throw them into the Thames on the other side of Waterloo Bridge. On one occasion a portion of a load fell off in the street, and the crowd picked a human skull out of it. Howse resorted to various other means of disposal including the use of quicklime to get rid of the corpses. One witness testified before the Committee: 'I have seen the man and his wife burn them, it is quite a common thing.' Samuel Pitts was a regular attendee at the Chapel who testified:

> the smell was most abominable and very injurious; I have frequently gone home myself with a severe headache ... there were insects, something similar

to a bug in shape and appearance, only with wings ... I have seen in the summertime hundreds of them flying about in the chapel ... we always considered that they proceeded from the dead bodies underneath.

The case of Enon Chapel was not an isolated incident. St Martin's in Ludgate, St Anne's in Soho, St Clement's on Portugal Street and many others were guilty of similar practices. The gravedigger at St Clement's testified that the ground was so full of bodies that he could not make a new grave. He said, 'we have come to bodies quite perfect, and we have cut parts away with choppers and pickaxes. We have opened the lids of coffins, and the bodies have been so perfect that we could distinguish males from females and all those have been chopped and cut up.' Other gravediggers gave similar accounts, one describing his experience as 'more horrible than ever Dante saw in Hell.'

At least the incident led to reform and the government were sent many weird and wonderful suggestions for ways of improving the burial of the dead. For example, one architect proposed the use of catacombs shaped like pyramids with each outer stone containing a coffin. Despite such ideas between 1837 and 1841, Parliament approved a plan for seven privately-operated 'Gardens of the Dead' to be laid out in London's outer suburbs at Highgate, Brompton, Nunhead, Kensal Green, Tower Hamlets, Abney Park and West Norwood.

Ostentatious funerals, by the mid-nineteenth century, were beginning to be looked upon with some degree of disdain by various Victorian publications. *The Times* had been critical of the expense, pomp, 'plumes' and 'undertaking millinery' at the funeral of the Duke of Northumberland in 1865. *The Lancet* in 1894 expressed relief that the expense of funerals had been reduced, hailing the fact that 'elaborate funerals of the past generations are almost as extinct as the dodo.'

The mourning industry started to decline after the 1880s and the death of Queen Victoria in 1901 marked the passing of an age in which the rigidity of mourning and all its regulations were dictated by the Victorian code of etiquette. The working classes could at least manage, by the assistance of death insurance from funeral clubs, to have a reasonable 'send-off'. The trappings of the funerary industry became simpler and writers were still criticising what they saw as the shabbiness of the cheap undertaking trade. In an attempt to improve the status of their profession the British Undertakers Association was established in 1905.

The term 'wake' stems from an old tradition of watching over the body in the hope that life might return. Later the practice became particularly associated with the aftermath of the funeral service when food and drink are served. The wake has a long history in Ireland and many Irish immigrants who came to London continued this tradition, as depicted in illustrations and satirical cartoons in the eighteenth century such as *The Humours of an Irish-Wake as celebrated at St Giles London*. The picture shows the deceased still laying on his deathbed surrounded by fifteen people in various states of grief: some praying, others sobbing and two drinking.

As early as 1180, William FitzStephen commented upon the way in which Londoners were famed for their celebrations, which included 'their care in regard to the rites of funerals and the burial of the dead.' The Drapers Company in 1523 recorded the death of Sir William Roche, alderman. After the pomp and ceremony of the funeral, guests came back to the home where they drank wine, beer and ate spiced bread. The following day they attended church, which was followed by a meal at the Draper's Hall consisting of 'First, brawn and mustard, boiled capon, swan roast, capon and mustard'. The second course consisted of pigeons, tarts, bread, wine, ale and beer. In addition, Lady Roche provided them with 'four gallons of French wine, a box of wafers and a pottell [measure equivalent to two quarts] of ipocras'. The latter was a rare sweet wine reserved for royalty or special ceremonial occasions.

Henry Machyn recorded many funerary feasts in the sixteenth century, such as that in November 1550 held in honour of 'Lady Judde, Mayoress of London and wife of Sir Andrew Judde, Mayor of London, and buried in the parish of St Helen in Bishopsgate Street'. After the burial, Machyn commented that the 'lord mayor and his brethren ... and all the street and the church were hanged with black' and there followed 'a great dole and a great dinner'. In May 1551, he noted that on the following day of the burial of Lady Huberthorn, there was a sumptuous dinner. In the same month the funeral of Lady Morris, wife of Sir Christopher Morris, knight and the master of the ordnance by King Henry VIII, there was 'a great dole and a great dinner as I have seen of fish and other things'. In July 1553, at the funeral of Ralph Warren, Knight, mercer and alderman, 'there was as great a dinner as I have seen.'

Funeral feasts in the sixteenth and seventeenth centuries were important aspects of the funeral and often entailed half of the total cost. Thomas Sutton (1532–1611) was a civil servant, businessman and moneylender and one of the richest men in England. On his death in December 1611 his body was embalmed and his funeral procession from Paternoster Row to Christ Church in Newgate Street took some six hours. His funeral feast took place in May 1612, as it was often the custom to celebrate the funeral of eminent persons some time after their internment. The feast took place at the Stationers Hall and it was a sumptuous affair consisting of:

32 neat's [cow's] tongues, 40 stone of beef, 24 marrow-bones, 1 lamb, 40 capons, 32 geese, 4 pheasants, 12 pheasant pullets, 12 godwits [large wading bird], 24 rabbits, 6 hernshaws [heron], 43 turkey-chickens, 48 roast chickens, 18 house pigeons, 72 field pigeons, 36 quails, 48 ducklings, 160 eggs, 3 salmon, 4 congers, 10 turbots, 24 lobsters, 4 mullets, 9 firkin and a keg of sturgeon, 3 barrels of pickled oysters, 6 gammon of bacon, 4 Westphalia gammons, 16 fried tongues, 16 chicken pies, 16 pasties, 16 made dishes of rice, 16 neat's and tongue pies, 16 custards, 16 dishes of bait, 16 mince pies, 16 orange pies, 16 gooseberry tarts and 6 grand salads.

Such lavish expense did not go down very well with the puritans who campaigned against such excesses of pomp and display and many requested that their own funerals be kept frugal. One such was William Ambler, who was buried in Bunhill Fields. He asked that no more than 'twelve persons be invited to my burial because the most of what I have is in other men's handes.' There were many others beside puritans who did not spend lavishly on food and drink after the funeral. In March 1664, twenty guests attended the funeral of Tom Pepys, brother of Samuel, and were served 'six biscuits a-piece and what they pleased of burnt claret'. Ned Ward (author of *The London Spy*) wrote before his death in 1731:

No costly funeral prepare,
Twixt sun and sun I only crave,
A hearse and one black coach to bear,
My wife and children to my grave.

An irreverent depiction of an eighteenth-century wake is Hogarth's series of illustrations, *The Harlot's Progress*, which tells the story of Moll, a twenty-three-year-old prostitute. The last engraving in the series is a funeral wake which depicts a telling mixture of grief and indifference. Many of those assembled have been fuelled by drink. The parson has a glass of brandy in one hand whilst his other hand is up the skirt of a girl. Another girl can be seen stealing the undertaker's handkerchief. Moll's madam is appropriately drunk whilst other prostitutes are distracted in various activities which include admiring themselves in the mirror or showing off their sores. The only one demonstrating any grief is Moll's maid who is disgusted at the use of Moll's coffin as a bar for drinks.

Although Christianity introduced some new festivals, there were many customs and rituals in existence before the Christian period. However, by the eighteenth century the rituals surrounding death combined a mixture of secular, folklore and religious practices with a growing commercial involvement. The custom of eating after the funeral is an ancient one but the custom of sin-eating seems to be more recent. Sin-eating as a funeral custom is mentioned in records from the seventeenth to the nineteenth century and was practiced in parts of England, the lowlands of Scotland and the Welsh borders. For a small payment of money a local person was paid to take upon him or herself the sins of the deceased and their consequences in the afterlife by eating and drinking near the deceased body. The writer and English antiquary John Aubrey (1626–1697) noted that the ritual was performed when the deceased was being removed from the house for burial. A loaf of bread and a jug of beer were passed over the deceased, or actually briefly placed on the body, and then the sin-eater consumed them. By this action the sin-eater was assumed to have taken on the sins of the deceased and to have brought peace to the departed soul.

Other examples of giving out food after the death of an individual are those associated with medieval Requiems and the custom of giving alms (including food) to the poor in exchange for their prayers. In late Elizabethan London there were at least sixty-two separate distributions of bread to the poor every Sunday. For some of the benefactors it was a way in which they could sustain memories of themselves by the reading of their names before the distribution. In St Giles, Cripplegate, a stone slab commemorates the brewer Charles Langlie who died in 1602. Langlie donated annual gifts to the poor of the parish as well as an accompanying sermon hoping that others might 'follow Langlies waies.' Sir John Milborne, draper and mayor of London in 1521, required that his thirteen bedesmen (poor people living in his almshouses) displayed their gratitude for his charity by insisting that they attend mass every morning at 8.00 a.m. near the tomb of their benefactor. Nicholas Wilkinson, a Shakespearian actor who lived in Holywell Street, was given recognition by an altar erected in St Leonard's Church, Shoreditch as a benefactor who gave an annual six pounds and ten pence to the poor inhabitants of the parish.

Sixteenth- and seventeenth-century funeral feasts were an important element of the whole ritual of death and, for the wealthy, they could be on a very grand scale. By the nineteenth century, the feast continued and many working-class families made the most of giving the deceased a good 'send-off'. However, for many middle- and upper-class families, the feast diminished in its scale and extravagance and became much more sedate.

The century after 1780 witnessed the distinct emergence of a mourning industry accompanied by a whole paraphernalia of pattern books, invitation cards, mourning dress, commemorative keepsakes, the commercialisation of undertakers and a complex set of rules regarding what to wear and the period of time spent in mourning. The growth of this industry created a demand for mourning fashions such as black hats with knotted bands, black woollen suits and dresses, which stimulated the tailoring industry. In addition, technological developments in printing assisted the placing of announcements and notices in newspapers regarding deaths and funerals. They also assisted the growth of advertising and promoted funerary fashions in the growing number of magazines.

The widespread expression of mourning reached its apogee in the nineteenth century. This century saw a continuation of some of the practices established in the eighteenth century as well as expansion and change in other practices. The period spent in mourning became more prolonged. This was particularly evident when Prince Albert died in 1861 and Queen Victoria undertook her long passage of grief. The regulations concerning mourning became more complex and rigid. The attempt to regulate what should be worn on these occasions had similarities to the old sumptuary laws, which had also tried to dictate what people should wear (and the number of courses they were allowed to eat). Mourning dress, as with other forms of dress, had been circumscribed in the old sumptuary laws, which tried to ensure that a person's social class was identifiable by their dress. Edward III (1327–1377) has been described as 'the King who taught the English how to dress' by providing the first national sumptuary laws in 1336, 1337 and 1363. An example of the complex laws during the reign of Henry VIII (r. 1509–1547) stipulated that 'None shall wear ... cloth of gold or silver, or silk of purple colour ... except ... Earls, all above that rank, and Knights of the King' and so on down each rank of society. Although the penalties were harsh, very few people were prosecuted under the laws and James I (r. 1603–1625) repealed them.

Similarly, mourning dress from the eighteenth century was the subject of convoluted regulations. Etiquette dictated the wearing of different attire depending on the family relationship as well as the appropriate length of time spent in mourning. Mrs Humphry, a popular London writer and journalist, wrote in *Manners for Women* in 1897:

> Widows' weeds used to be worn for a year and six months. It was then reduced to a year and a month, the vulgar reading of which was a year and a day. During the last few years deep crepe and distinctive headgear have been dropped at the end of six months, the period known technically as 'black silk' then setting in, this lasting for six months instead of three, as used to the case when the very deep weeds were worn for a year.

If there was any doubt that these rules seemed trivial, Mrs Humphry quickly pointed out that 'they are a crystallisation in externals of kindheartedness and those good manners that are the fruit of noble minds.' However, wearing mourning dress did not commence until a week after the death for fear of the suggestion that the dress had been prepared in advance.

Fashion magazines such as *Queen* and *The Gentlewoman* advised on many aspects of mourning including the strict dress code to be followed. The New York magazine, *Harpers' Bazaar*, of April 1886 mockingly noted that we do not have 'the mutes, or the nodding feathers of the hearse, that still forms part of the English funeral equipage.' Mourning attire was regarded by many as an ideal way to display wealth and respectability. The *Englishwoman's Domestic Magazine*, started in 1852 at two-pence a copy, was founded by Samuel Beeton, the husband of Isabella who as Mrs Beeton was the author of the extraordinarily successful *The Book of Household Management*. It was the first cheap magazine for women and included colour plates of fashion and cut-out paper patterns. It advised many widows 'never to put on their colours again.' Although the thought of wearing black clothes must have seemed dull, many women went to great lengths to appear fashionable in times of mourning. There were changes by the mid-nineteenth century in the style of skirts, shawls, shoes, fans, gloves and small displays of defiance by wearing hair beneath the bonnet. By 1875 the women's magazine industry was well established. As more magazines started to appeal to lower middle-class and working-class women they marked a rejection of the more literary and elitist style of late eighteenth-century feminine literature.

Such prolonged and visible displays of mourning could be interpreted as a sign of respect for the departed, as help in coping with grief, the result of society's expectations or a recognisable symbol that invited sympathy. Etiquette manuals and magazines gave some advice, as Pat Jalland points out in her book *Death in the Victorian Family* (1996). In *Manners and Social Usages* (1884) it was suggested that: 'a mourning dress does protect from unwanted intrusion on private grief against the untimely gayety of a passing stranger. It is a wall, a cell of refuge.' The *Queen* magazine in 1875, however, tempered the wearing of mourning dress against the unnecessary cost involved and advised women 'to use common sense' suggesting that 'a plain black dress is by no means inordinately costly.' Not everyone approved of mourning dress and there were those who either criticised it for the embarrassing pressure it placed on women or those who felt it was both wasteful and indulgent sentimentality. One reformer was Katherine Hume-Rothery who, in her 1876 publication *Anti-Mourning*, made a scathing attack on those who perpetuated and promoted elaborate mourning rituals. She argued that this 'miserable custom' was a burden imposed on the less wealthy classes who, 'are, in the senseless slavery imposed by fashion [and] driven, to spend their last farthing, or worse, to incur debt they cannot pay ... in this foolish mockery of supposed respect to the dead.'

Class distinctions prevailed through funeral attire but industrialisation made possible the production of cheaper dresses which found a market among people of limited income. In addition, magazines provided dressmakers with a template for copying expensive fashions at a lower cost. This was emphasised by Mrs Humphry in *Manners for Women*:

> The making of mourning dresses is now conducted at such speed, as compared with the deliberate and leisurely mode of procedure of long ago ... At first sight fashion would seem to have as little to do with mourning as it has with grief, but as those who wear the garb of woe are not invariably mourners in the strict sense of the term, fashion influences this form of dress very appreciably.

The proliferation of magazines and papers in the nineteenth century brought with it an increase in advertising and there was fierce competition between companies that offered services in relation to mourning. George Shillibeer (1797–1866) ran London's first omnibus service which commenced on 4 July 1829 and shuttled between Marylebone and the Bank of England. Shillibeer was something of a maverick and he decided that meeting the needs of the bereaved made more business sense than running buses. In 1851 he advertised in the *Daily News* that he could save customers 'one half' if they used his company instead of any other undertaker. Large shops such as Jay's of Regent Street opened as the London General Mourning Warehouse in 1841. Within a decade other shops along Regent Street were quick to follow. Pugh's Mourning Warehouse (1849), Peter Robinson's Court and General Mourning Warehouse (1853) and Nicholson's Argyle General Mourning and Mantle Warehouse (1853) were all advertising and advising customers on what apparel to wear. Catalogues displayed illustrations of dinner dresses and mourning dresses for bereavement occasions. By 1862 Jay's advertised 'A complete Suit of Domestic Mourning for 2½ guineas'. Peter Robinson's of Regent Street advertised in the *Illustrated London News* in January 1873: 'Mourning for Families in Correct Taste.' Robinson's promoted 'Skirts, in new Mourning Fabrics, trimmed crepe' from thirty-five shillings to five guineas. Jay's could boast the royal crests of arms above their window display as well as making the claim in advertisements in the *Queen* in 1890 that, 'Messrs Jay are constantly receiving new millinery from the first houses in Paris, and the most approved forms are at once copied to suit every degree of Mourning.'

Manuals such as *Cassells Household* Guide (1880) offered advice and guidance on how to proceed after bereavement from registering the death, the costs of the funeral and the expense of burial in the various metropolitan cemeteries. It also added in volume 3:

> The blinds of the windows of the house should be drawn down directly the death occurs, and they should remain down until after the funeral has left the house, when they are at once to be pulled up. As a rule, the females of the family do not pay any visits until after the funeral. Neither would it be considered in good taste for any friends or acquaintances to visit at the house during that time, unless they were relatives of the family.

With some alertness to the sensitivities of class it also stated:

> It sometimes happens among the poorer classes that the female relatives attend the funeral; but this custom is by no means to be recommended, since in these cases it but too frequently happens that, being unable to restrain their emotions, they interrupt and destroy the solemnity of the ceremony with their sobs, and even by fainting.

In a similar condescending tone the *Lady's Magazine*, commenting on the widespread mourning which accompanied the death of Princess Charlotte in November 1817, stated that 'Considerable distress has always been occasioned by a general mourning', especially to 'the labouring class of manufacturers'. Giving more practical guidance, *Mrs Beeton's Book of Household Management* (1861) advised on the best approach to condolence visiting:

> Courtesy would dictate that a mourning card should be used, and that visitors, in paying condoling visits, should be dressed in black, either silk or plain-coloured apparel. Sympathy with the affliction of the family, is thus expressed, and these attentions are, in such cases, pleasing and soothing.

The culture of mourning was changing by the late Victorian period. Acknowledging concessions to fashion as well as a decline in the display of mourning, Mrs Humphry wrote:

> Of late years the periods for wearing [mourning dress] have been very much abbreviated, and many other changes have taken place in what may be called … the etiquette of mourning … We have all been wearing black crepe for so long that things have become rather mixed … Even widows do not wear their weeds nearly so long as was usual and they are seen in places of amusement … while still wearing deep mourning – a thing that would not have been tolerated by society ten years ago. The whole matter is undergoing a revolution.

Although some widows continued the practice of wearing mourning dress in the twentieth century, the 'revolution' Mrs Humphry wrote about was unstoppable and the Victorian rituals of mourning began to be observed less and less.

2

Resurrectionists and Bodysnatchers

If one crime above all others can be guaranteed to evoke an immediate shudder and sense of revulsion, it is probably the illicit seizing of unburied corpses and especially the exhumation of corpses for sale to teachers of anatomy and surgery. It intrudes on some of our most primeval and deeply-felt fears and taboos. It is a crime that we associate with the eighteenth and early nineteenth centuries and late-Georgian society. By no means unique to the capital, it is, however, a crime that was associated with London!

Even in the present largely secular age, dinned into us and firmly rooted is the belief that the remains of the dead should be treated with respect. From earliest times, however, there has been a tension between this reverence and the needs and interests of wider society. Man's innate sense of curiosity and desire to push back the boundaries of what is known, has led him to try to find out how the body works or what happens when it malfunctions. As far as doctors, surgeons and scientists are concerned, it has provoked a desire to understand bodily functions and be able to treat disease and malfunctions more effectively. The research needed to bring about developments which might benefit mankind as a whole has frequently conflicted with the powerful forces of established religion. Here we trace how and why the issue came to a head in England and how it manifested itself in London, particularly in the period from 1750 to 1830.

The robbing of graves was not a new activity. For example, thieves had eagerly plundered the untold riches to be found in the burial chambers of the ancient Egyptian Pharaohs. Corpses have always attracted that minority of the population given to the black arts and to necrophilia. In England exhumation was occasionally used as a form of aggravated punishment. John Wycliffe (*c.* 1330–1384) was regarded as a heretic by the hierarchy of the Church and many years after his death his remains were taken out and burnt. King Richard III's body was hastily buried in the abbey of the Greyfriars at Leicester after his death at the Battle of Bosworth in 1485. At the Dissolution the building was ransacked and his body removed and supposedly thrown into the nearby River Soar. Richard III is the only English monarch to have no known grave. Two years after Oliver Cromwell, the Lord Protector died, his remains were removed from their resting place in Westminster Abbey. In 1661, during the reaction against the execution of Charles I, Cromwell and two other regicides were posthumously found guilty of treason. They were exhumed and their remains were dragged on hurdles to Tyburn where they were ritually hanged. After several hours their heads were hacked off and taken away while the bodies were supposedly dumped in a pit next to the gallows. The heads were displayed at Westminster Hall.

In the Middle Ages, knowledge of human anatomy and physiology was minimal. In 1300 the Church had outlawed the dissection of human bodies for the purposes of research or demonstration on the grounds that they were images of God and that a body that was incomplete would not be able to be reunited with its soul at the Last Judgement. Dire penalties faced those who dared to defy the ecclesiastical authorities. The Church taught that nothing could justify the dissection of humans, even if they were criminals who had committed heinous crimes.

For hundreds of years, men training to be physicians had to make do with the teachings of Galen (AD *c.*130–201), the great Greek anatomist. His observations, although unquestionably acute and profound, were based on the dissection of a wide range of mammals and what we now know as the incorrect assumption that the information derived from such sources was also applicable to human anatomy. While Galen's teachings were acceptable to the Church, their continuance stood in the way of human progress.

A restless soul who could not reconcile what he knew empirically with what was being taught, was the Flemish anatomist Andreas Vesalius (1514–1564). His enormously-detailed, finely-illustrated and seminal work published in 1543, generally known as *De Humani Corporis Fabrica,* outraged the religious establishment, not least because it was clearly the product of its author's extensive and systematic dissection of human bodies. Perhaps he started the whole thing because the first body that he systematically dissected was stolen to order. It was the remains of a felon dangling from a gibbet!

The contribution of Vesalius cannot be exaggerated and he more than anyone else can be said to have started the movement which put the study of human anatomy on a scientific basis. One effect of this was to increase the demand for anatomical subjects for demonstration and teaching purposes. Conflict was inevitable between the forces of religious, legal and social orthodoxy and those of scientific enquiry. The Renaissance polymaths Leonardo and Michelangelo eagerly seized every opportunity that presented itself for minute examinations of the internal disposition of the human organs. Leonardo is thought to have dissected over thirty human corpses. A new approach to the study of natural phenomena was being created. It was to prove unstoppable but England lagged behind Italian and Dutch practice so far as the study of medicine and surgery were concerned.

In England in 1540 Henry VIII created the Company of Barber-Surgeons. He granted them the right to secure the bodies of four executed felons a year. They were entitled to use these as object lessons in public lectures and demonstrations. The King thereby unknowingly created an unholy alliance which was to cause enormous controversy over the years. This was between medicine, science and the apparatus of the State in the form of the law and the judiciary on the one hand and the world of crime, criminals and exemplary punishment on the other. In the reign of Charles II (1660–1685) two additional corpses per annum were made available.

Surgeons before the nineteenth century were not held in high esteem. They were rough-and-ready men who treated injuries and wounds, often without great success, performed amputations, frequently with fatal results and bled patients thought to be suffering from all manner of ailments. If the patients lived it was frequently in spite of, rather than because of, the surgeons' ministrations. They also cut hair and treated piles, in-growing toenails and various other unglamorous conditions sadly all too common among their patients, most of whom were from the poorer sections of society. The role of the physicians was more prestigious and they worked with better-off patients, although there is little evidence that their efforts were any more effective.

William Cheselden (1688–1752) can fairly be described as the father of English surgery. In 1711 he started giving private anatomy classes and obtained his necessary visual aids by openly buying the bodies of executed felons. Cheselden's initiative was disapproved of by both the Company of Barber-Surgeons of which he was a member, and by the public as a whole. They rejected the idea that publicly anatomising executed felons was an activity that would ultimately improve the human condition. Understandably, they found the whole idea creepy and repulsive. In 1745 Cheselden was instrumental in setting up the negotiations that led to the creation of the Company of Surgeons, which in 1800 became the Royal College of Surgeons. Its headquarters, Surgeons' Hall, was located in Old Bailey, a street right on the doorstep of Newgate Prison which housed many condemned felons and other prisoners. This was very handy because any prisoners who died and whose bodies were unclaimed, were easily obtainable for demonstration purposes. Unofficial practice was for the unclaimed bodies of felons hanged at Tyburn also to be obtained by the London surgeons.

The Royal College was the only body that could award qualifications in surgery in England and Wales and anyone wishing to become a surgeon had to meet the requirements of the College and become a member. In 1823 the controversial decision was taken that anyone who wanted to be recognised as a member of the College would have to submit certificates of attendance from one of four London teaching hospitals. These were St Thomas' and Guy's which were then known as the 'United Hospitals', St Bartholomew's and the London Hospital.

The courses they provided were extremely expensive and often of poor quality. For that reason there was a role for private schools of anatomy and surgery because they gave students the opportunity to practice dissection relatively cheaply, rather more informally and under the supervision of lecturers who often had superior didactic skills to those in the hospitals.

The man who can be fingered for putting the crime of body-snatching onto an established basis was William Hunter (1718–83), an immensely energetic Scotsman who had moved to London and numbered among his numerous activities lecturing on human anatomy. His classes were very much 'hands on' and he prided himself on being able to provide every student with the opportunity to practice on human cadavers. Firmly pushing legal issues and moral scruples into the background, he paid associates to rob graves and they in turn bribed sextons, hospital porters and others to provide information and practical assistance. In 1767 William moved into a house in Great Windmill Street. To these premises considerable numbers of corpses enclosed in baskets and hampers were wheeled in hand barrows, and sometimes left in the middle of the night inside the railings to await his attention in the morning. He never asked how or from where these specimens had been obtained. William eventually specialised in obstetrics and it was known that he would buy female corpses at different stages of pregnancy but also that he would pay particularly high fees for cadavers exhibiting especially interesting abnormalities of gestation.

William was joined by his brother, John (1728–1793), who went on to even greater eminence as an anatomist, surgeon and physiologist and is considered by many to be the founder of scientific surgery. John, whose contribution to improving the human lot cannot be overstated, also put the pursuit of knowledge before other considerations and not only employed men to obtain a large and steady supply of illicit 'specimens' for him, but seems to have positively enjoyed socialising with these nefarious operators. Perhaps this was evidence of the 'common touch' for which he was well known.

Still the demand for specimens for demonstration and practice continued to grow. The Act to Prevent the Horrid Crime of Murder (usually called the 'Murder Act') was passed in 1752. It allowed the courts, at their discretion, to submit the bodies of convicted murderers to the surgeons for dissection and public exhibition. This was a form of aggravated punishment because such deceased felons would not be accorded Christian rites of passage. For the superstitious at least, this meant that they would be unable to enter Heaven at the Second Coming, a situation further confirmed by the fact that after dissection they would not be anatomically complete. As well as hopefully acting as a deterrent to murder by wickedly turning the screw on convicted murderers, this act offered the further advantage of generating an additional supply of cadavers for the advancement of science. As Peter Linebaugh ('The London Hanged', 1991) commented, 'it appears that a precondition of progress in anatomy depended upon the ability of the surgeons to snatch the bodies of those hanged at Tyburn.'[1]

The Murder Act was a much-hated piece of legislation. The preamble to the Act specifically stated that 'in no case whatsoever the Body of any Murderer shall be suffered to be buried'. It was seen as a spiteful aggravation of the dreaded judicial punishment of death by hanging. It intruded cruelly on the bereaved relations when they were at their most vulnerable. Dissection of the corpse and its subsequent public display was regarded as an affront to accepted religious norms and to folk beliefs and practices which were every bit, if not more, deep-rooted. Attitudes to death were a curious mixture of Christian and semi-pagan beliefs. It was for this reason that relations, friends, workmates and members of the crowd frequently fought with the surgeons' men around the scaffold at Tyburn in order to prevent the body of the executed felon being taken away to be publicly dissected. Anyone convicted of rescuing or attempting to rescue a corpse from the custody of the surgeons was liable to transportation for a term of seven years.

Death by hanging was not always instantaneous. There were cases of felons who had been hanged, cut down and placed in their coffins only to come around later. In 1709 John Smith was hanged at Tyburn. Two hours after he had supposedly died, he was cut down and taken to a nearby house where he made a complete recovery and for the rest of his life was known as 'Half-Hanged Smith'. In 1736 Thomas Reynolds was hanged at Tyburn. He was cut down when all signs of life were judged extinct. His mourning relations had just reverentially placed his body in the waiting coffin and were about to put the lid in place when, with an air of understandable indignation, the deceased started moving and then remonstrating with them. The hangman, stung by such public evidence of his poor workmanship, wanted to have another go at Reynolds but the crowd carried him off as if he was a trophy. Unfortunately all this excitement was too much for Reynolds and he died shortly afterwards.

It is understandable that even the most hardened of murderous criminals would blench at the prospect of being hanged and then recovering consciousness only to find that a surgeon was poised over them about to make the first incisions of the anatomical demonstration. This was no empty fear. It actually happened in 1740 to a rapist called Duell who had been hanged shortly before and then recovered consciousness just at the critical moment.

In 1751 William Hogarth (1697–1764) published his series of engravings called *The Four Stages of Cruelty*. This set of four pictures was intended by Hogarth to confront the contemporary popularity of activities which involved cruelty to animals. He does so by tracing the criminal career of his anti-hero figure, Tom Nero. His start on the road to perdition is shown in the first illustration where he tortures a stray dog held down by one of his friends. Other examples of the cruel abuse of animals are shown elsewhere in this animated but repellent scene. Nero's career embraces further unedifying activities but is terminated when he is tried and found guilty of murder and then hanged. The final scene is called 'The Reward for Cruelty' and depicts Nero's corpse lying on a slab in the lecture room of Surgeons' Hall. The hangman's rope is still round his neck and three surgeons' assistants in aprons are working on different parts of his body. The lecturer is seated and demonstrating various points to his audience. He is identifiable as John Freke, a well-known surgeon and former friend of Hogarth with whom the artist had quarrelled, a common event in Hogarth's life. Two skeletons stand in niches: one is that of James Field, a notable pugilist, the other being James Maclean, a 'gentleman highwayman' who was hanged at Tyburn in 1750.

Occasionally adventurous surgeons themselves went to burial grounds and obtained freshly-buried corpses, but the profession as a whole had its reputation to uphold. Generally they found others to do their dirty work and they had few qualms about the origins of the 'subjects' they bought or how they had been obtained. The field was open for the emergence of a specialist sub-stratum of the criminal fraternity. This was the 'resurrection man', 'resurrectionist' or 'sack-'em-up man' generally but somewhat misleadingly known as the 'bodysnatcher'. Strictly speaking, bodysnatchers were the people who opportunistically seized unburied corpses and tried to sell them to the schools of anatomy. In addition, there were the 'burkers' who killed in order to obtain corpses for the same reason. Doubtless there were some who tried all three methods of making a living.

It was this form of criminal low-life that took the risk of punishment and the singular social disapproval attached to the whole idea of robbing graves and defiling the dead. They were true pariahs and frequently could only inure themselves to the horrors of their work by being permanently inebriated. However, the surgeons who bought the 'subjects', the fresh corpses, did so with total impunity. The learned men of science and the dregs of the criminal world united in a bizarre but mutually beneficial symbiosis. Both parties were widely loathed. However, as long as desecrated graves were restored tidily so that no offence was given or there was no threat to public health, official policy seems to have been to turn a blind eye to the surgeons and anatomists who bought the subjects – after all they were from a superior social class to the majority of the 'subjects' themselves.

During the heyday of the resurrectionists, in legal terms the disinterment of a body was a misdemeanour. It was defined as breaching 'common decency' and was punishable by a fine or a term of up to six months' imprisonment. A human cadaver could not belong to anyone and was therefore not regarded as being property. This greatly offended public opinion because it meant that what was regarded as one of the most heinous of crimes was punished in such a trifling way. Additionally there was a perception that those who made and implemented the law were largely immune from the activities of the resurrectionists. In modern society, the law has always tended to be more rigorous and comprehensive in the defence of property than the person. It seemed an insulting anomaly that the theft of a shroud, for example, was regarded as a felony while taking a body away was merely a misdemeanour.

Gravediggers, sextons, the drivers and porters of hearses and general handymen in hospitals frequently either provided 'insider information' about 'subjects' for which they were paid. Sometimes, because it was a very lucrative criminal activity, they became resurrectionists or bodysnatchers themselves. Charles Dickens in *A Tale of Two Cities* has a character called Jeremiah Cruncher who is an apparently respectable bank porter by day but a resurrection man by night.

Resurrection men needed an unusual combination of skills if their careers were to prosper. They had to be physically strong, they required strong stomachs and they needed to be able to ignore the normal human fears and taboos concerning the dead, burial places and darkness. Nauseating and noxious gases were released on those occasions when resurrectionists accidentally broke open older coffins while engaged in their nefarious handiwork. A sharp eye had to be kept for any items that might have been specially placed on or around the grave to provide clues as to whether the contents had been disturbed. Equally, they wanted to ensure that they would not fall foul of any of the booby traps, such as spring guns, that might be set up in order to deter their activities. Sometimes relatives of the deceased might guard the grave or pay watchmen to do so. In an understandable state of nervousness given the place, the time and the task they were engaged in, it was all too easy for them to loose off at random with any firearms they might have. It was also handy if the resurrectionists possessed effective negotiating skills in order to get a good price for the cadavers they obtained.

Robbing graves was a complex and demanding operation and could only be done by a gang of at least three or four. The usual method of recovering the body was for the gang to start by removing the fresh soil with spades and mattocks which were usually made of wood and surrounded by sacking to muffle the sound. The soil was then placed carefully on sheets brought along for the purpose. When the coffin was exposed, the lid was broken in two with a special device something like a grappling iron. One of the gang went down into the grave and tied a rope around the neck of the corpse which was then unceremoniously hauled up to the surface. The corpse was stripped and the shroud and any other minor items that had been buried with it would generally be put back. This was done so that the resurrection men, if apprehended, could not be charged with stealing any burial items. The corpse was usually placed in a sack and the grave refilled with great care so as to make it look as if it was undisturbed. The body, suitably covered by sacking, would then usually be wheeled through the streets in a hand barrow. Such was the attention to detail with which this work was done that many grieving relatives visiting the grave the next day would have been unable to find any signs that it had been tampered with. The disinterment was almost always done at night with shaded lanterns and as quickly as possible. Perfectionists generally reckoned that they could remove the body and restore the grave to pristine condition in about half an hour.

It was indeed a lucrative enterprise for the resurrection men. In the early years of the nineteenth century there were about 300 students a year in London engaged in studies involving dissection of human corpses and a subject could be had for just one or two guineas. By the 1820s the number of students in London had grown to at least 1,000. A resurrectionist could expect to earn considerably more than a skilled working man. Demand rose and 'subjects', especially those that were fresh and showed particularly interesting evidence of disease or any abnormalities, could change hands for as much as fifteen guineas. Sometimes even an unusual arm or leg might fetch a good price. Foetuses were always in demand. Male corpses tended to be valued more highly on account of their musculature. Little interest was evinced in a corpse after putrefaction had set in. Teachers of anatomy and surgery reckoned that each student needed to have had exclusive practise on a minimum of two cadavers before he could be considered competent at surgery.

Sir Astley Cooper (1768–1841) lectured on anatomy at St Thomas' Hospital from 1789 and at the College of Surgeons in 1793. In 1800 he became Surgeon at Guy's Hospital and in 1813 Professor of Comparative Anatomy at the College of Surgeons. Historians regard him as a crucial figure in the transformation of surgery into a science. In 1820 he removed a tumour from the head of King George IV. His career never looked back. Well-respected professionally and a darling of fashionable London society, enjoying the patronage of the rich and well-connected, Cooper at the same time was the 'Godfather' of the unholy alliance between the medical profession and the criminal underworld. He exemplifies the double standards whereby elite society ignored the complicity of their own in this partnership but stigmatised those who seized and sold the cadavers. Cooper spent much of his own money supporting the families of those resurrection men who worked for him but who had been caught, prosecuted and imprisoned. He did this not out of kindness but because he valued skilled resurrectionists and wanted to maintain good relations with them. On a personal level, like most other people, he despised them.

He was immensely self-assured and famously once told the Select Committee on Anatomy (see below) that the law was completely powerless to prevent him from obtaining any specific corpse once he had decided that he wished to dissect it. He enjoyed being in the limelight and provided the committee with lurid revelations about the unpleasantness of which the resurrection men were capable. He revealed that one gang leader, if and when he found rivals on his patch, would break into their headquarters and mutilate any corpses he found so as to render them useless for selling to the anatomists. If he was unable to gain entry to the gang's premises, he would quickly whip up a mob eager to give vent to their collective hatred of the bodysnatchers. In one 'turf war', a gang got hold of a corpse in an advance state of putrefaction, chopped it into pieces and deposited these gory items in and around the premises used by their rivals.

A surgeon named Brookes who appeared before the same committee related how he once forgot to give a gang a tip and they responded by dumping two putrefying corpses near his house. In the darkness, two young ladies stumbled over these gruesome obstacles and their horrified screams precipitated a riot. The morality of the London mob, rough-and-ready as it may have been, required absolutely that the dead should be treated with reverence. Brookes had to take refuge in Great Marlborough Street Police Station to avoid the possibility of being lynched.

The deference and legal immunity extended to men like Astley Cooper is shown by the occasion one night when three hampers were on their way to Cooper's premises in a cab. The driver suspected that the hampers contained dead bodies and he stopped to alert a watchman. Together they confirmed the grisly nature of the cab's cargo. The watchman called at Cooper's premises to warn him that he would have to report the matter to the Lord Mayor first thing next morning. Cooper was up betimes. He hurried to the Mansion House where the Lord Mayor went to great length to assure him that he had already been apprised about the matter and that his visitor could be certain it would go no further.

Professional surgeons in the teaching hospitals tended to look down on those who ran and taught in the private anatomy schools of which there were seven in London in 1825–6. An example of the latter was Joseph Carpue who ran his own school in Dean Street, Soho. Carpue caused a storm of controversy when he crucified the body of an executed felon so that an artist could provide a realistic portrayal of the way in which the body hung. It cut little ice with his critics when he assured them that the painting he had commissioned was a teaching aid. It should be mentioned that the private anatomy schools had no right under law to receive the bodies of executed felons for teaching and demonstration purposes.

In 1810 a roistering medical student at a private medical school attracted a hostile crowd when he climbed onto its roof brandishing a human leg which he then dropped down the chimney of a nearby building. There it fell into a cauldron of stew that was cooking on the hob. An outraged crowd only dispersed after the lecturer paid them to go away. In 1820 a surgeon had his house burnt down because the mob thought, wrongly as it happened, that he had mutilated or dissected the corpses of the Cato Street Conspirators.

Some bodysnatchers went to hospitals or the poor law authorities posing as the caring relatives of the deceased who simply wanted to take the body of the dear departed away in order to give it a good funeral. They made sure first that the deceased was unlikely to have any people who really cared for them. The officials were usually only too happy to get rid of the cadaver because it saved them the cost of a funeral. For this reason they tended not to be too fastidious in checking out the credentials of the 'caring relatives'.

Those who obtained specimens for the surgeons by whatever means needed an effective intelligence network, an 'ear to the ground' as it were. They also needed to be audacious and opportunistic. In October 1831, a scapegrace by the name of Williams realised that the widow who occupied a hovel just off Hackney Road had popped out and would be gone for a few minutes. He broke in easily knowing that the house contained the body of her fourteen-year-old son who had died a couple of days earlier. He swiftly trussed the body up in a sack and made his escape. He was seen and arrested but he quickly managed to find an illicit buyer for the boy's body.

The stakes were high in the resurrection game. The demand for cadavers was such that the resurrection men and bodysnatchers were to some extent able to dictate their own financial terms from the anatomists and they were not averse to playing dirty tricks on them. One ploy was to deliver a subject to the home of an anatomist, take payment and then return a couple of hours later to burgle the anatomist's premises and carry the cadaver off to sell it to another anatomist. One surgeon took delivery of a subject in a sack one evening and retired to bed shortly afterwards only to be woken some time later by noises from his cellar. Upon investigation he found that the 'subject' was a severely confused man who had been sacked up while befuddled with drink.

Perhaps London's leading resurrectionist was Ben Crouch. His business reached its peak from 1809 to 1813 when he had a virtual monopoly of the supply of bodies to the hospitals on the South Bank and to St Bartholomew's. He was tough, aggressive and ruthless but he also possessed a sound business sense. His intention was to eliminate rivals and corner the London market for specimens so that he could dictate prices. Like the gangsters of the Prohibition in the USA in the 1920s, he built up a network of informers in privileged positions who had inside information and put them on his payroll. Rivals either joined him or risked violent measures when Crouch sent his enforcers to pay them a call.

The anatomists attached to the hospitals resented Crouch's resourcefulness and tried to take him on by creating a cartel called the Anatomical Club, which in turn would be able to dictate prices. Their innate snobbery, however, meant that they could not bring themselves to include the private anatomy schools. Crouch exploited this weakness by delivering only to the private schools which meant that the hospitals were faced with a dire shortage of specimens. Any other gang trying to do business with the cartel was threatened with reprisals. An uneasy working compromise was eventually reached.

Josh Naples was a busy resurrectionist who kept a detailed diary of his activities in 1811–1812. This provides a unique insight into the ways in which the resurrectionists operated. Not the least interesting item in this diary is that describing the rivalry between Ben Crouch's Gang and Israel Chapman's Jewish Gang based in the Saffron Hill district close to Clerkenwell. This reiterates information elsewhere about the systematic bribery of officials, the emphasis on effective intelligence, surveillance of the activities of rivals and even working agreements between rivals to exclude those they considered outsiders.

Many people criticised the anatomists. Some thought that their work did nothing to advance medical science. Others favoured it in principle, just so long as the specimens used were not their own nearest and dearest. Some of those who objected to anatomisation, even ostensibly on religious grounds, seemed to have no objection if surgeons dissected the imported corpses of foreigners. Even those people who thought that dissection was beneficial because it enhanced scientific knowledge demanded that the bodies be treated reverentially and be given the normal rites of passage when the anatomists had finished with them. In practice, cadavers were treated as commodities and teaching aids; reverence for the dead was never uppermost in the minds of those who had dealings with them. Surgeons had a habit of removing organs and preserving them and so a cadaver was unlikely to remain complete, even if it was eventually buried with due respect.

Thomas Hood (1799–1845) picks up on these concerns in his poem 'Mary's Ghost':

'Twas in the middle of the night
To sleep young William tried;
When Mary's ghost came stealing in
And stood at his bedside ...

The arm that used to take your arm
Is took to Dr Vyse,
And both my legs are gone to walk
The hospital at Guy's.

I vowed that you should have my hand,
But Fate gives us denial;
You'll find it there at Mr Bell's
In spirits and a phial …

I can't tell where my head is gone,
But Dr Carpue can;
As for my trunk, it's all packed up
To go by Pickford's van.

The cock it crows, I must be gone.
My William, we must part;
And I'll be yours in death although
Sir Astley has my heart.

Don't go to weep upon my grave,
And think that there I be;
They haven't left an atom there
Of my anatomie.

Those hostile to the work of the anatomists circulated wildly sensationalist allegations about their activities. What happened to corpses while they were in the care of the anatomists? Those cadavers displaying anatomical peculiarities were examined and scoffed at by audiences of gaping students and the bodies of attractive young women were defiled, or so it was alleged. Bodily parts were abused. Drinking cups and sugar basins were fashioned out of skulls and it was even claimed that some surgeons kept vultures which were usefully employed disposing of such parts of the cadavers as they themselves had no use for.

The mass graves in which paupers were sometimes interred always interested resurrectionists. If several inmates of a poor law workhouse died in a short space of time, say about a week, they might be placed in a common burial pit. This could contain a dozen or more corpses, some relatively fresh, others in an advanced state of decomposition. If the resurrectionists were not too squeamish, they might obtain several corpses with little more effort than what was required for seizing just one.

Those readers already disgusted by the activities of the resurrectionists may recoil in greater horror on learning that even lower forms of criminal life lurked in burial grounds. Some desperadoes opened up graves in order to obtain bones which could be ground down and sold for fertilizer. Others left the bodies behind but salvaged the wood from the coffins to be sold as kindling. Some removed teeth to sell for reuse as dentures for fashionable people. A female corpse with unusually luxuriant hair might be scalped. Everything had a market value. Could anything be worse than the lowlife that exhumed and dragged away newly-buried bodies in order to remove the fatty tissue for sale as raw material for candle-makers?

As the activities of the resurrection men and bodysnatchers increased, public concern led to the establishment in 1828 of a Select Committee on Anatomy. It enquired into how the schools of anatomy obtained the cadavers which they used as specimens. The Committee questioned a large number of witnesses including leading anatomists and professional resurrectionists. It commented on the anomaly that under the law of the time, virtually all teachers and students of anatomy were guilty of a misdemeanour for buying exhumed cadavers but only those who actually dug them up were ever prosecuted. It also learnt that in 1827 more than 1,000 inmates of workhouses in London had died with no known friends or relations, their bodies therefore being unclaimed and going on to receive pauper funerals. A trifle callously, it concluded that if only these bodies were made available on a regular basis, the abhorrent activities of the resurrectionists would no longer be required.

The understandable fear generated by the activities of the resurrectionists and their close kindred, the bodysnatchers, led Edward Bridgeman to invent and market his 'Patent Iron Coffin' in 1818. This was made of cast iron and designed so as to be almost impossible to reopen once sealed. About a hundred were sold but they were greatly disliked by clergymen and sextons because although they were somewhat smaller than conventional coffins, they did not eventually break down in the same way as wooden ones did.

In 1819 a parishioner of St Andrew's in Holborn by the name of Gilbert, wanted his wife to be buried in a Bridgeman coffin. The incumbent of St Andrew's, however, greatly disliked these coffins and demanded an extortionate fee to discourage the interment. Gilbert, incensed by the rector's action, took him to an ecclesiastical court. Rather inconveniently the rector then died and with Mr Gilbert remaining unbowed and his wife unburied, the case dragged on in an uneasy limbo. The Bishop of London, anxious to pour oil on troubled waters, suggested that while the dispute was sorted out, Mrs Gilbert should be placed temporarily in a wooden coffin. However, the cadaver was securely sealed in a Bridgeman coffin and was therefore quite irretrievable. Five months passed with Mrs Gilbert remaining unburied and her husband was threatened with prosecution. Bridgeman had been waiting and watching and he now perceived an opportunity for free publicity for his product. He led a funeral party bearing Mrs Gilbert in her patent coffin to St Andrew's looking to force the issue with the parish authorities. A confrontation occurred as the participants postured, jostled and even threw a few punches. All concerned were egged on by the large crowd that had gathered, keen for entertainment. Mrs Gilbert, cosy in her coffin and totally oblivious to the chaos going on around her, was placed on a convenient stone block nearby. To the onlookers' chagrin, the outcome was something of an anticlimax as Bridgeman was led away charged with causing a breach of the peace. The coffin containing Mrs Gilbert was placed in the church's charnel house as a temporary measure.

Those who could afford them hired mortsafes. These consisted of a strong heavy iron framework lowered with a block and tackle and fixed over the grave until such time as the body concerned was too putrefied to interest the resurrectionists. Normally the mortsafe was then removed. None are known to have survived in situ in Greater London but one can be seen in the churchyard at Henham, Essex, not far from Saffron Walden. In a few cases the huts or small rooms used for watching over burial grounds have survived. One can be seen in the churchyard of St John's, Horsleydown, Bermondsey. Another stands in Giltspur Street just to the east of St Sepulchre's and close to the site of Newgate Prison.

The evidence put before the Select Committee on Anatomy in 1828 made it quite clear that the corpses surreptitiously obtained by the anatomists almost all belonged to what we now call the 'disenfranchised'. Predictably they were executed criminals or those who died in prison, suicides, 'unclaimed' inmates of hospitals and workhouses and men from the 'other ranks' in the army and navy.

In early November 1831, a gang of men were trying to hawk the body of a youth around a number of London anatomy schools without much success. It was a nice, fresh cadaver and should have fetched a good price. Its teeth had been removed. The surgeons did not usually cavil when such a specimen came their way. They did this time because it looked very much as if it was the body of a murder victim. The authorities were alerted and the gang members were quickly arrested. They were habitués of the Fortune of War public house in Giltspur Street, a known resort of resurrectionists and close to St Bartholomew's Hospital. The corpse was eventually identified as that of a youth of Italian extraction whose name was Carlo Ferrari, or Ferriere, who soon became known as 'The Italian Boy'. It seems that he obtained a frugal living working the streets equipped with a tray containing plaster or wax busts of well-known people which he offered for sale.

The case of the 'Bethnal Street Gang' and 'The Italian Boy' attracted enormous voyeuristic interest and spawned the publication of innumerable catchpenny ballads and broadsides. Within days of the execution of two of the gang, a stage play was showing at a theatre in Curtain Road, Shoreditch. This was not far from the misleadingly rural-sounding but squalid slums known as Nova Scotia Gardens which were the base for many of the gang's activities. This location became almost a tourist attraction for a while and rejoiced in the nickname 'Burkers' Hole'.

Those convicted of the murder of the 'Italian Boy' were hanged before a huge crowd outside Newgate Prison. This had become the main site for executions in London after they ceased at Tyburn in 1783. With ironic justice, their bodies were then passed on to the surgeons for public dissection.

The case of the 'Italian Boy' followed the lurid revelations surrounding the activities of the bodysnatchers Burke and Hare in Edinburgh and the disclosure that mass deaths from cholera in 1832 had provided an unusually large number of specimens for the lecturers in anatomy and their students. There was a growing public determination that the trade in illicit bodies had to stop – and immediately! Parliament was compelled to take action. The first Anatomy Bill presented in 1829 failed to get through the House of Lords and fell again in 1830 because

Parliament was dissolved. In 1832 a further bill slipped through almost unnoticed during the furore about parliamentary reform.

In 1832 a bill known generally as the Anatomy Act virtually ended illicit exhumations and bodysnatching. Executors and others such as the poor law authorities, having legal charge of those who died unclaimed, could donate their bodies to licensed surgeons and teachers of anatomy as long as the deceased had not previously and specifically stated an objection to being dissected. Regulations were made to ensure that the remains were decently buried after they had ceased to be used as subjects.

The Anatomy Act of 1832 and the Poor Law Amendment Act of 1834 were evidence of the stark social and economic realities of the developing industrial society. Gone were considerations of responsibility on the part of the rich and powerful for the poor and powerless. Relations between individuals and between classes were now primarily defined in terms of money, the 'cash-nexus'. The Anatomy Act was a piece of class legislation. In the first hundred years that the Act was in operation, almost 57,000 bodies were dissected in the London anatomy schools alone. All but a few of these came from the institutions of the Poor Law.

There is an old Arab proverb that 'barbers learn their trade on the heads of orphans'. This implies that being orphans, the infants had little option but to comply with the needs of the barbers. From the early 1830s, the medical profession developed its anatomical knowledge and honed its surgical skills on the inanimate bodies of many of society's most deprived citizens. They too had little alternative. It would have been cold comfort to them to know that in their tens of thousands they contributed, each in a small way, to the revolution in medical and surgical practice which so much increased life expectancy in the twentieth century.

Before leaving this subject let's have an excerpt from 'The Surgeon's Warning' by Robert Southey (1774–1843), which captures the loathing felt for the surgeons, teachers of anatomy and their associates:

> All kinds of carcasses have I cut up,
> And now my turn will be;
> But brothers, I took care of you,
> So pray take care of me.

I have made candles of dead men's fat,
The Sextons have been my slaves,
I have bottled babes unborn, and dried
Hearts and livers from rifled graves.

All night long let three stout men
The vestry watch within;
To each man give a gallon of beer,
And a keg of Holland's gin;

Powder and ball and blunderbuss,
To save me if he can,
And eke five guineas if he shoot
A Resurrection Man.

And let them watch me for three weeks,
My wretched corpse to save;
For then I think that I may stink
Enough to rest in my grave.

The desecration of graves did not completely end with the passing of the Anatomy Act of 1832. In 1869 Dante Gabriel Rosetti obtained the permission of the Home Office to open up the coffin of his wife. This is because he had placed some unpublished poems in her grave when she died seven years earlier; maybe his love for her had worn a bit thin or perhaps he wanted to sell them because he had a cash-flow problem. So in the hours of darkness Rossetti and a small party made their way into Highgate Cemetery and recovered the poems. The book in which they were written had to be disinfected and then every page had to be dried. It was a legal but extremely macabre way of increasing one's published literary output.

NOTES

1. Linebaugh, P., *The Tyburn Riot against the Surgeons,* in Hay, Linebaugh *et al,* 1977, p. 68.

3
Controversies

Infanticide, Suicide, Cremation and Euthanasia

Attitudes towards illegitimacy have a long history of stigma. The 1624 Act to 'prevent the destroying and murthering of bastard children' remained in force until the early nineteenth century and was aimed essentially at unmarried mothers. Infanticide was viewed as the most common form of murder in the seventeenth century and was one of the reasons for the creation of London's Foundling Hospital in 1739. There were high levels of infant urban mortality in the early nineteenth century. The bodies of babies were regularly discovered in streets or rivers. Some of them had not died of natural causes.

Life was especially cheap for illegitimate children. A consistent stream of cases came to the Old Bailey involving young mothers who had killed their children, normally by strangulation. Others sought different methods. In 1675 a woman from St Martin-in-the-Fields threw her infant into the fire and 'then threw the Coals upon it, where it was burned to Death.' In 1681 Ann Price locked her new-born baby in a box. The *London Post* in July 1700 reported on a woman who was sent to Newgate for murdering a three-year-old child. The father was a married man who pressured the woman to kill the child.

In the most painful fashion the woman shoved red-hot 'Knitting-kneedles up the Child's Fundament ... by which he Languished and Dyed.' The following year *The Post* covered the story of a pregnant woman who, in Ratcliff Highway, strangled her four-year-old son and, 'causing his Tongue to hang out, she cut it off; and afterwards cut his Throat.' A new-born child was found with its throat cut, in a muddy ditch near Lambeth Church in 1718 and the mother cut her own throat the next morning. In August 1730 a young mother was committed to Newgate for the murder of her one-month-old bastard child. She cut off the child's head and hurled the body into a field near Enfield. In 1733 Frances Deacon murdered her child by throwing it into a pond – a common method of disposing of babies. At Moorfields in 1735 Elizabeth Ambrook threw her baby son from a window two stories high. It died.

The *Marylebone Mercury* reported a number of cases of infant deaths between 1857 and 1859 including a baby found by two young men in a basket in Regents Park, by no means an uncommon event, and a housemaid who found a parcel containing a dead baby wrapped in it during a visit to a church. *The Times* noted in 1861 that within the past five years 278 infants had been murdered in the metropolis. This was among the lower of the estimates for infant deaths.

In 1867 Central Middlesex was the location of over half the infanticides carried out in Britain. This appalling record was highlighted and publicised by a small group of coroners and doctors. Between 1861 and 1865, responses to the issue of infanticide included the establishment of the Association for the Preservation of Infant Life, the National Society and Asylum for Prevention of Infanticide and in 1870 the Infant Life Protection Society. Despite these initiatives, there was no effective legislation until after the First World War.

As thousands of children were at risk of being abandoned, there was no shortage of louche people ready to exploit the situation, notably through the practice of baby farming. This involved 'relieving' mainly unmarried mothers of their babies for a fee, taking them into care and then later killing them. Rapacious owners of 'lying-in' houses preyed upon both infants and their unmarried mothers. The owners of many of these houses placed advertisements in newspapers stating that they would offer good care of infants for a specified period of time. Newspapers must have known what was going on and bear some responsibility for indirectly assisting this awful practice. A young mother could easily find up to a dozen advertisements in some papers. Desperate and vulnerable, they responded to these ads, made the necessary arrangements with the baby farmers who took the infants in and often they never saw their children again. Many did not want to.

The *London Times* of 25 February 1834 showed little compassion when it fulminated to the effect that poor relief should be for the destitute and that the provision of relief to mothers of illegitimate children was detrimental to female morals. Many young pregnant women had limited employment opportunities which exacerbated the costs of keeping a child from starvation. The options were stark: they could place their children in a workhouse, commit infanticide or resort to baby farmers. In the latter case the child would be 'adopted' for a set fee and then disposed of as soon as possible, usually by poisoning. Dumping children in the street or in a river saved on burial costs.

Frederick John Wood was fourteen months old when farmed out to a house at No. 24 Swayton Road, Bow. When he died ten months later, the coroner reported that the cause of death was fluid on the brain and a malformed chest. The owner of the house, Mrs Savill, like many others who were involved with this awful crime, was not charged. In January 1868, the *Pall Mall Gazette* exposed a Mrs Jagger of Tottenham, who was reported to have had from forty to sixty infants in her care in a three-year period, the majority of whom had died of starvation. An informant tipped off the authorities that no fewer than fifty-five babies had died in an eighteen-month period whilst under the 'care' of a Mrs Martin of No. 33a Dean Street, Soho. Martin had made a very comfortable living by charging between £10 and £50 per child. However, without sufficient evidence from witnesses and mothers, many of whom were reluctant to come forward, she escaped prosecution and eventually moved from the area. Fate did serve up some degree of justice, however, when she died from apoplexy in November 1869.

Some lying-in houses in the Brixton and Peckham district came under surveillance the following year after sixteen infant bodies had been discovered. A policeman, Sergeant Relf, was alerted when he saw an advertisement in the newspaper stating, 'good home, with a mother's love and care, is offered to a respectable person, wishing her child to be entirely adopted.' Relf replied to the address which was in Goar Place, Brixton, using a false name. Having gained access he found ten infants, five of whom were seriously malnourished. The owners, Sarah Ellis and Margaret Waters, were charged with conspiracy to obtain money by fraud as well as the murder of one of the infants, John Cowan. The trial attracted much interest and was covered extensively by the newspapers as the 'Brixton Farming Case.' Graphic and ghoulish descriptions appeared of how babies were poisoned, their bodies wrapped in old rags and then dumped in the streets. One witness at the trial stated that Ellis and Waters often left the house with infants and later returned with only the children's clothing. It is difficult to know the actual number of children who died whilst in their 'care', but it is thought that they murdered between sixteen and nineteen babies in the Brixton area. Ellis, who administered narcotics to the children, was released from prison but Waters was hanged at Horsemonger Lane on 11 October 1870.

Unfortunately reform was slow and the awful practice continued. Public attention was alerted in the 1890s to such cases as those of Joseph and Annie Roodhouse where it is known that at least ten children died in their care. Another was Alice Reeves from Lambeth. Upon investigation, the clothes of over three hundred children were found in her house. Asa Chard Williams was tried and executed for throwing a baby into the Thames in 1900. At least two more executions for infanticide followed in the next seven years.

By the turn of the century a whole range of developments began to take place such as the changes to the Infant Protection Act in 1897, a more systematic approach to child protection, a decline in child poverty and a decline in births.

Until the Suicide Act of 1961 abrogated a law that had been in force in England and Wales since 1554, it was a crime to commit suicide and anyone who attempted and failed could be prosecuted and imprisoned. For centuries suicide was considered to be a mortal sin in the eyes of the Church and was punished by a refusal to bury the victim in consecrated ground. Until 1823 the bodies of suicides were buried at crossroads with a stake through the heart. Burial at a crossroads was chosen for two particular reasons: not only did the sign of a cross have religious connotations, but burial there also made sure that the ghost of the deceased would be kept firmly in its place by the constant passing of traffic, or would be confused, not knowing which direction to take. In addition to the denial of burial in consecrated ground, the property and goods of the deceased was forfeited until the law was repealed in 1870. This had been a product of early English laws governing the punishment of suicide and developed by medieval judges to enrich the royal treasury.

More men committed suicide than women and this has been consistent throughout the centuries. At the beginning of the twenty-first century, men still account for the greater number of suicides across all age groups, but particularly the 25–44 age range where men are almost four times more likely to kill themselves than women.

The word *suicida* was in use from at least 1178 although it was a term not generally used in the Middle Ages. Details for suicides in the medieval period are limited by the absence of the sources associated with later periods such as censuses, registers of deaths or burials, bills of mortality and newspaper reports. What records do survive tell us that hanging was the most common form of suicide and drowning the second most frequent method. A high number of suicides resulted among those with mental illness as the later Bills of Mortality testify. Suicide was a very private act which was often difficult to prove and equally difficult to talk about. In England suicide was unique in that it was considered a crime against the monarch and a matter for royal justice. Suicides in the period prior to 1500 were predominantly from among the poor and destitute and the reasons for this were madness, disease, imprisonment or fear of punishment. From the sixteenth century there was a dramatic rise in suicides although this is mainly a result of recording them more efficiently. It could also be related to the social tensions of the time, a fall in living standards and the impact of the Reformation. However it was still the poor who made up the vast majority of reported suicides, particularly during the hungry months of late winter and early spring.

The Bills of Mortality for London from the seventeenth century show the number of people committing suicide in London each year.

For example, in 1632 the Bills record that fifteen people 'Made away with themselves', whilst in 1775 there were twenty-nine deaths by suicide for London. It was not always easy to determine the cause of death, however, and many suicides might have been categorised under 'drowned' (104 in 1775), 'fools, etc.', 'Lunatick' (the combined figure for deaths of fools and lunatics in 1775 was 136), 'found dead', 'kil'd by several accidents' (74 recorded for 1632) or 'dead in the street'. In 1839 the *Journal of the Statistical Society of London* recorded 656 suicides in Westminster between 1812 and 1836. This was about twenty-five per cent of the annual total for Great Britain in that period.

Throughout the eighteenth century, newspapers regularly reported on deaths by suicide. In April 1701, the *London Post* noted that a 'sober and honest' old man hanged himself in his lodging room near Whitechapel Church. In 1718 the *Weekly Journal* told of a porter who hanged himself by the church in Stepney because he had been dismissed from his job. A barber from the Strand in 1719 committed suicide in a terrible fashion when he cut open his body with razor blades, 'then cut off his privy parts, and at last cut his throat from ear to ear'. In 1722 the *Daily Post* reported that John Moor of Paternoster Row was so reduced to poverty that he hanged himself at the Bear Alehouse in Covent Garden. Three years later in Eagle Court, St John's Lane, a quack doctor cut his throat but took three days to die. A rat-catcher from Cripplegate in 1726 had the means of death at his disposal and took a dose of rat poison to commit suicide. An apprentice from Smithfield in the same year took the advice of a girl literally when she told him to go and hang himself. In 1730 the mother of a one-year-old child was found hanging from a tree near Woolwich.

It was common practice for condemned inmates in Newgate and other prisons to commit suicide – often to the disappointment of the scaffold crowd who waited in anticipation, eager to see them executed. The murderer, John Williams, committed suicide by hanging himself in the House of Correction in Cold Bath Fields in 1811. The authorities were not to be outdone, however, and the following day the body of Williams was dressed in blue trousers and a white and blue striped waistcoat, placed in open view on a cart and taken through the streets of London. Thousands turned out to view the procession which ended at the intersection between St George's Turnpike and Cannon Street. There, he was lowered into a grave and a stake was driven through his body.

In *Old and New London* (1878), Walter Thornbury stated that 'certain spots in London have become popular with suicides. Waterloo Bridge is chosen for its privacy; the Monument used to be chosen for its height and quietude.' Waterloo Bridge was certainly a popular choice providing privacy with its one-penny toll. Olive Anderson in her book on Victorian and Edwardian suicides noted that, 'In 1840 around 30 suicides a year, about 15 per cent of London's registered suicides were committed from this bridge.' Thomas Hood's 1844 poem *The Bridge of Sighs* was based on suicides from Waterloo Bridge:

One more unfortunate,
Weary of breath,
Rashly importunate,
Gone to her death!

Take her up tenderly
Lift her with care;
Fashion'd so slenderly,
Young, and so fair ...

Who was her father?
Who was her mother?
Had she a sister?
Had she a brother?
Or was there a dearer one
Still, and a nearer one
Yet, than all other?

Visitors seeking reasons for London's high suicide rate often commented that depressing conditions such as the 'fogs' contributed to the extent of self-slaughter. The writer Fyodor Dostoevsky (1821–1881) commented that the 'gloom never forsakes' the Londoner.

The Monument provided a pretty foolproof setting for some dramatic suicides. Between 1750 and 1842 a number of people jumped from the top and succeeded in killing themselves. They included William Green in 1750. He was a weaver and wearing a green apron he arrived at the door of the Monument, left his watch with the doorkeeper and a few minutes later was heard to fall. Thomas Craddock, a baker, fell to his death in July 1788 while Lyon Levi, a diamond merchant in 'embarrassed circumstances', killed himself in January 1810. Two well-reported cases were those of Margaret Moyes, daughter of a baker who committed suicide on 11 September 1839, and fifteen-year-old Richard Hawes in October 1839.

In the tradition of Victorian sensationalism, the broadsheets and other cheap literature reported on suicides in melodramatic fashion. Broadsheets, which were often single sheets, were sold in the streets and public houses. The most popular was the 'gallows literature' which gave vivid, even lurid, accounts of crimes and the punishments they attracted. Headings such as 'Dreadful Suicide of a Young Woman by Throwing Herself off the Monument' (1839), 'Another Dreadful Suicide at the Monument, by a Young Woman' (1842) and 'Another appalling catastrophe at the Monument!!, horrible suicide of a youth' (1839) helped to excite and titillate curiosity. One particular example of this type of a single-sheet Broadside, 'Copy of verses on the melancholy death of Margaret Moyes, who committed suicide by throwing herself off the Monument on Wednesday, September 11, 1839', read:

> From strangers oh! What awful shrieks.
> When she let go her hold,
> Like lightning she descended.
> T'was dreadful to behold;
> With a heavy crash upon the rails,
> The shock was most severe,
> Which cut off her arm and it was found,
> Near the centre of the square.

Margaret Moyes's 'extraordinary suicide' received wide coverage. She was twenty-three years of age when she went to the Monument from Charing Cross to meet friends. After waiting some twenty minutes she paid her sixpence, and then ascended the Monument stairs alone. Reports stated that her 'fall ended miserably'. The case caught the imagination of the public as well as tapping into a particular Victorian psyche of the fear of suicide. The day after her death crowds flocked to the scene and Monument Yard was packed with people attempting to gain access to the stairs of the Monument. Similar scenes took place for the inquest at the Swan Tavern, Fish-Street Hill, where people were desperate to hear any morsel of information they could get. The newspapers cashed in on the public thirst for knowledge of Moyes's suicide. Even though the cheap press of the day had been criticised some years previously for pandering to a readership with graphic accounts of suicides and 'tales of wonder and horror', it was not only the cheap press that satisfied the appetites of people. On 15 September 1839 the *Observer* reported:

> Her left arm, near the shoulder, came in contact with the bar, and was so violently severed that the part cut off flew over the iron railings several yards into the square. After striking the bar, the body fell onto a tub containing a lilac plant, which it broke in pieces, as well as several flower-pots, placed on the right side of the door. Not a sign of life, except some contortions of the muscles of the legs and arms, was discernible on the body when it was picked up.

The Registrar-General, William Farr, appealed for some control of the sensationalised tales of murder and suicide in the newspapers. This fell on deaf ears when the year following Moyes's death, a fifteen-year-old boy leapt to his death from the top of the Monument. Richard Hawes was clearly imitating Moyes's suicide as he had often spoken about her death and had threatened to commit suicide. Hawes's father had committed suicide and on the morning of his own death Richard had been sacked from his job for being idle whereupon he threatened to jump out of a window. At the inquest many details of Hawes's life were revealed. He was quiet and impressionable, could be violent and he read widely – particularly the Bible, which he had with him when he jumped to his death. All of this information found expression in the press which did not spare any salacious detail of Hawes's death and his motives. A Middlesex Magistrate and Lord Mayor of London, Sir Peter Laurie, campaigned against suicide. He took a hard line on sentencing those who had attempted suicide. In 1841 he said: 'I shall look very narrowly at the cases of persons brought before me on such charges [of suicide].' He favoured imprisonment and a month on the treadmill for such attempts.

Pleas of insanity persisted in the case of attempted suicides. On 9 March 1894, *The Times* reported that James Doggrell and his wife, of Acton Lane in Willesden, were found with their throats cut. Doggrell survived to be charged with attempted suicide and murder. After he had cut his wife's throat he cut his own but failed to kill himself. Doggrell claimed that he was not in his 'right mind'.

The last suicide from the Monument was that of a seventeen-year-old servant girl, Jane Cooper, from Hoxton. In August 1842, Jane climbed over the top of the iron railings, tucked her clothes between her knees and jumped headlong. One broadsheet recorded:

> It is with feelings of horror we have to give publicity to another dreadful affair ... At about half-past ten o'clock the neighbourhood of Fish Street Hill, Eastcheap, and their Vicinities, were thrown into a state of the greatest alarm and agitation, in consequence of a report having been circulated that a young woman had committed suicide by throwing herself off the Monument. It added that Jane, 'in her descent struck the coping stone with her head, and fell into the street, a little beyond the curb.'

The issue of the disposal of the body of the victim of suicide took on a particularly controversial dimension in 1822–3 and effectively led to legislation which stopped the practice of burying the deceased at a crossroads. On 12 August 1822, Viscount Castlereagh, the Foreign Secretary and leader of the House of Commons, committed suicide by cutting his throat with a letter opener. By law he should have been buried at a crossroads with all the indignity that went with such a ritual. However there were always exceptions to the rules, particularly when it came to a leading member of the establishment. It was announced that he had been under such 'a grievous disease of mind' that a 'state of mental delusion in manner, led him to kill and destroy himself.' The British establishment could retire having resolved this moral dilemma of what to do with one of their own. Public outrage followed with demands insisting that no suicide victim could be buried in Westminster Abbey. Lord Byron wrote in savage terms of the hypocrisy of it all in the preface to cantos VI–VIII of *Don Juan*:

Of the manner of his death little need be said, except that if a poor radical had cut his throat, he would have been buried in a cross-road, with the usual appurtenances of the stake and mallet. But the minister was an elegant lunatic – a sentimental suicide – he merely cut the 'carotid artery,' (blessings on their learning!) and lo! the pageant, and the Abbey! and 'the syllables of dolour yelled forth' by the newspapers – and the harangue of the Coroner in the eulogy over the bleeding body of the deceased … and the nauseous and atrocious cant of a degraded crew of conspirators against all that is sincere and honourable. In his death he was necessarily one of two things by the law – a felon or a madman – and in either case no great subject for panegyric.

Insult was added to injury by the fact that Castlereagh was a deeply hated political figure by many. His funeral on 20 August was greeted with jeering and insults along the processional route to Westminster Abbey. Lord Byron's Epitaph to Castlereagh summed up the level of hatred:

Posterity will ne'er survey
A nobler grave than this:
Here lie the bones of Castlereagh:
Stop, traveller and piss.

A year later Abel Griffiths, a twenty-two-year-old law student, committed suicide after murdering his father. A witness told the coroner that Griffiths had been suffering from a 'depression in the brain', however, the jury concluded that Griffiths had killed himself 'in a sound state of mind.' He was interred at the crossroads of Eaton Street, Grosvenor Place and the King's Road. The undignified ceremony, in which constables and watchmen were stationed about the neighbourhood to keep back the crowds, involved Griffiths being wrapped in a piece of Russian matting, his bloodied and unwashed body being dropped into a hole about five feet deep. The Annual Register for 1823 reported that 'the disgusting part of the ceremony [was the] … throwing [of] lime over the body and driving a stake through'. Abel Griffiths was the last known London suicide to have been buried at a crossroads as the law made it illegal for coroners to issue a warrant for burial in a public highway; suicides were henceforth allowed to be interred in a churchyard or public burial place.

However, old superstitions persisted and the 1823 Act contained punitive clauses which made clear that anyone dying through an act of suicide must still be buried without Christian rites and at night, between the hours of nine and midnight. Their goods and chattels still had to be turned over to the Crown. Middle-class families were at pains to conceal suicide because, as it was illegal, they stood to lose their property to the Crown. In addition, a suicide's body could not be buried in consecrated ground so clergy became complicit in certain cases in the cover-up.

The controversy regarding insanity in relation to suicide continued. As the nineteenth century progressed, the definitions of physicians in the cases of suicide led to a whole range of debates while Victorian literature found an outlet for many melodramatic tales involving suicide. For example, Mr Merdle's suicide in Dickens's *Little Dorrit* (1857); in *Jane Eyre*, Jane's cousin, the cruel John Reed takes his own life; Captain Brierly in Joseph Conrad's *Lord Jim* (1899) commits suicide by jumping overboard from his ship; a striking worker commits suicide in Elizabeth Gaskell's *North and South* (1854); after the disappointment of his bitter first marriage, Jude hears of his mother's suicide by drowning and tries to imitate her in Thomas Hardy's *Jude the Obscure* (1895); Tom Jarndyce attempts suicide in *Bleak House* (1852) by Charles Dickens.

The term 'assisted suicide' has been often been used in relation to euthanasia. However, the history of euthanasia presents difficulties because the term previously meant something different to how it is commonly understood today. In the thirteenth century Henry de Bracton, an English judge and writer, observed in the *Laws and Customs of England,* that 'just as a man may commit felony by slaying another so may he do so by slaying himself.'

Sir Thomas More in his book *Utopia* made one of the earliest references to euthanasia in 1516:

> They console the incurably ill by sitting and talking with them and by alleviating whatever pain they can. Should life become unbearable for these incurables the magistrates and priests do not hesitate to prescribe euthanasia

> ...When the sick have been persuaded of this, they end their lives willingly either by starvation or drugs, that dissolve their lives without any sensation of death. Still, the Utopians do not do away with anyone without his permission, nor lessen any of their duties to him.

Sir Francis Bacon (1561–1626) believed that the duty of the physician was not only to improve the health of people but also to 'mitigate pain and dolours; and not only when such mitigation may conduce to recovery, but when it may serve a fair and easy passage'. David Hume in his essay *On Suicide* argued: 'death alone can put a full period to misery ... that a man who [is] tired of life, and hunted by pain and misery, bravely overcomes all the natural terrors of death, and makes his escape from this cruel scene.'

The history of cremation is a long one and it is referred to in the Book of Genesis. Pagan Anglo-Saxons practised cremation from the fifth and sixth centuries, but its occurrence as an official practice in Britain is more recent. The practice of cremation had been debated two hundred years earlier when Sir Thomas Browne (1605–1682), an English physician born in Cheapside, put forward the idea in 1658. One of the first recorded cremations in Britain was that of Honoretta Pratt in 1769. Pratt was the daughter of Sir John Brooks of York and the widow of the Hon. John Pratt, Treasurer of Ireland. She was burnt in an open grave at St George's Burial Ground, Hanover Square in London, at her own request. A stone was erected in the burial ground with the following inscription:

> This worthy woman believed that the vapours arising from graves in church yards in populous cities must prove hurtful to the inhabitants and resolving to extend to future times, as far as she was able, that charity and benevolence which distinguished her through her life, ordered that her body should be burnt in the hope that others would follow the example, a thing too hastily censured by those who did not enquire the motive.

Debates, essays and writings about euthanasia were generated from the seventeenth century, and interest continued down until the nineteenth century. From the mid-nineteenth century there were significant changes relating to death. Reforms in public health were contributing to the fall in the death rate and a decline in Christian faith affected changes in mourning as well as witnessing the beginnings of a growth in cremations.

It was between 1873 and 1875 that two particular developments influenced the beginnings of cremation in Britain. The first of these involved Sir Henry Thompson, Surgeon to Queen Victoria, who had been influenced by a visit to the Vienna exhibition where he saw a demonstration of equipment used for carrying out cremations. On his return to England he wrote a paper in *The Contemporary Review* entitled, 'The Treatment of the Body after Death.' Thompson became an enthusiastic spokesman of cremation arguing that it was a 'necessary sanitary precaution against the propagation of disease among a population daily growing larger.' There were other arguments in favour of the practice, such as the prevention of premature burial and the fact that cremation would be cheaper than burials. Thompson's article generated much support as well as criticism, particularly religious bigotry. Sir Henry was so encouraged by the degree of support for his idea that he called a meeting at his house at No. 35 Wimpole Street in Marylebone on 13 January 1874. He, along with a number of friends, drew up a declaration which read:

> We, the undersigned, disapprove the present custom of burying the dead, and we desire to substitute some mode which shall rapidly resolve the body into its component elements, by a process which cannot offend the living, and shall render the remains perfectly innocuous. Until some better method is devised we desire to adopt that usually known as cremation.

Amongst the signatures were those of John Everett Millais and Anthony Trollope. As a result of this gathering, the Cremation Society of England came into existence. It later purchased land from the London Necropolis Company next to the cemetery in Woking with the intention of building a crematorium. However, the Society soon faced objections from some locals led by their vicar who resented such a practice taking place on their doorstep. In addition, the Society also faced legal obstacles. The Home Secretary, Sir Richard Cross, refused to endorse the practice until Parliament had given legal authorisation.

Ten years later a particular event helped their cause. The eccentric Dr William Price (1803–1893) of Llantrisant was a vegetarian, republican, ex-Chartist, anti-smoker and had rejected the institution of marriage for much of his life. At the age of eighty-three he took Gwenllian Llewellyn of Llanworno, who was in her twenties, as his 'lawful wedded wife'. His eccentricity can be gauged by the fact that he thought nothing of taking walks in the nude. When he wasn't naked he often wore a fox pelt on his head, a green pixie-like jacket and trousers and a sash and sword. Prince claimed to be the Archdruid of a lost Celtic tribe. He cremated his five-month-old son, Jesus Christ, on a local hillside (he also had two more children before he died at the age of ninety-two). Conducting his own defence at Cardiff Assizes, Price was acquitted of the charges against him. Cremation was deemed lawful, provided that it did not constitute a public nuisance. This important ruling opened the way for the legalisation of cremation. Another historic precedent came the following year at Woking in 1885 when Mrs Jeannette Pickersgill became the first official cremation.

The first provincial crematorium was built in Manchester in 1892, and was followed by Glasgow (1895) and Liverpool (1896). The Council of the Cremation Society after searching for land in north London, eventually found a site for a crematorium adjacent to Hampstead Heath and in 1900 the London Cremation Company Limited was founded. Funds were raised to buy and develop the site and architect Sir Ernest George was appointed to plan the famous crematorium at Golders Green. It opened in 1902. Significantly, Sir Henry Thompson performed the opening ceremony. Amongst those whose ashes are kept at Golders Green are Sigmund Freud, Ivor Novello, H.G. Wells, Bram Stoker, Alexander Korda, Sid James, Peter Sellers and Kingsley Amis. From the turn of the century cremation became more acceptable but it was still far from the desired choice of the vast majority of the population.

Cremation was given a higher public profile when well-known people chose to be cremated, such as the Duchess of Connaught in 1917 who was the first member of the Royal Family to be cremated. Nonetheless, the move to cremation was slow with about 800 cremations per year in 1908 and less than one per cent of corpses being cremated in 1918. The number of crematoria rose from one in 1885, to 249 in 2005. Between 1902 and 2005 Golders Green has had more than 300,000 cremations – more than any other crematorium in the UK.

4
Bizarre Deaths

One of London's fascinating aspects is its diversity. This is reflected in the death of its citizens and this chapter considers a range of curious or otherwise interesting cases and ways in which Londoners have died.

Smithfield was one of many sites in London where executions formerly took place. One who died there in a particularly excruciating manner was Richard Rose, a cook in the household of the Bishop of Rochester. In 1532, he was blamed for the death of two people who consumed gruel that he had prepared. His punishment, designed to fit the crime, was to be boiled to death in a cauldron of water suspended over a fire.

A number of religious offenders went to their death at Smithfield. One such heretic was a man named Collins who, in 1538, mimicked the officiating priest when he elevated the host during a service of worship. Collins lifted his pet dog above his head. This incident came to the notice of the authorities and in spite of the fact that Collins was clearly deranged, he was condemned to be burnt as a heretic. His accomplice the dog died with him, by no means the first or last occasion on which animals have been judicially executed for their alleged criminal offences.

Edwin Bartlett was something of an eccentric. He had his own distinctive view of the hallowed institution of marriage which held that a man should be allowed two wives. One should be a companion, the other should be there for his sexual delectation. Bartlett's wife, Adelaide, was French and a woman of considerable beauty, but she soon discovered to her chagrin that she had been cast in the 'companion' category. Bartlett, however, showed no sign of being in a hurry to go off in search of a woman to perform the sexual role. In 1885 the Bartletts became friendly with a young Methodist Minister named Dyson. They discussed all sorts of matters including Bartlett's views on matrimony. During one of these chats, Bartlett revealed that if he was to die, he would like Adelaide and Dyson to marry. He went further: he encouraged them first of all to kiss and cuddle and then to have sex while he watched. Dyson fell head over heels in love with the lovely Adelaide. On 1 June 1886, Bartlett was found dead in the lodgings he shared with Adelaide in the Pimlico district of London. The post-mortem revealed death by chloroform poisoning. What a can of worms now opened up. Just as Dyson was falling for Adelaide, Bartlett for the first time had started taking a sexual interest in her as well. This made Dyson insanely jealous and police enquiries showed that he had bought a considerable amount of chloroform. In court Adelaide insisted that the chloroform was taken regularly by her husband to help him to get to sleep. A murder trial followed and Adelaide and Dyson clearly had both the motive and the means. What was never established was whether Bartlett was actually murdered. If it was suicide or poisoning by mistake, how had he managed to swallow such a large amount of the fiery poison? When Adelaide was acquitted, pathologist Sir James Paget remarked that she really ought to reveal how she did it, even if only in the interests of science. But she didn't.

Short-bladed, sharp-edged weapons have frequently been used for the purpose of murder; but cases involving swords are less common. However, in the 1880s, London found itself rapt with interest in one such murder case. The marriage of Mr and Mrs Sweet had had its ups and downs and they constantly rowed about all manner of apparently trivial issues. Things literally came to a head when Mrs Sweet told her husband, who unluckily for him had been christened Sylvanus, that she objected to his habit of anointing his hair with pomade. What exactly happened next was never fully established, but the outcome was all too evident. Mr Sweet ran his wife right through the head and out the other side with a sword. The defence was able to convince the court that Sweet had committed the offence whilst suffering an epileptic fit.

Thankfully it is only rarely that someone is killed by a coffin. Henry Taylor managed this unusual achievement in 1872, although he was obviously unable to enjoy the celebrity that might have gone with it. He was a pallbearer at a funeral at Kensal Green Cemetery. The coffin and its contents were unusually heavy and the ground was slippery after excessive rain. When the funeral party approached the grave, Thomson suddenly stumbled and his fellow pallbearers had no option but to drop the coffin. Unfortunately it fell on his head and chest, inflicting fatal injuries.

Thomas Britton (1644–1714), a coal-merchant, stands foursquare with many of London's unsung minor celebrities. For many years he ran a shop in Jerusalem Passage in Clerkenwell, above which he held musical events which attracted figures as prestigious as the composer Handel. Something of a polymath, Britton also studied chemistry and the occult and was one of the founders of the Harleian Collection of the British Library. In spite of the fact that he continued to trudge the streets hawking coal, Britton hobnobbed with well-known aristocrats and even went on expeditions with them looking for bargains in antiquarian bookshops. An inoffensive man, he was deeply superstitious and died prematurely as a result of a practical joke. A new acquaintance of his, a ventriloquist, tried out his skills on the unsuspecting Britton. A voice apparently boomed forth from a sack of coal telling him that he would die within a few hours if he did not immediately fall on his knees and say the Lord's Prayer. Clearly terrified, Britton sank to his knees to do exactly as the voice instructed. Traumatised by this experience, the poor man died a few days later.

In April 1782, a Mrs Fitzherbert from Northamptonshire was visiting London and decided to take in a performance of *The Beggar's Opera* at the Drury Lane Theatre. This highly popular work combined burlesque of Italian opera with political satire and some scenes of genuine pathos. It was perhaps gently comical in places but Mrs Fitzherbert found the work so irresistibly funny that she had to leave the theatre before the performance was over with tears coursing down her face and she proceeded down the street howling and wailing in transports of uncontrollable and manic hilarity. These outbursts continued unabated until terminated abruptly by her death less than forty-eight hours later.

In the late nineteenth century, a publican in Clerkenwell achieved the dubious distinction of being burnt to death by his own whisky. He was down in the cellar tapping a large cask of this liquor when the bung came loose and the contents shot out over the walls and over everything else including him. It was then that he made the fatal mistake of lighting a candle so that he could get a better idea of how much damage had been caused by the leak.

Robert Naysmith died in 1906 in an Islington workhouse, alone and penniless. Born into a well-off Scottish family, he was the 'black sheep' who went off the rails and made some sort of a career for himself as a travelling showman with the stage name of 'The Human Ostrich'. His act lacked subtlety, consisting as it did simply of swallowing hatpins, marbles, small pieces of glassware, stones and other generally unpalatable items. Unsurprisingly, making a living in this way took a severe physical toll and Naysmith was forced to retire from the stage. With no qualifications, he tried a new career selling bootlaces but poverty and sickness forced him into the workhouse. Doctors called to attend him thought he was joking when he told them about his stage career and they only took him seriously when he developed an abscess which burst revealing the cause to have been a small brass nail. Naysmith's health deteriorated very quickly and he died aged just thirty-four. A post-mortem revealed over thirty items that he had swallowed while doing his acts and which had lodged in his liver, kidneys and intestines. His death was certified as being due to gastritis and peritonitis. A verdict of death by misadventure was passed on the unfortunate 'Human Ostrich'.

Commercial Road was opened in 1803 having been built through the East End to provide a direct route from the East and West India Docks to the City. It was always busy and cosmopolitan, as befitted the districts through which it passed and many apparently exotic sights were to be glimpsed by those who used it regularly. In 1875 bystanders and others were treated to the extraordinary spectacle of a full-grown tiger stalking along Commercial Road in the sensuously feline yet infinitely threatening manner of such creatures if they are on the loose. A crowd gathered and, following at a respectful distance, watched aghast as the beast picked up a small boy and carried him off, presumably looking for a suitable spot in which to make a meal of him. The child, obviously a gutsy little East End street-urchin, was screaming blue murder and was determined not to go down without a fight. One zealous spectator, doubtless full of good intentions, picked up a crowbar hoping to prize the tiger's jaws open and thereby allow the infant to escape. His good intentions came to naught because in wielding the crowbar he managed to deal the luckless infant a fatal blow. The tiger, incidentally, had escaped from a shop for exotic pets on the nearby Ratcliff Highway.

To the twenty-first-century mind, there can be few activities that seem more futile than duelling for the sake of honour. If a man of rank had been publicly slighted before the seventeenth century, redress would probably have been achieved by hiring a few thugs to give the offender a thorough going-over. If the insult was deeply felt, a slit throat or a knife in the ribs would probably have done the trick. In the early seventeenth century, however, the idea emerged that a more honourable way of settling such issues among those who now saw themselves as 'gentlemen' was by means of a fair fight in the presence of seconds. One of the earliest recorded duels of so-called honour was that fought at Islington in 1609 between two courtiers who were favourites of James I. The cause of the duel is not recorded, but with supreme skill they managed to kill each other. The King was saddened and somewhat irked when he heard of the affair and decreed that they be buried in one grave. It can still be seen in the churchyard of St Mary's, Islington.

After the restoration of the monarchy in 1660, duelling became very prevalent, especially among the more violently-inclined younger members of the gentry. Covent Garden and Lincoln's Inn Fields became favoured places for the settling of differences. Hyde Park also had its moments, including the famous duel between Lord Mohun and the Duke of Hamilton in 1712. Mohun was widely regarded as a blackguard and few mourned his passing. Both assailants received many frightful wounds which proved to be fatal.

Shortly afterwards an unsuccessful attempt was made in Parliament to make duelling illegal. Some people condemned the practice of duelling outright, while others felt that each duel should be evaluated according to the seriousness of the slur or slight involved. Duelling was given an almost respectable veneer when in 1809 two Cabinet ministers, George Canning and Lord Castlereagh, fought with pistols on Putney Heath, in this case without fatal consequences. In certain circles it was felt that a young gentleman had not proved his manhood until he had fought a duel or two. In 1829 even the Duke of Wellington fought a duel, in this case in Battersea Fields. He survived.

The years 1763, 1764 and 1765 marked a high-point for duels. The irascible John Wilkes fought Samuel Martin in Hyde Park over the issue of how the phrase 'cowardly scoundrel' should be interpreted. Wilkes received an injury coyly described as being 'below his navel'. Later a surgeon was shot dead also in Hyde Park by an officer of the marines. Soon afterwards, Epping Forest was the scene for a duel between an army captain and a military chaplain who died later from the wounds he sustained. The fifth Lord Byron, related to the famous poet, killed William Chaworth in a duel arising out of a drunken brawl. This was in the back room of a tavern in Pall Mall in January 1765.

There was a tacit understanding that duels were only fought between gentlemen, those of refined birth and breeding. This is probably why there was such a row about the duel fought on Wimbledon Common in 1838 between a draper and the nephew of a tavern-keeper. Many of those who expressed their horror ignored the fact that Mirfin, the draper, was shot and killed, and instead directed their indignation at the fact that people of humble origin had dared to ape their social superiors in trying to settle their differences in a duel with pistols.

Duels were sometimes fought over matters which today seem absurdly trivial such as that which took place in April 1803 when Captain McNamara met Lieutenant-Colonel Montgomery at Primrose Hill: the Captain believed that the military man had insulted his dog. As an officer and a gentleman there was only one possible way of obtaining redress. The duel resulted in the death of Montgomery. Some duels were fought over what were little more than drunken squabbles. Occasionally they were initiated by men seeking to liquidate their debts by finding an excuse to fight a duel with a creditor. What is so generally striking, however, is the politeness and punctiliousness that usually seems to have marked the proceedings and the sincere regrets that were often expressed when one duellist killed his adversary.

Duelling was against the law but juries were markedly reluctant to convict the survivor of a duel in which one of the participants died. The high-born pedigree of many who participated in duels may have had something to do with this, but until the 1780s duelling seems to have been accepted by juries as a perfectly acceptable way for gentlemen to settle their differences. It was viewed as the logical successor to the medieval idea of trial by combat and there were even those who argued that victory in a duel was always won by the participant who had God on his side. By 1800 public opinion had changed and those who fought duels were likely to receive less sympathy from the courts.

No one has computed how many people died in London as the result of duels, but the issues over which they fought had little to do with real 'honour' and much more to do with affronted pride, drunken belligerence and the boredom and general pointlessness of life experienced by many of those who fought them. While undoubtedly there were some real rotters who were killed, duelling led to many completely pointless premature deaths. It is perhaps a blessing that in duels fought with firearms, marksmanship was generally very poor. It was another matter where swords were used: frightful injuries and death often ensued.

Cremorne Pleasure Gardens were situated on a twelve-acre site in Chelsea between the King's Road and the River Thames. They opened for business in 1843 and although starting promisingly, they (like many of London's other pleasure gardens) went into a decline as they attracted disreputable visitors whose vulgar tastes and boorish behaviour deterred more discerning patrons. Cremorne gained a reputation for the daring balloon ascents that took place there. In 1874 a well-known Belgian balloonist by the name of Vincent de Groof announced that he would provide spectators with an additional thrill by not only ascending in a hot-air balloon, but also jumping from it and descending to the ground wearing an outfit with bird-like wings and a tail. To the delight of the crowd all was going according to plan until the wind suddenly changed direction and his colleague in the basket was forced to cut de Groof free. Some of the more callous onlookers cheered even more loudly as de Groof plumetted earthwards, frantically flapping his wings for all he was worth, but to no effect.

Being charitable to the spectators, perhaps they thought it was part of the show. The sexton of St Luke's Church in Chelsea was watching and shouted to de Groof to land in the churchyard. Quite how this would have helped the stricken aeronaut is not clear, even if he had been able to act on the undoubtedly well-meaning advice. It was all in vain anyway because the intrepid balloonist and bird man crash-landed in Sydney Street, Chelsea. He died of his injuries shortly afterwards. Cremorne Gardens shut down three years later.

One of the most notable of London's unburied must be the first wife of Martin van Butchell. The man himself was a successful dentist who became disenchanted with teeth and went on to make a second career as a truss-maker. Although a large percentage of his clients were fashionable and wealthy, he refused to visit them in their homes and insisted that they came to him instead. When not ministering to the rich, he gave his services gratis to the woebegone inmates of Newgate Prison. His first wife died in 1775 and he had her embalmed so skilfully that she looked very lifelike and almost as good as new. He put her on display in his house in Mayfair and charged visitors, of whom there were plenty, to view her. Rumours were rife about why he chose to preserve her in this way but the truth never came out. When showing his strange exhibit to visitors, he always referred to her as 'my dear departed'. Something of an eccentric, van Butchell rode around London on a pony which he painted with either purple spots or black stripes, depending on his mood. His son inherited his mother's cadaver but being unable to find a use for it, he donated it to the Royal College of Surgeons. There it remained until scattered to the four winds by an exploding German bomb in 1941. It never was buried.

The arm of the Grand Junction Canal which runs from Paddington to the River Thames at Limehouse is usually known as the 'Regent's Canal'. Work on it began when the future George IV was acting as regent while his father was indisposed. Along part of its route it skirts Regent's Park. In the early hours of the morning of 2 October 1874 a steam tug set off from the City Road Basin not far from the Angel,

Islington. It was hauling five barges, one of which, the third, was carrying five tons of blasting gunpowder. At five minutes to five, the tug and its attendant barges were passing under Macclesfield Bridge which joins Avenue Road to the circular road inside Regent's Park. There was a blinding flash followed by an eruption of flame, smoke and sparks. Bridge and barges disintegrated. Mud, pieces of timber and lumps of iron took off in all directions. Trees were uprooted and windows were blown in as far as a mile away. People ran, panic-stricken and screaming, hither and thither around the neighbouring streets, thinking the end of the world had come. Three bargemen died and their remains were never found. Questions were asked in Parliament about the transporting of such potentially dangerous cargoes as gunpowder through densely-populated built-up areas. The immediate cause of the explosion was never established.

One of London's most tragic citizens was Joseph Merrick, universally known as 'The Elephant Man'. He was grotesquely disfigured by multiple neurofibromatosis and was forced to earn a demeaning living as an exhibit in a freak show. Despite having an appearance which struck those who looked at him with a mixture of revulsion and pity, he was gentle and sensitive and only wanted to be accepted and liked by his fellow humans. The story of how an eminent surgeon, Sir Frederick Treves, found him and took him under his wing and gave him a home is well-known. Merrick's head was so huge and heavy that he had difficulty holding it up and he was obliged to sleep sitting up in bed with his head resting on his knees. One night he must have achieved what he had always wanted – to sleep in the normal fashion of other people with his head on a pillow. After a life of much suffering, but borne with a great deal of dignity, Merrick died in his sleep. His skeleton has been preserved at the Royal London Hospital.

Another famous preserved skeleton is that of Charles Byrne, the 'Irish Giant'. This may be viewed in the Hunterian Museum housed in the building of the Royal College of Surgeons and Physicians in Lincoln's Inn Fields. Born in 1761, his parents were of normal stature and there was nothing about his appearance as an infant to suggest his future stature. Local salacious gossip, however, had it that his prodigious growth was because his parents had conceived him during a bout of frolicking on the top of an extremely tall haystack.

He was bullied as a child and did not enjoy robust health. As a teenager he was exhibited first around Irish towns and villages and then in various parts of mainland Britain. In Edinburgh he caused a sensation by lighting his pipe directly from a gas street lamp. His manager was one Joe Vance who knew a good product when he saw it and he soon headed off to London with Byrne. Here he proved to be a great draw as a human curiosity being advertised as 8 feet 4 inches tall when in fact he was probably 'just' 7 feet 10 inches. Although he was only twenty-two years of age, some of those who paid good money to view him noted that he was stooped and unhealthy-looking. The public were capricious and soon drifted off in search of alternative titillations. Byrne was particularly galled when he found that he had spawned imitators. One was a fellow countryman called Patrick Cotter who had the effrontery also to call himself the 'Irish Giant'.

Byrne's best days were soon over. The world was a cruel place for a man who had little to offer the world apart from being a giant. Known neither for his razor-sharp intellect nor his fund of witty repartee, Byrne's health, which had never been good, now began deteriorating because of heavy drinking. By the spring of 1783 it was evident that he was a dying man. Many London surgeons were licking their lips at the prospect of obtaining his corpse – what a specimen that would be! The most determined of these was John Hunter who already had a collection of preserved human oddities and Byrne would be its crowning glory if he could only lay his hands on him. Where the advancement of science was concerned, Hunter had few scruples and he employed a man to trail around in Byrne's wake so as to be on hand when the giant died.

Byrne was not too inebriated to be jittery about the fate that might befall him. He knew that Hunter intended to get hold of his remains and he wanted to be allowed to rest in peace and in one whole piece! It must have dawned even on Byrne's befuddled senses that he was worth more dead than alive. He knew that Hunter and various other surgeons were in league with the resurrection men and that no resting place would be safe from their attentions. By now Byrne was a rather pathetic figure forced to spend the last of what little savings he had by making a secret arrangement with some fishermen to take his body when he died and have it buried at sea. Where serious money is concerned, secret arrangements count for little and Byrne's wishes were soon common knowledge. There are various stories of what happened when Byrne obligingly died. The upshot, however, was that Hunter had to spend a large amount of money but he got what he wanted. Byrne's body was delivered to his house in Earl's Court whereupon Hunter, needing to work quickly, boiled the corpse in an enormous kettle. He disposed of the body tissue and all Byrne's other remains because it was the skeleton he was after. To this day the skeleton shows the staining caused by the boiling.

A certain additional poignancy is lent to Byrne's skeleton because close-by stands the skeletal remains of Caroline Crachami. She was born in 1815 and became widely known as the 'Sicilian Fairy'. When she was born she weighed a mere one pound after a full-term gestation. At the age of nine when she died unexpectedly, she was just over 19 inches in height. Her remains too were eagerly sought after and her father was involved in an unseemly wrangle with the doctor who had been exhibiting her and was looking to obtain a good price from the anatomists. Imagine his anguish when, after a diligent search, he found his minute daughter's body already in the process of being anatomised! A scandal blew up but the tiny skeleton eventually went on exhibition in the museum attached to the Royal College of Surgeons. Even before that it had been made the subject of a learned paper by the eminent surgeon Sir Everard Home who used it as an object-lesson in the horrible effects of what was known as 'maternal impression'. This was the theory that some severe trauma experienced by the mother while pregnant could account for physical abnormalities in the child. In the case of Caroline, Home 'explained' that when her mother was four months pregnant, a monkey had secretly entered the caravan in which she was sleeping. When its movements woke her, she moved suddenly and the creature bit her. A similar explanation was offered for the appearance of Joseph Merrick: his mother while pregnant had been nearly run down by an elephant which stampeded out of control during a circus parade. The shock of this had impressed itself on the luckless unborn infant and led to the formation of his singularly pachyderm-like features, or so it was asserted.

Probably the only Londoner to die as the result of trying to stuff a dead chicken was Francis Bacon (1561–1626). He was a politician, writer, philosopher and fatally as it was to prove, an amateur scientist. One very cold, snowy morning he was riding in a coach on Highgate Hill with some friends when he abruptly ordered the driver to stop. Without offering any explanation, he jumped down and rushed into a nearby hovel and bought a chicken from its bemused occupant after giving her an offer she couldn't refuse. Eagerly he killed and disembowelled the fowl before stuffing it with snow. Quite what his friends made of all this is not recorded but Bacon didn't care anyway – he was a zealot in pursuit of scientific knowledge. He wanted to know whether freezing would help to preserve meat. He never did find out because he suddenly felt poorly and was put to bed with a chill. Unfortunately the bed in which he was placed was damp and unaired and Bacon caught pneumonia and died.

When it comes to malicious shenanigans and bizarre deaths among the upper crust, there can be little to beat the murder of Sir Thomas Overbury in 1613. A scheming, ambitious but able man, he was a trusted and probably intimate friend of the vapid Robert Carr, Viscount Rochester, who himself was the favourite, and possibly a lover, of King James I. Carr was bisexual and fell for Frances Howard, the Countess of Essex. At first Overbury encouraged their passion but was greatly put out when the Countess initiated proceedings to dissolve her marriage to the husband she hated, at which point Carr revealed his own intentions of marrying her. In vain did Overbury plead with Carr that Frances was unscrupulous and ruthless, a necromancer and sexual libertarian. She was also exceptionally beautiful. The Howard family was extremely ambitious and resented Overbury's close relationship with Carr which made him privy to much sensitive 'insider' information. Frances especially hated him for trying to prevent her marriage to Carr. The Howards used their influence with the King to get Overbury out of the way by securing a diplomatic appointment for him overseas. But Overbury was no fool – he knew a bribe when he saw one – and refused the job. This made Carr turn against him and he easily persuaded the King to order Overbury to be detained in the Tower of London.

Now the really nasty bit started. The Howards decided that Overbury needed to be silenced permanently. They succeeded in having the existing Lieutenant of The Tower dismissed when they found they could not corrupt him and managed to get Sir Gervase Elwes, an unprincipled crony of theirs, appointed in his place. With his connivance they had another of their creatures, Richard Weston, appointed as Overbury's gaoler with a brief to murder him with poison. Frances had some shady associates who provided a variety of poisons with which his meals were laced. They put arsenic in his salt, mercury in his pork, catharides in his pepper and various acidic substances and metallic poisons in other meals. It did not take long for these potent ingredients to start making their presence felt and Overbury began displaying various distressing symptoms. For fear that the poisons might be discovered, they were administered in smallish doses which only prolonged Overbury's agonies. When he realised what was being done to him he bravely, but perhaps unwisely, threatened to expose those he believed were behind the poisoning. He even hinted that he knew things about the King that would cause a sensation if he made them known. His enemies, by now extremely concerned to save their own skins, kept a close guard to prevent him receiving or despatching any messages. Overbury was tough but the poisons he had assimilated took their toll. Understandably cautious about eating and drinking, he wasted away into a human skeleton covered in sores. Still he did not die and only succumbed excruciatingly when mercuric chloride was administered with an enema.

The Howard faction decided that the evidence needed to be disposed of as quickly as possible and Overbury was interred before the day of his death was out. The Howards were jubilant and Frances got what she wanted: her first marriage was nullified on the grounds of non-consummation by a jury of middle-aged ladies of dubious probity who were easily bribed to attest to Frances' virginity after they had examined the relevant parts of her anatomy. That little technicality being dealt with, Frances then married Carr who had just been made Earl of Somerset in a splendid ceremony paid for by the King. Then the rumours started. The Howards and Carr had plenty of enemies. Elwes and various minor players in this grisly drama were arrested, questioned and summarily hanged. Frances decided on pre-emptive action. She made a full confession – she was pregnant and pregnant women were not executed – and she and Carr were placed in the

Tower. There were widespread calls for them to be executed for their dastardly crime and they were condemned to death but James, never one to allow justice to get in the way of his friends, let them stew for a while before ordering their release. Anyway, James had never liked Overbury, probably being jealous of his friendship with Carr. Perhaps there was divine retribution because the evil Frances, Countess of Somerset, died soon afterwards of cancer. It was an agonising death.

Edward III (r. 1327–1377) was everyone's idea of how a king of the age of chivalry should have looked. He was a fine upstanding man around 6 feet in height, well-built, muscular and sinewy. He was an avid if sometimes reckless devotee of jousting and a formidable opponent at that sport. Inevitably he received some injuries while participating in tournaments, including head injuries, which may account for the mental deterioration that he suffered late in life. He had a happy marriage with Philippa of Hainault, but as was the way at the time, he took advantage of his social pre-eminence by taking various lovers. The most prominent of these was Alice Perrers who some accuse of giving him a venereal infection. Distraught after the death of his mother Isabella in 1369, a terminal decline seems to have set in, especially when his son, the Black Prince, developed a debilitating disease from which he died. During his last months Edward was greatly enfeebled and he died at Sheen, just outside London. He had grown a luxuriant beard and long flowing hair probably because he had simply lost interest in his appearance. A wooden effigy was made of him after his death. The face was lifelike and showed the mouth twisted with a facial paralysis. This supports the theory that the King had a stroke in his latter years and helps to explain his sudden and severe physical and mental decline. This man, so warlike in his youth, lies in Westminster Abbey and is depicted in a superb bronze effigy. His appearance is that of an old man of peace with flowing locks and beard and an expression of great serenity.

Mary I (r. 1553–1558) has not generally had a good press and has frequently been portrayed as an embittered and vindictive religious bigot. A judgement on the role she played in history is outside the remit of this book and suffice it is to say that her death was not accompanied by great outpourings of grief from most of her subjects. Attractive and vivacious when young, she had become careworn and somewhat shrewish by the time of her marriage in 1554 at the age of thirty-eight. Within months, Mary was displaying many desperately wished-for signs of pregnancy. No wish-fulfilment was achieved on this or a later occasion and she was totally bereft when her husband, with ill-disguised haste, returned to Spain for the last time. Everything was going wrong for Mary in her personal life and in her role as Queen. She lost weight and appetite but developed considerable enlargement of the abdomen in a grotesque parody of her fervent wish to pass on her genes. Current medical opinion is that she probably had cancer of the ovaries or possibly of the uterus. She was forty-two when she went into a final decline with long bouts of semi-consciousness interspersed by brief periods of lucidity during which she seems to have come to terms with her imminent mortality. There was little love lost between Mary and her half-sister, Elizabeth, who succeeded her on the throne. It is perhaps to Elizabeth's credit that she paid for Mary to be buried in an appropriately fine tomb in Westminster Abbey. Mary's heart was removed and placed into a casket where it was later joined by Elizabeth's heart. Elizabeth's tomb is adjacent. The two women, related by blood but disparate in so many other ways, are united in their last sleep.

Charles I (r. 1625–1649), was a small man imbued with an enormous sense of his own importance. This was a natural accompaniment to his concept of the divine role and rights of kings. The stages by which the events unfolded that led to his being condemned to death for high treason have been examined and re-examined by historians and are not relevant to the present discussion. Anger reverberated around Europe about the heinous crime of commoners condemning God's anointed to death. There were rumours of punitive interventions from overseas and many at home found the whole prospect an appalling one. However, having gone so far, his enemies had little option but to go ahead with the execution. The King displayed both courage and dignity on his way to and at the scaffold. The date was 30 January 1649 and the place was Whitehall. A low block was used for humanitarian purposes – it places the neck in such a way that it should be cleanly severed with one blow of the axe. This is indeed what happened and the King died instantaneously. The watching crowd emitted an eerie groan when the deed was done and then several people who had paid large sums of money for the privilege, came forward and soaked items of clothing in the King's blood and even prized off pieces of blood-stained timber from the scaffold. An item imbued with the King's blood was considered to be a powerful talisman. In 1813, when the tomb of George III was being erected in Westminster Abbey, workmen accidentally broke into the vault of Henry VIII where the body of Charles had been placed back in 1649. The opportunity to view the remains of the executed King was too good to miss and one of the royal physicians, Sir Henry Halford, examined the contents of Charles's coffin. Somehow, Halford obtained the King's fourth cervical vertebra and had it mounted for use as a salt cellar. If this was not indignity enough, it seems that one of the workmen managed to remove one of Henry VIII's finger bones which he made into a knife handle.

William III (r. 1689–1702) was not a merry monarch. He never seems to have found life in England very congenial and he always preferred the company of Dutchmen to that of his own subjects. William was a lifelong sufferer from asthma and although he seized the opportunity to be joint ruler of England very eagerly, he soon found that the damp climate of the British Isles exacerbated his respiratory problems. The death of his wife Mary from smallpox in 1694 affected him badly and he descended into a more-or-less constant state of gloom. He developed swellings in his legs, his breathing deteriorated and he became extremely irritable. In February 1702 he was riding from Kensington to Hampton Court when his horse stumbled on a molehill and he was precipitated to the ground, breaking his right collarbone. Complications ensued including pneumonia which made an existing heart condition more chronic and he is likely to have undergone a terminal pulmonary embolism. His death went largely unlamented, but the maker of the molehill which started the process gave rise to what became the traditional Jacobite toast: 'To the little brown gentleman in the velvet waistcoat.'

George II (r. 1727–1760) was a dapper little man who carried himself well. He married Caroline of Ansbach with whom he seems to have been genuinely in love but he had an eye for the ladies and would probably have had even more affairs had his health been better. The complaints that he suffered from were of the sort that he really wouldn't want to tell new sexual partners about. He had a disease of the gall bladder with sporadic bouts of severe pain, recurrent excruciating piles and a fistula which involved an infected track from the rectum to the buttock. Problems in the same general area were eventually to bring him down. He got up at six in the morning on 12 October 1760 in St James's Palace and, as was his custom, drank some chocolate before heading straight into what was coyly called his 'close-stool'. His valet, used to hearing his master making straining noises on account of his constipation, was surprised to hear what he thought was a louder then usual royal breaking of wind. He was then thoroughly alarmed to hear loud groans coming from the close-stool. Increasingly concerned for the King's welfare, the valet eventually decided to enter the private chamber. He found that the King had collapsed unconscious and cut his face badly as he did so. He was lifted and carefully placed in his bed but it was clear that he was beyond help. George II had died from a ruptured ventricle of the heart caused by aortitis. The King's medical attendants believed that the condition was probably syphilitic in origin. George II was by no means the only British King to have syphilis. Technicalities apart, however, he remains the only King of England to have died while sitting on what is colloquially known as 'The Throne'.

Only a handful of commoners, and even fewer of those of royal blood, have been killed by a cricket ball. This is the doubtful distinction that befell Frederick, Prince of Wales, the eldest son of George II. Frederick, who was known to all and sundry as 'Poor Fred', never really had a chance in life. His father and mother hated him from birth. George described his son as a 'half-witted coxcomb' and on another occasion as: 'the greatest ass, the greatest liar, the greatest canaille and the greatest beast in the whole world and we would heartily wish he was out of it.' For his part, Frederick described his father as 'an obstinate self-indulgent miserly martinet with an insatiable sexual appetite.' Given this antipathy, it must have come as a great relief to all concerned when in 1751 Frederick unwittingly accorded with his father's wishes. The Prince was a keen cricketer and owned his own pitch at Cliveden in Buckinghamshire; it was while playing there that he received a hard blow on the chest with a cricket ball. An abscess developed which later burst and brought about his death.

It is said that when his father was told of Frederick's death, he didn't even look up from his card game.

There may seem to be a disproportionate number of members of royalty whose deaths were odd, but of course their deaths tend to be better documented than those of commoners. We hope, however, that we have managed to provide enough examples from other elements of London's population as well to give at least a flavour of the strange circumstances under which they died.

5
Churchyards and Other Burial Places

> 'Tis now the very witching time of night,
> When churchyards yawn, and hell itself breathes out
> Contagion to this world.
>
> William Shakespeare, *Hamlet*

Churchyards elicit strong emotional responses. What may be a haven of peace and serenity amidst the hurly-burly of the metropolis, alive on a hot sunny day with the lazy buzz of insects and the soporific cooing of pigeons, changes, for atavistic and barely understood reasons, into a place that most of us shun during the hours of darkness.

The churchyards and burial places of London stand as evidence of the capital's past and also of its continuity. Old London contained around 140 medieval places of worship of which over half still exist in some form today. While some churches have lost their churchyards, examples can be shown of churchyards that have survived their churches. An example is St Botolph in Aldersgate, EC1.

How to dispose satisfactorily of the dead has been a problem that has always exercised the minds of human beings. The first inhumations or burials in the ground in Britain are thought by archaeologists to have been in about 24380 BC, at a time when cremation was by far the more common practice. In the Neolithic era (*c.* 4000–2400 BC) bones were often interred in chambers inside mounds known as long barrows. In the Bronze Age (*c.* 2000–500 BC) individual burials became more common and the size of some of the sites and the quality of the grave goods they contain are clear evidence of the existence of class and social status, factors which are evident throughout the history of funerals and dealing with death. By the time of Roman settlement in Britain, inhumation seems to have become the usual method for disposal of the dead.

The origin of churchyards is obscure. Many of them undoubtedly stand where pre-Christian forms of worship took place. Ancient burial sites were frequently used by missionaries as places for spreading the Christian word. In AD 601 Pope Gregory stated that pagan shrines should not be destroyed but instead should be sanctified by the Church; pre-Christian altars were to be replaced by Christian ones. It was natural that many of them would develop permanent buildings in which a variety of religious functions could be performed and many were located adjacent to or actually within land that had been used previously for non-Christian burials. Sometimes crosses were erected to mark the place at which Christian worship regularly took place before a church was built on the site. Later on in medieval times virtually all churchyards would have possessed a cross and these symbolised the sanctity of the churchyard and acted as a collective memorial to the anonymous dead buried there.

The churchyards of London today are largely isolated from the communities in which they are located. It often requires a deliberate effort to enter a churchyard and in so doing one may feel cut off from the surrounding clamour, but this was not always the case. In medieval times the church, or at least its nave, and the ground surrounding the church were at the absolute heart of the community. The churchyards of London and everywhere else in England were the place in which the spiritual and indeed much of the secular activity of the populace took place. In fact churches and their immediate environs would have been positively bustling and noisy for much of the time. Markets were frequently held in churchyards and inside the nave of the church in inclement weather. Hucksters bawled their wares and bargain-hunters haggled noisily over prices. The flat tops of table tombs made excellent places for vendors to display their goods. People negotiating financial transactions often bargained in the churchyard and then finalised the deal in the porch, which was considered to be an appropriate place for making a binding agreement.

Some London parish churches housed the activities of the local guilds. One example was St Helen's in Bishopsgate which had strong connections with the Merchant Taylors. Sometimes the archery butts were located in the churchyard. The longbow was medieval England's ultimate deterrent and men were required to practice their skills regularly. Itinerant entertainers performed in churchyards. Miracle plays were staged. Football, wrestling and other sporting activities took place there. On feasts and festivals, the place was *en fête* and virtually the entire population would converge on church and churchyard. There would be much merrymaking and bawdy behaviour of the sort that accords ill with what we regard, even in a secular age, as the sanctity of hallowed ground. The Church authorities frowned on much of this activity although the local priest often encouraged it because he might be able to do some fundraising, by providing refreshment, for example. Certain parts of the rituals associated with baptism, marriage and burial took place in the churchyard. All in all, there was never a dull moment.

Class and status have been factors in death as much as in life. Although Death has been described as the 'Great Leveller' and the Church made pious statements about the equality of all in the eyes of God and about the sanctity of poverty, the reality was more hardnosed. Both the place of burial and the nature of the memorial commemorating the deceased closely reflected his or her wealth and influence. Members of the medieval lay social elite were keen to be buried within the precincts of a religious establishment and they were prepared to 'buy their way in' with generous benefactions. Very senior clerics would also expect to be interred intermurally, that is, within the main church building of the cathedral, church or monastery with which they were associated. Their relative status can often be gauged by their proximity or otherwise to the high altar or to any prominent reliquaries. The grandeur of their funerary memorials is of course another factor reflecting status. Most lay people were buried in the churchyard in what by later standards were shallow graves. They were usually unmarked until the fashion for headstones developed.

There may have been as many as fifty monasteries inside and outside the walls of the City of London before the Dissolution in the late 1530s. Many had cemeteries largely for the interment of the deceased members of their communities. Of these burial grounds, few traces survive although spaces which may have once been used for burials can still be seen at Christ's Hospital in Newgate Street and at St Bartholomew the Great in Smithfield. The churchyard of St Catherine Cree, Leadenhall Street, is the successor to the burial-ground of Holy Trinity Priory. The little churchyard of St Martin Outwich, Camomile Street, covers some of the space allotted for burials at the former Priory of St Augustine Papey. St Helen's churchyard on Bishopsgate Street probably stands on a site previously used for interments in St Helen's Priory. The churchyard of St Mary Magdalene, Bermondsey, may cover parts of the cemetery attached to the great Bermondsey Abbey of the Cluniac order.

From the Reformation, churchyards began to be used much less for secular purposes and almost exclusively for burials. By the sixteenth century the churchyard was being used for the burial of the rich as well as the poor and funerary memorials, where they survive, provide much evidence of the social distinctions and the mores of their time. There were favoured sites within churchyards: the rich had a preference for their burial places to be close to the main paths so that they could be seen. Their family members were often interred in close proximity to each other. The north side of the church was known as 'the Devil's side' and considered unlucky. Before the nineteenth century when the overcrowding of churchyards became a major problem in London and elsewhere, these parts were usually reserved for strangers, paupers, unbaptised infants, those who had died a violent death and for suicides.

To remind people of the imminence of the afterlife, the gates to churchyards were often decorated with various gruesome devices. St Nicholas, Deptford and St Olave, Hart Street displayed skulls; those at St Olave being impaled on spikes. St Catherine Cree had a skeleton lolling malevolently in a pediment. St Olave is believed to be the church mentioned by Dickens in *The Uncommercial Traveller*. What he must have seen sounds daunting:

> As I stand peeping in through the iron gates and rails, I can peel the rusty metal off, like bark from an old tree. The illegible tombstones are all lopsided, the grave-mounds lost their shape in the rains of a hundred years ago ... One of my best loved churchyards, I call the churchyard of St Ghastly Grim ... It is a small, small churchyard with a ferocious strong spiked iron gate, like a jail. This gate is ornamented with skulls and crossbones, larger than life, wrought in stone; [and] thrust through and through with iron spears.

Churchyards need to be differentiated from cemeteries. Many parish churches date back at least in part to as early as AD 1000. The churchyards in which they stand may be even older as sites of worship. Cemeteries, on the other hand, are a later attempt, usually from the nineteenth century, to solve the problems of shortage of space for burials in churchyards and the desire of Nonconformists, Jews and others to run their own burial grounds.

Before the rapid growth in population and the great expansion of the urban areas which we associate with the Industrial Revolution, churchyards had been able to deal with the normal rate of burials. In the eighteenth century, the birth-rate and the population may have grown at unprecedented speed, but there was also, paradoxically, a marked increase in death rates. Existing churchyards were becoming grossly overcrowded. Some, such as St Paul's, had been in continuous use for the best part of 2,000 years. Bodies were piled one on top of the other and the increasing use of coffins meant that interments took up considerably more space. The ground level of many churchyards was well above that of the foundations of the church and of adjacent streets. A handful of Jewish burial grounds and others attached to Nonconformist chapels had come into use in London, but with about 40,000 deaths occurring each year, matters had literally reached breaking point and the situation was not just an administrative scandal but a potent health hazard. One contemporary expert reckoned that 2,572,580 cubic feet of noxious gas was emitted annually from the putrefying corpses buried in London. Miasmic theories about the spread of disease were still prevalent and so there were many people who believed that the loathsome stench emanating from so many burial grounds was at least partly responsible for the scourge of cholera.

One response to the overcrowding of burial places was the removal of human remains to charnel houses or bone holes, sometimes known as ossuaries. There was an ossuary and chapel in the churchyard of Old St Paul's; another was at St Bride's on Fleet Street. Sometimes associated with them were endowed charnel-chapels where prayers were offered for the souls of the human remains interred there.

As early as the seventeenth century, John Evelyn (1620–1706), the famous diarist, expressed his concern that burials in London would eventually exceed the space available for interment and he proposed the creation of an extensive, purpose-built burial ground north of the City. Sir Christopher Wren (1632–1723) advocated the building of a number of well-designed cemeteries around the periphery of London.

After the English Reformation, intermural burials became fashionable. Sometimes the burials were in family vaults. Headstones came into use in the sixteenth century and could be afforded by people of relatively humble social status. This drove many of those who were better off to emphasise their affluence by being buried inside the church. Intramural burial became virtually synonymous with social superiority. This in turn meant that not only was the churchyard overcrowded but the church as well. Sometimes recourse would be made to burial in vaults under the nave (the main body of the church). Enterprising clergymen used intramural burial as a source of income. At St Alphege in Greenwich, relatives paid for no fewer than 400 coffins to be placed in the rector's vault between 1718 and 1800. At the church of St Peter le Poer in Broad Street EC2, which was demolished in 1907, the intramural burial fees in 1838 ranged from the most basic accommodation at £18 5s 6d to 100 guineas for a vault with accommodation for four. Further intramural burials were forbidden by national legislation in 1850.

English burial practices lagged well behind those employed on the Continent and they were put to shame when the vast landscaped and splendidly appointed Pere Lachaise Cemetery was opened outside Paris. Three grand schemes for London were proposed. The first was largely a copy of the Pere Lachaise Cemetery and included special provision against the depredations of the resurrectionists. This cemetery was to be in the Primrose Hill area. The second scheme was for a huge 'Grand National Cemetery' in the vicinity of either Primrose Hill or Shooters Hill. A major feature of this proposal was a series of grandiloquent buildings modelled on examples from ancient Greece and Rome, such as the Erectheum on the Athenian Acropolis. The allocation of burial space in this cemetery would have constituted a celebration of the class system: the centrepiece was to be a space reserved for the so-called great and good. Placed around them would have been a larger area given over to the burial of people of middling rank. The largest section of all, around the periphery, would have been devoted to those in humbler social positions. The third proposal was the most extraordinary. It envisaged an enormous pyramid, the top of which would have been higher than St Paul's Cathedral. This was to be located in the Primrose Hill district and would have contained 5,167,104 alcoves in an enormous structure not unlike a honeycomb. It was believed that such a building would virtually eliminate issues of security and provide a dignified and hygienic solution to the question of how to dispose of the dead. This building which would have totally dominated the north London skyline was, of course, never built, nor indeed were the other two, but the fact that they were put forward as serious suggestions is evidence of the debate that was taking place on what was seen as an increasingly urgent matter.

A prominent critic of the existing situation was George Walker, a doctor with a surgery in Drury Lane, who systematically visited, observed and noted what he regarded as bad practice in London's graveyards. In his district there were a number of grossly overcrowded burial grounds crammed in cheek-by-jowl with slum housing and small industrial premises. With the exception of Jewish and Quaker burial grounds, the Anglican, Nonconformist and private sites were overcrowded, unseemly and presented health hazards. Walker's findings were published in 1839 in a book with the rather ponderous title: *Gatherings from Grave-Yards, Particularly those of London with a concise History of the Modes of Interment among different Nations, from the earliest Periods; and a Detail of dangerous and fatal Results produced by the unwise and revolting Custom of inhuming the Dead in the midst of the*

Living. He recorded all manner of bad practices and laced his report with such horrors as:

> In making a grave a body, partly decomposed, was dug up, and placed on the surface, at the side, slightly covered with earth; a mourner stepped upon it, the loosened skin peeled off, he slipped forward, and had nearly fallen into the grave.

Of a churchyard in Whitechapel, he wrote that 'the ground is so densely crowded as to present one entire mass of human bones and putrefaction'. St Anne's churchyard, Soho, was no better:

> Here in this place of 'Christian burial', you may see human heads, covered with hair; and here, in this 'consecrated ground', are human bodies with flesh still adhering to them. On the north side, a man was digging a grave; he was quite drunk, so indeed were all the grave diggers we saw ... a child's coffin, which had stopped the man's progress, had been cut, longitudinally, right in half; and there lay the child ... wrapped in its shroud, resting upon the part of the coffin which remained. The shroud was but little decayed.

For sheer unadulterated horror, nothing equalled what Walker found in the burial place beneath Enon Chapel in Clement's Lane EC4, a private speculative venture set up in 1823. The burial chamber was separated from the chapel above only by floorboards. Walker graphically described repellent black flies living off the putrefaction of the bodies, which appeared in untold numbers in the summer during which the stench was simply intolerable. The children attending the Sunday school held in the chapel called them 'body bugs'. Rats by the hundred infested the neighbourhood. There were rich pickings for them.

Walker and other critics spotlighted the activities of private speculative cemetery companies as being especially heinous. To attract business they undercut the burial charges of the parish churches. In doing so, they stooped to such dubious practices as using men to officiate at funerals who were not in holy orders, employing gravediggers who could only work when inebriated and placing bodies in graves so shallow that it was simple for thieves to steal the metal handles and lead components of coffins, to remove wood for sale as firewood, and worst of all, to remove bones which were ground down and used as fertilizer.

In 1846 Walker published evidence that undertakers at the Spa Fields burial site in Clerkenwell clandestinely but regularly burnt corpses and coffins so as to free up more space for new interments.

For Walker, the solution was clear: what was needed was the total removal of the dead from the proximity of the living. In 1844 he established the Metropolitan Association for Abolition of Burials in Towns. No wonder he became known as 'Graveyard Walker'.

Charles Dickens found a macabre source of interest in burial places. In *Bleak House* he has one of his characters, 'Jo', gazing appalled through the iron railings into a graveyard:

> 'There!' says Jo, pointing, 'Over yinder, among them pile of bones, and close to that there kitchen winder! They put him very nigh the top. They was obliged to stamp upon it to git it in ... Look at that rat! Hi! Look! There he goes! Ho! Into the ground!'[1]

Provincial cities had led the way with the establishment of privately-funded cemeteries for those who could afford to pay; Liverpool had gained one in 1825 and Glasgow in 1832. In 1830 the London Cemetery Company was formed. The first result of its enterprises was the great cemetery at Kensal Green, founded in 1832, measuring 54 acres and then well outside the built-up parts of London. Its services were not cheap. A mausoleum could be secured for at least £1,000, a brick vault was available for £50 and even the most basic burial plot cost 30 shillings. What followed was a battle of architectural styles for funerary buildings which reflected the contemporary battle among those designing churches and public buildings between the advocates of what can loosely be described as the Greek Revival and the Gothic Revival styles. The Cemetery Company applied to the commemoration of the dead the same laissez-faire practice that prevailed in the world of economic and social policy. So the funerary architecture at Kensal Green is itself a monument to economic individualism as well as to stylistic eclecticism. Ecumenicalism was also evident at Kensal Green, not, it must be said, from motives of religious idealism, but out of a desire to maximise income by widening the potential clientele while restricting it to those who had the depth of pocket necessary to reserve a site. Some of the later private cemeteries provided burial plots at prices affordable to the less well-off. All may have been equal in the eyes of the Almighty, but inevitably social distinctions were honoured and there were clear demarcations between those parts given over to the burial of the commonality and the interment of those who had enjoyed greater material success in their lives.

The original plan for Kensal Green envisaged an exercise in medieval fantasy with a huge Gothic chapel, walls with towers and crenellations and even a working mock Gothic water gate. The intention was that funeral parties would be able to arrive at the cemetery on a branch of the Grand Junction Canal. Kensal Green became one of the sights of London and remains the *sine qua non* for those who are fans of Victorian funerary architecture.

The building of Kensal Green by no means eliminated the issue of how to bury London's dead, a problem which intensified daily because of the growth of London's population and also because of the mass deaths which occurred as a result of the outbreak of epidemic diseases through the 1830s and 1840s. Cholera was particularly prevalent and in 1832, for example, 196 bodies were interred in a burial ground opened up in Davenant Road, Whitechapel, after a localised but extremely virulent outbreak.

Edwin Chadwick (1800–1890), famous as the author of the ground-breaking *Report on the Sanitary Condition of the Labouring Population of Great Britain*, published in 1842, argued in a subsidiary report, 'Interment in Towns', that the disposal of the dead must not be left to private enterprise. He brought his usual thoroughgoing and meticulous scrutiny to bear on what developed into an examination of the whole issue of urban mortality, especially among the working class. He recorded many cases of corpses being kept unburied for ten days or a fortnight while the bereaved relations tried to scrape together the money for a funeral. Chadwick drew on the evidence of many witnesses, one of whom was an undertaker in the Blackfriars district. He described graphically the appalling health hazards that could occur where a cadaver was kept for some time in the one living room of a working-class hovel:

> In cases of rapid decomposition of persons dying in full habit there is much liquid; and the coffin is tapped to let it out. I have known them to keep the

corpse after the coffin has been tapped twice, which has, of course, produced a disagreeable effluvium. This liquid generated animal life very rapidly; and within six hours after a coffin has been tapped, if the liquid escapes, maggots ... are seen crawling about. I have frequently seen them crawling about the floor of a room inhabited by the labouring classes, and about the tressels on which the tapped coffin is sustained. In such rooms the children are frequently left whilst the widow is out making arrangements connected with the funeral. And the widow herself lives there with the children. I frequently find them altogether in a small room with a large fire.

Another witness, an undertaker from Whitechapel, varies the theme:

When the corpse is uncovered, or the coffin is open, females will hang over it. A widow who hung over the body of her husband, caught the disease of which he died. The doctor told her she must have kissed or touched the body: she died, leaving seven orphans ... A young man died not long since, and his body rapidly decomposed. His sister, a fine healthy girl, hung over the corpse and kissed it; in three weeks she died also.

While some of the conclusions of this undertaker might not be scientifically verifiable, Chadwick was clearly concerned not just with the physical but also the psychological effects of this ongoing close relationship between the living and the dead. He was perceptive enough to identify poverty as the main villain of the piece and as far as he was concerned, the prices of the services provided by undertakers were exorbitant and scandalous.

Chadwick's proposed remedy was a radical one. He wanted central government to provide national cemeteries as part of a programme whereby the State would take responsibility for the nation's dead from the deathbed until they were safely interred in their graves. His report dealt with the issue on a national scale but as far as London was concerned he argued that future burials in London should be in what he called 'National Cemeteries'. An enlarged Kensal Green would become the 'Great Western Metropolitan Cemetery'. This was very appropriate because it was just a stone's throw from the Great Western Railway's main line into and out of Paddington. A 'Great

Eastern Metropolitan Cemetery' would be established at Abbey Wood, to the east of Woolwich. Access to this cemetery would be via the River Thames and Chadwick spoke airily about the building of a fleet of steamboats which would be able to transport up to ninety-six corpses a day to Abbey Wood. While Chadwick was respected for his hard work and undoubted integrity, he was disliked for his dogged persistence and because he could be extremely boring. He lived up to his reputation by bombarding all those in influential positions with letters or, when possible, personal harangues outlining the virtues and the minutiae of his scheme. Chadwick's excessive zeal made his critics and enemies determined that he was not going to get his own way on this issue. They cited medical 'experts' who pointed out that if the proposals were to go through, the decomposing corpses buried at the Great Eastern Cemetery would produce over three million cubic feet of toxic gases or miasmas which could easily poison the inhabitants of London, so close by. A minimum of twenty-four miles from the metropolis was needed as a safety margin, they argued.

Chadwick's scheme did not go ahead. Nevertheless, he was a powerful advocate of statism and the 'force' was with him, as they say. Private enterprise was under pressure because it had clearly failed to provide answers to the burial issue as well as to so many other aspects of public health or the 'sanitary question'. Chadwick was a leading force behind the first Public Health Act which was passed in 1848. This provided for the creation of a central board of health with powers to create local boards up and down the country which would deal with public health issues in the areas under their jurisdiction. These issues included the disposal of the dead. Initially it was a permissive act. The act was not well-received and did not apply to London, extremely powerful vested interests seeing to that. Instead London was placed under the authority of the Metropolitan Commission of Sewers. For all that, the Public Health Act was immensely important as official recognition of the existence of social problems that could only be tackled through agencies of central government.

In 1849 London suffered a particularly severe visitation of cholera which only emphasised the inadequacy and inefficiency of existing methods of dealing with the dead in the metropolis. The state of burial places continued to be an issue and in 1850 the Metropolitan

Interments Act was passed which gave the Board of Health powers to create new cemeteries, and to forbid further burials in churchyards which were full up. Remarkably, given the economic philosophy of the time, the Act had provision for the compulsory purchase of private cemeteries. In practice, the act was not very effective. Approaches were made to buy Brompton and Nunhead cemeteries but in the event only Brompton was purchased and therefore went on to have the distinction of being the only London cemetery to be owned by the State. Chadwick's dreams lay shattered – he had ruffled too many feathers. In 1854 even the Board of Health lost its identity.

The problem of burying London's dead did not go away just because Chadwick was put out to grass. Ironically, it was private enterprise that soon came forward with a scheme for an absolutely enormous cemetery to be built on a greenfield site at Brookwood near Woking in Surrey. In 1852 the London Necropolis and National Mausoleum Company bought the 2,000-acre site and planned, laid out and landscaped what to this day remains the largest cemetery in Britain. Most of those laid to rest at Brookwood were, at that time, from south and east London.

Also in 1852 what became known as the Metropolitan Burial Act was enacted. This abolished the Metropolitan Burial district and the responsibility of the General Board of Health for burial in London. Powers were instituted to prevent interment in any place in London where it was considered that such burials might be inimical to public health. No new burial ground could be opened in, or within two miles of, London without ministerial approval. Parishes could establish Burial Boards funded from the Poor Rate to buy land for use as cemeteries including unconsecrated ground for nonconformists. The City of London was given its own Burial Board and intramural burial was prohibited. A locally-devolved system of public cemeteries was put into place as opposed to the centralised system which Chadwick had so tirelessly advocated.

The Burial Boards soon got to work. The vestry of St Pancras was first off the mark and the result in 1854 was the purchase of a site at Finchley Common which in 1877 was extended to become the St Pancras and Islington Cemetery. This went on to become the largest of the Burial Board cemeteries in London. Shortly afterwards, also in 1854, the St Marylebone in East End Road, N3, the Westminster in Uxbridge Road were established, and the South Metropolitan Cemetery Company's premises at Norwood were extended. In 1899 the Local Government Act created twenty-eight metropolitan borough councils under the umbrella of the London County Council and they took over responsibility for burials within the metropolis.

The success of Kensal Green spawned many imitators including, among the best known, Norwood, Brompton, Highgate, Nunhead, Abney Park and Tower Hamlets. Each of these is enormously interesting and has its own distinctive character, but no detailed historical or architectural description of these cemeteries will be attempted here because there is a wealth of published material dealing with Victorian burial in general and with individual cemeteries. The best general surveys are probably those by Curl[2] and Meller,[3] while a good example of the second genre has been written by Barker.[4]

An influential voice in cemetery design was that of John Claudius Loudon (1783–1843). He was a landscape designer who brought his skills to bear on the planning of 'gardens of rest'. In 1843 he published *On the laying out, planting and managing of Cemeteries and on the improvement of Churchyards*. He recommended a systematic approach to the number of graves to be provided per acre and to the drainage and upkeep of cemeteries. As far as he was concerned, Kensal Green had paid insufficient attention to drainage and this was having a damaging effect. He praised Abney Park for its trees and indeed he laid a great emphasis on designing and maintaining London's cemeteries as public amenities, to be enjoyed in much the same way as Londoners enjoyed their existing royal parks.

Not all religious groups wanted their burials to take place on land consecrated by the Church of England. Nonconformists had their own burial sites and these were often small and attached to the places where they worshipped. Most have disappeared but one of the largest remaining and most interesting is Bunhill Fields. An added distinction is that it is the only cemetery within the City of London. It seems that in the sixteenth century it became a repository for bones from the charnel house of Old St Paul's Cathedral, at which time it became known as 'Bonehill'. In the seventeenth century it became a burial ground for dissenters. Among its most illustrious occupants is William

Blake (1757–1827), poet, mystic and artist. He has a monument but the specific location of his interment at Bunhill Fields is unknown.

London's many Jews required their own burial places and some of them appeared very early on. In Alderney Road, Whitechapel E1, for example, is a cemetery dating back to 1697 which catered for the local Ashkenazi community. Another close by, surrounded by a forbidding high brick wall topped with broken glass and easy to miss, is in Brady Street. This was opened in 1761. Judaic law required space between coffins and insisted on graves being at least 6 feet from the surface and meant that their burial grounds never became as overcrowded and hazardous to health as those of the Church of England. London's Sephardic Jews also had their own places of burial and there are two, both tiny, in Mile End Road, E1. One of them, the Jewish Old Sephardic Cemetery, was opened in 1657 and is the oldest surviving Jewish cemetery in Britain.

A common practice was the re-interment of human remains from earlier burial places in later cemeteries. Many churches in the City of London and in inner-city areas elsewhere around London suffered from depopulation and declining congregations and were demolished, their burial grounds being closed and their contents removed and relocated to purpose-built cemeteries. An example is the City of London Cemetery in E12, a huge place founded in 1856. It contains human remains from the churchyards of St Andrew, Holborn; St Sepulchre, Newgate; Christ's Hospital Burial Ground, Newgate Street and Newgate Prison, which was demolished in 1900. The New Southgate Cemetery, N11 has the reinterred remains of bodies previously buried at the Savoy Chapel in the Strand and St Michael Bassishaw in Basinghall Avenue, EC2.

Special burial places were needed during serious outbreaks of pestilence. When the Black Death was at its height in London in 1349, the need to inter the huge numbers of dead led to new sites being brought into use in the form of communal burial pits. It is known that one of these was where the Charterhouse now stands in EC1 not far from the Church of St Bartholomew the Great in Smithfield.

The Great Plague reached its height in August and September 1665. Daniel Defoe, in *A Journal of the Plague Year*, estimated that 100,000 died during this outbreak. He mentions Londoners afflicted by the plague wandering out of the City in despair and confusion and sometimes collapsing and dying after only a mile or two. The people nearby would then dig a rough-and-ready grave and push them into it unceremoniously with long-handed poles which enabled them to keep the victims at a distance. This meant that many unrecorded burials took place in the environs of London. Some certainly took place at Stoke Newington. Generally, however, huge pits were dug and bodies simply thrown into them without coffins or grave-clothes. One of the most important of these pits was in Aldgate Churchyard. It was over 20 feet deep and 1,114 bodies are known to have been placed in it between 6 and 20 September 1665. Other sites where plague pits existed include Seward Street, EC1; Holwell Row, EC2; Moorfields, EC2; Park Street, SE1 and another close to the present Golden Square, W1. Dozens of others existed, some recorded and others unknown. From time to time, excavations for new buildings reveal human remains in quantities suggesting the presence of a plague pit.

In the 1850s there seems to have been a general sense that the nation needed a more appropriate last resting place for its most illustrious citizens than that afforded by Westminster Abbey and its motley and overcrowded collection of memorials and interred remains. Various suggestions were put forward including one by Sydney Smirke for a 'National Edifice to Receive the Monuments to Illustrious Men', to be sited close to the Serpentine in Hyde Park. This building would have borne some resemblance to a scaled-down version of Salisbury Cathedral. Nothing came of this proposal nor of the suggestion that part of the new Palace of Westminster should be devoted to commemorating the lives and housing the remains of the country's most worthy citizens.

The feeling that Westminster was an appropriate location for a national mausoleum did not go away and debates continued. The Golden Jubilee of Queen Victoria in 1887 came and went and still no decision had been made so recourse was had to that stalwart bastion of indecision, delay and obfuscation – a Royal Commission. The Commission's deliberations were prolonged and came to nothing because of the country's preoccupation with the Boer War. In 1903 a proposal for a 'National Monument' in the shape of a pyramid emerged once again. Artists' impressions show a structure of truly monumental ugliness, which was to be located in Hyde Park. More interest was generated by the 'Imperial Monumental Halls', the name tentatively proposed for a scheme that was the brainchild of John Pollard Seddon and Edward B. Lamb. Apart from the proposed name, there was nothing else tentative about the proposal. The building would have been dominated by a great Gothic steeple with an openwork spire reaching 550 feet and totally overpowering Big Ben and the Victoria Tower of the Palace of Westminster nearby. Funeral services for the country's most eminent citizens would be held in Westminster Abbey from which it would be a simple matter to move them in solemn procession and lay them to rest in the 'Imperial Monumental Halls'. These had the space for not only the remains of all foreseeable future worthies and their memorials, but they could also be used for relieving some of the overcrowding in Westminster Abbey itself. Truly this would have been a national mausoleum.

A mausoleum can be defined as a purpose-built, substantial structure intended to contain one or more tombs. The earliest English mausoleums date from the first half of the eighteenth century and tend to be found in the grounds of private estates where they were designed not just to house the dead, but also to be looked at and to be a sublime feature of the landscape.

In the garden cemeteries established around London, starting with Kensal Green, those who bought burial plots were allowed to erect more-or-less whatever monument they desired. This led the rising middle class, the *nouveaux riche* whose social status did not necessarily match their financial means, to spend conspicuously on their memorials. What better way to impress the living than to build a mausoleum that clearly cost a lot? Good taste was not always uppermost in the minds of those who were to occupy these places. Consequently, the great Victorian cemeteries of London witnessed the appearance of an eclectic farrago of funerary buildings taking their inspiration from the Gothic, the Italianate, the Greek, the Egyptian, the Byzantine and random mixtures of any of these or other buildings that quite simply defy categorisation. Building materials included a variety of stone, polished marble, brick, the terracotta so beloved of the Victorians and even cast iron. Major architects were sometimes employed to design these structures.

As might be expected, London has a large number of fine mausoleums. There are many published guides and gazetteers to the London cemeteries and no attempt therefore is made to list these buildings here. Most of the cemeteries opened in the nineteenth century contain examples which will reward the efforts of those who go looking for them.

The prize for containing perhaps the oddest mausoleum of all might very well go to Mortlake Roman Catholic Cemetery which is coyly hidden away in an obscure part of SW14. Here lovers of the eccentric seek out what at first glance looks like an Arab tent. This is exactly what it is meant to look like. It takes the verisimilitude to the extent of making a good job of imitation guy ropes and creases in the fabric. It is, however, made of stone, not of canvas, and is a mausoleum containing the remains of Sir Richard Burton (1821–90) and his wife, Isabel. They were a real oddball couple. Burton was a ferocious-looking man who had a mastery of an amazing number of little-known languages and dialects and a passion for exploring remote and seldom-visited parts of Asia, South Africa and South America which often involved him 'going native'. When not engaged in exploration, he earned a crust doing translations and he is credited with the first English version of the *Arabian Knights*. He went on to translate *The Perfumed Garden* which his wife destroyed in a frenzy of prudishness. Eager to make amends for this censorious action, she had his body shipped back to England after he died at Trieste. She had little money but somehow managed to persuade friends to pay for a mausoleum in which he, and then she in due course, could be laid to rest. This mausoleum she designed herself, which is perhaps blindingly obvious. It was a dual-purpose building. Lady Burton sometimes conducted séances inside the mausoleum.

The idea of a huge cemetery serving London but sufficiently distant to preclude the possibility of it ever being subsumed within suburban development, first surfaced at the end of the 1840s. Enough land would be bought to provide for the burial needs of London into the foreseeable future and the distance from the metropolis would ensure that the land would be cheap and the site would pose no health hazards to Londoners. The place chosen was Brookwood near Woking in Surrey and the venture went ahead in association with the

London & South Western Railway Company. They were interested in what looked like regular and steady business. The London Necropolis and National Mausoleum Company (later the London Necropolis Company), for its part, was interested in the cheap means of transport that the railway company offered. The idea of this giant necropolis took on added urgency following the cholera outbreak of 1848–49 which killed close on 15,000 Londoners.

It would not be true to say that the concept of this rail-served necropolis met with universal approval. The Bishop of London found the idea of cadavers from widely differing social classes all travelling in the same train from London quite offensive. Considerations of social class pervaded the practices of the Necropolis Railway. Tickets and services for three classes were available and had to be bought for all travellers – living and dead. The deceased of course needed only a one-way ticket. The coffins appropriate to the different classes of travel were readily distinguishable by the quality of workmanship and ornamentation, and also by the degree of care shown by the Necropolis Company's staff when loading and unloading them. To attract business, fares for coffins and mourners needed to be cheap. In fact, the fares were so cheap that it was quite common for London golfers who liked the golf-courses around Woking, to disguise themselves as mourners and travel in the necropolis trains to save money. How they disguised their golfing paraphernalia does not, unfortunately, seem to have been recorded.

A special annexe was built at Waterloo station. This consisted of two platforms, one for mourners and the other for coffins. It lay on the southern side of the station and from it trains ran down the main line of the London & South Western Railway Company to Woking where a short branch line took them directly into the necropolis. This had two stations. One was for Roman Catholics, Jews, Parsees and the various nonconformist sects and the other for Church of England customers. At Waterloo, the station had a decorative entrance arch with ornamental gates and an iron parapet bearing the words 'Cemetery Station'.

A brochure issued by the Necropolis Company invited the bereaved, when the service was finished, to pause and admire the rustic scenery, to be invigorated by the fresh country air and to contemplate the 'noble site of which their departed relative or friend had become a tenant'. A daily train started to operate on 13 November 1854 and the service was well used for many years. The Necropolis Company's station at Waterloo was destroyed in an air raid during the Second World War.

The Brookwood Necropolis Railway is well known. A similar service which has received less attention was that established by the New Southgate Cemetery and Crematorium Company which opened a cemetery at Colney Hatch in 1861. This company had the admirable objective of helping those people who could afford only the most simple of funerals. An agreement was reached with the Great Northern Railway Company for the building of two stations, one at Maiden Lane in the Copenhagen Fields area just north of Kings Cross, the other at New Southgate. The railway company agreed to put on special trains for the conveyance of coffins and mourners.

The building at Maiden Lane was designed partly as a mortuary and partly as a railway station. The body could lie in hygienic conditions until the time of the funeral and mourners were allowed access at reasonable times to pay their last respects. On the day of the funeral, instead of the normal lugubrious procession through the streets, the coffin and its accompanying party were conveyed directly to the necropolis station on Maiden Lane. The journey took fifteen minutes. A charge of 6d was made for transporting the coffin, necessarily a single ticket, while returns for the mourners cost 1s 6d. Unlike the Brookwood Necropolis Railway, this venture was never a success and trains ran for less than ten years. Part of the necropolis station at the London end was still visible in the 1950s. At one time the Corporation of London and the Eastern Counties Railway Company were planning a branch line and special station at the City of London Cemetery at Aldersbrook, E12, but nothing came of this scheme.

The Royal Hospital Chelsea Burial Ground, SW3 is little known. It only covers one acre and was founded in 1692. Around 10,000 people were laid to rest there before it closed as a burial ground in 1854. This may be a small site but there have been some interments with appeal for lovers of the curious. Three old soldiers now buried at

Chelsea lived to the ages of 112, 111 and 107 respectively. One of these centenarians must have been a lusty old fellow because he married when aged over one hundred. Equally piquant is the fact that among other interments are those of two women, one of whom died in 1739 and the other in 1792, who served in the army for some years before their true sex was discovered.

Mention should be made of catacombs. Nine London cemeteries including Highgate, Abney Park, Brompton and Kensal Green possessed these modular houses of the dead. They were below ground and usually consisted of a vaulted passage built out of brick. Some had cells in which only the coffin ends were visible. Others, deliberately more ostentatious, had shelves on which the coffins were readily visible. These coffins were of lead, often elaborately decorated and draped in velvet. These were meant to be viewed and admired. There was a short-lived, rather mawkish vogue for paying admission to visit these grisly surroundings.

New provision for the burial of the dead could be an attraction to the still living. In 1831 new vaults were constructed at St Martin-in-the-Fields on which the *Sunday Times* of 12 June 1831 reported:

> The new vaults under St Martin's burying ground are the most capacious structure of the sort in London ... they consist of a series of vaults, running out of one another in various directions; they are lofty, and when lighted up, as on Tuesday, really presented something of a comfortable appearance ... crowds of ladies perambulated the vaults for some time, and the whole had more the appearance of a fashionable promenade than a grim depository of decomposing mortality.

Tucked away in the north-east corner of Hyde Park is a pet cemetery. In the 1880s, the dog belonging to the Duke of Cambridge was run over by a carriage near Hyde Park and he had the animal buried there, starting a fashion which meant that up to the 1950s, something like two hundred other pets were laid to rest there, each with an individual headstone. As might be expected, there are more dogs than any other animal buried there but a few cats and even the odd parrot, goose and monkey make up the numbers.

NOTES
1. Dickens, C., *Bleak House,* quoted in Meller, *see below*, p. 7.
2. Curl, J.S., *The Victorian Celebration of Death,* revised edition, 2000.
3. Meller, H., *London Cemeteries. An Illustrated Guide and Gazeteer,* 3rd edition, 1999.
4. Barker, F., *Highgate Cemetery: Victorian Valhalla,* 1984.

6
Death and the Afterlife in the Arts

Death has been depicted in art for thousands of years. In England Christian art represented death through a range of forms including wall paintings, stained glass, effigies, manuscripts, tapestries, carved tombs and headstones. As the commemoration of death became more secular, other artefacts accompanied the process of grieving: jewellery, mourning rings, brooches, lockets, furnishings, sculptures, paintings, memorial cards, song sheets and funeral apparel such as gloves, hats, handkerchiefs and fans. The living were reminded of their own mortality by the presence of burial grounds and the *memento mori* ('remember you are mortal') on tombs, in music and chants and in funeral art and architecture especially after the recurring bubonic plague pandemics from the 1340s onward.

We are fortunate that so many monuments have survived because they inform us about the social, religious and economic circumstances of past eras and the ways in which our ancestors not only dealt with death, but also about how they wished to be remembered. The term 'monument' covers a diverse range of artefacts such as monumental brasses, incised stone slabs, effigies, tomb chests and grave markers.

Monumental brasses provide an interesting source of evidence for the styles and fashions of the past, or at least of the clothes worn by that minority who could afford to be commemorated in this way. The earliest memorial brasses date from the thirteenth century and often depicted a family group. The people they commemorate were usually represented on life-size plates with incised lines, surrounded by architectural and heraldic inscriptions and accessories such as coats of arms, religious emblems and scrolls with biblical texts. Memorial brasses reached their peak of artistic excellence in the fourteenth century and then declined through neglect and destruction from the sixteenth century.

These brass plates have survived better than wooden effigies or painted wooden boards and can be found in many London churches including some fine examples in St Helen's Church in Bishopsgate, which has monumental brasses of Sir William Pickering, a faithful soldier; Sir Thomas Gresham, founder of the Royal Exchange and Sir John Crosby, a successful City merchant. A brass plate in a stone frame to John Stow (1625–1605), the author of the *Survey of London*, is in St Andrew Undershaft. St John the Baptist Church in Croydon has numerous fifteenth- and sixteenth-century memorial brasses while St John the Baptist in Hillingdon has the brasses of Lord John L'Estrange (d. 1479) and his wife Jacquette who was the aunt of the two princes who died in the Tower. The London Brass Rubbing Centre is based in St Martin-in-the-Fields Church in Trafalgar Square and has ninety replica brasses. Southwark Cathedral contains only one brass, which was erected during the Commonwealth (1649–1660) and is dedicated to ten-year-old Susannah Barford. The charming epitaph reads: 'This world to her was but a tragedy play, She came and sawt, dislikt and pass'd away.'

The impact of the religious changes during the Reformation in the sixteenth century wreaked much damage and destruction to the fabric of churches including their memorial brasses and tombs. An Act of Parliament in 1550 ordered the destruction and defacing of carved or painted church images and, although it tried to exempt 'any image or picture set ... upon any tomb in any church, chapel, or churchyard', this was often ignored. During the reign of Edward VI (1547–1553), London churches suffered a great deal of iconoclastic damage, losing many of their altars, paintings, relics and virtually all their statuary. Some opportunists saw the potential for making money out of these materials, especially the metal which was particularly valuable. Not surprisingly, large quantities of brass in churches were stripped away and sold. At St Leonard in Shoreditch in the 1580s the vicar Meredith Hammer 'plucked up many plates fixed on the graves, and left no memory of such as there had been buried under them.' The churchwarden at St Andrew in Holborn gained 36 shillings from a hundredweight of copper taken from the tombs and gravestones. Gravestone plates from St Mary Aldermary were sold for £3 13s and metal from monuments was selling at 3 pennies per pound at All Hallows, London Wall. Two centuries later in 1732, the pickings from coffins still proved to be tempting. In Bow Church vault the gravedigger of Aldgate and his assistant helped themselves to lead and plate from a coffin and sold it to a Robert Moore in King Street who gave them 'the rate of nine shillings and four-pence a hundred for it.' They had previously sold coffin handles and lead.

The impact of the Black Death in the middle of the fourteenth century, killing as it did up to 30,000 of the city's population of 70,000, intensified the ways in which death was thought about as well as the manner in which it was portrayed. There was a greater emphasis on the macabre and morbid images of Death as the destroyer who was often depicted as a skeleton with a spear attacking the living. The fifteenth-century monk, John Lydgate, wrote in his poem, *Death's Warning*, 'my dreadful spear that is full sharp ... Doth yow now lo, here thys manace.' This image of death endured over the centuries and can be seen in many illustrations and sculptures such as the monument to Lady Elizabeth Nightingale and her husband (d. 1731) in Westminster Abbey, which contains an elaborate representation of death preparing to throw his spear. The figure of death looming over its victim is shown in a painting in Westminster Abbey. This late thirteenth-century image portrays a young man on his deathbed with death waiting at the bedpost.

Wall paintings in English medieval churches dealt with various themes about death although very few such paintings still exist in London's remaining churches. Paintings served as messages and stories. One morality tale entitled 'The Three Living and the Three

Dead' originated in Flanders and came to England where it became a popular theme in fifteenth-century paintings and murals on church walls. The story was about three kings who, while out hunting, came across three corpses. The corpses castigated the kings for their preoccupation with pleasure and worldly things. Their words of warning, which were shown in text scrolls, read: 'as you are, we once were; as we are, so shall you be'. As with similar tales, the message of the paintings was to be prepared for death and subsequent Judgement. Other illustrative messages appeared in the fourteenth century during the Black Death in the form of the Four Horsemen of the Apocalypse and the *Danse Macabre* (Dance of Death). The *Danse Macabre* personified the figure of Death leading dancers in a slow, stately procession. Such images helped people to express and share their grief as well as reminding each other that death is not only inevitable, but also the common denominator of all humanity.

The most famous Dance of Death in England was painted on the walls of the cloister at Old St Paul's Cathedral and it influenced other images of the dance in England after 1430. The author of the text which accompanied the image was the monk and poet, John Lydgate, who had been greatly impressed by seeing the famous *Danse Macabre* in the Churchyard of Holy Innocents in Paris in 1426. Lydgate made a translation of the text which was then included in the famous series in Old St Paul's. The painting, by an unknown artist, was destroyed in 1549 when the cloister and tombs were pulled down on the orders of the Duke of Somerset and only the poems by Lydgate were preserved. Thomas Rowlandson (1756–1827), the English caricaturist, produced a variation on the Dance of Death between 1814 and 1816. In traditional depictions of the Dance, Death does not care for the social position, or for the wealth, sex or age of the people it leads into its dance. Rowlandson's illustrations are rather different; his emphasis is on the activities of daily life and events rather than the view that all will die equally in front of Death.

Effigies of the deceased – stone, wooden, plaster or marble – developed from the twelfth century in England, although again this form of monument was reserved for the elite. One of the earliest in England was the marble effigy on the tomb of Abbot Gilbert Crispin of Westminster (1085–1117) in the south cloister of

Westminster Abbey. Temple Church off Fleet Street has nine effigies including those of William Marshall, 1st Earl of Pembroke and his sons dressed in full knightly attire. Marshall went to the Holy Land as a crusader between 1183 and 1186 where he first encountered the Knights Templar, although he did not join the order until a few months before his death in 1219. The medieval effigies in Temple Church mostly display the crossed legs which may or may not signify their Crusader status. In Southwark Cathedral there is a wooden effigy of a knight of 1280, one of less than a hundred such effigies in Britain.

The use of effigies as additions to funerary monuments became established by the late thirteenth century. The first recorded use of an effigy appears in 1327 for the burial of Edward II at what was then Gloucester Abbey. It was intended that the corpse of a monarch would be displayed during the funeral procession. However, given the time that sometimes elapsed between death and the funeral, the corpse was often so decomposed that an effigy was used instead. The significance of the occasion with the monarch dressed in elaborate clothes and holding the orb and spectre was to impress upon those in attendance the majesty and the mystique of kingship.

Artists attempted to provide as close a likeness of the deceased as possible with the effigy or 'representation of the body.' This likeness was further improved during the fifteenth century when masks were taken of the deceased immediately after death. By the late seventeenth and early eighteenth century, effigies were being made out of wax and they accompanied the funeral procession. Sometimes effigies were produced many years after the death of the person, an example being that of Elizabeth I which was remade in 1760. The final public figure to be honoured in this way was Nelson in 1806 whose waxwork was the last to be placed in Westminster Abbey. This was not a funeral effigy, however, as Nelson was buried in St Paul's Cathedral and the waxwork was used more as an attraction for visitors.

From the late thirteenth century onwards funeral effigies of a deceased monarch would be embalmed, dressed in the coronation robes before being exhibited while lying in state, and then during the funeral service and the procession. This custom continued for over three centuries until after 1660 when the effigy no longer accompanied the royal funeral. Excellent examples of effigies can be found in the Museum in the East Cloister of Westminster Abbey. Eighteen life-size waxen images including Elizabeth I, Charles II, Queen Anne and King William III and Queen Mary II, as well as non-royal figures, can be seen. These waxworks were modelled while the subjects, in the case of royalty, were still alive in order to obtain the best possible likeness and were dressed in their own clothes and with their own accessories. The Westminster effigies were made for every monarch over four centuries of British history and were carried on top of their coffins as they made their last journey through the streets of London. At the funeral of Henry VIII, the effigy carved by Nicholas Bellin lay on top of the coffin which was 'wonderful richly apparelled, with velvet, gold, and precious stones of all sortes.' The effigies were skilfully crafted works of art. There is a marked difference between the wooden manikin carved for the burial of Edward III in 1377 and the elaborate model made of Charles II where artisans made a skeleton from wood and iron wire and then fleshed it out with straw sewn into a canvas skin. The effigy was dressed in the King's clothes and decked out with wig, sword, jewellery and plumed hat.

The Reformation witnessed a diminution of religious imagery and a growing secularism, particularly in relation to images and ritual. This was reflected in paintings that portrayed the deathbed scene, which became a popular theme in Reformation Europe and Britain. An example of this is *Venetia Stanley, Lady Digby, on her Deathbed*, by Van Dyck (1633) in Dulwich Picture Gallery. Venetia Stanley (1600–1633), the wife of the diplomat and author, Sir Kenelm Digby, was celebrated for her beauty. She had been the subject of a great deal of scandal, having being the mistress of Edward Sackville, 4th Earl of Dorset. After nine years of marriage to Digby, she died suddenly. It was rumoured that she had drunk her husband's 'viper wine', a concoction reputed to preserve beauty. Her husband wrote of the painting:

> This is the only constant companion I now have ... It standeth all day over against my chaire and table ... and all night when I goe into my chamber I sett it close to my beds side, and by the faint light of candle, me thinks I see her dead indeed.

Another deathbed scene is the painting by an unknown artist of the *Memorial Portrait of Sir Henry Unton* (1596) in the National Portrait Gallery which depicts the life of Unton culminating in his death and burial.

Unlike the limited survival of medieval tombs, around 5,000 sixteenth- and seventeenth-century tombs in England have survived, although many of those in London were destroyed in the Blitz. Many fine sculptors and masons emerged in this period, such as Nicholas Stone (1586–1647) who has been described as a leading master mason and the single most important carver of funerary monuments in early Stuart London. He was apprenticed to Isaac James, a London mason, and later went to work under the sculptor Hendrick de Keyser in Holland. Stone returned to London and settled in Southwark and in 1619 he was appointed as master mason to James I, and then to Charles I. He designed many fine tombs including the effigy of Queen Elizabeth.

In death as in life status was important and the rich and wealthy were keen to display their past social rank through elaborate tombs and memorials. London churches and cathedrals contain many ornate tombs to the famous as well as the less famous. The elaborate medieval canopied tomb of John Gower (1325–1408) is located in the north aisle of Southwark Cathedral. Gower is credited with being the first English poet as well as a friend of Chaucer's. A recumbent effigy of Gower, with his head resting on copies of his three greatest works, adorns the tomb. However there were many who exaggerated their own importance and were determined to outdo their betters by having a more flamboyant monument. The rise of a wealthy merchant class from the sixteenth century produced men who were keen to portray themselves with shows of commemorative ostentation which they thought would impress the living. However, these efforts raised eyebrows in some quarters. One critic of this particular trend was the poet and antiquary John Weever (1576–1632), who had travelled extensively abroad and eventually settled in Clerkenwell. In his *Ancient Funeral Monuments* (1631) he commented: 'for some of our epitaphs more honour is attributed to a rich Tradesman or gripping usurer, than is given to the greatest Potentate.' Examples of this flamboyance can be seen in some of the tombs in Westminster Abbey.

The well-to-do and vain could buy the right to be buried there, a practice which continued until the mid-nineteenth century. A visitor might be forgiven for thinking they are viewing the monument of a well-known national figure of heroic status rather than a memorial dedicated to the vanity and wealth of a rich merchant.

In order that the sculptured image of the deceased was as near a likeness as possible, many monuments were built for individuals while they were still alive. The purpose of such memorial was the hope that it would enable the deceased to be remembered for ever. In 1574 Archbishop Sandys in a funeral service at St Paul's said: 'All these things, furniture of funerals, order of burying and the pomp ... are rather for the comforts to the living than helps to the dead.' Rememberance, however, is transient and the comment of a seventeenth-century rector, Timothy Oldmayne, was brutally correct: 'oblivion and neglect are the two principal handmaids of death'.

The development of capitalist society in the eighteenth century facilitated changes in the visual culture of death. New and cheaper production methods allowed the manufacture of coffins and furnishings to be available to a wider market. Southwark became a particular centre for the funerary and commemorative trades. A greater choice of memorials and other funerary items also became available.

Industrial developments contributed to the production and availability of sculptured headstones and outdoor monuments, many of which are among the most visible and impressive displays of death. Anyone who has visited one of the major London cemeteries cannot but be impressed by the decorative gravestones. Prior to the eighteenth century, graveyard monuments were mostly made from local stone if suitable, or from Portland stone. The growth of the canals made possible the utilisation of other types of material such as York stone and granite for the more prestigious tombs.

Some of the most common gravestone symbols were the skull and crossbones, which represented the decaying body; the hourglass indicating the passage of time, a tree stump or truncated pillar symbolic of a life cut short. Other common symbols included an anchor (hope), broken column, cherub, candle (loss of life), arrows, Father Time, scythe (life cut short), torch, urn, willow (grief) and angels in a variety of poses – flying, trumpeting or weeping. Many types of flowers and plants appear including the lily (purity), poppy (sleep), rose (sorrow), ivy (friendship), palm branch (victory), rosemary (remembrance) and laurel (heroism). Many religious themes were chosen such as the Bible or other holy book, chalice, cross, sacred heart (usually in Catholic graveyards), Star of David (symbol of Judaism) and crescent (usually Muslim). Animal symbols can be seen on headstones including birds (resurrection), butterflies (short life), lambs (innocence) and lions (courage).

The variety of designs and symbols on headstones provide some insight into the life of the deceased. Trades and occupations are often represented by a variety of symbols. A butcher might have a steel knife or cleaver; a farmer a hoe or a flail; a gardener a rake or spade; a mason a wedge or level; a sailor an anchor or sextant; a shoemaker a leather cutter's knife; a weaver a loom or shuttle and a smith, a hammer and anvil.

Around the mid-eighteenth century the art, architecture and sculpture of ancient Greek civilisation became increasingly popular. Examples of this movement, which was known as neoclassicism, can be seen in memorial sculptures on tombs and on the walls of cathedrals and mausoleums. Typical imagery included broken columns, a weeping mourner and cherubs. This genre also embraced painting, which was full of ancient gods and classical themes, as can be seen in the *Apotheosis of Nelson* (1807) by Benjamin West. West influenced other artists such as Scott Pierre Nicolas Legrand to produce a similar painting with the same title. Both are in the National Maritime Museum in Greenwich. Legrand depicts Nelson being received into immortality among the gods on Olympus witnessed by grieving men on the deck of a boat. Neptune, the god of the sea, leans down to support Nelson while above Fame is personified as a female figure holding a crown of stars over Nelson's head. Other popular themes included Hercules, Minerva and Jupiter.

Images of death were favoured themes of caricaturists who used the figure of Death in humorous and satirical ways. In William Hogarth's (1697–1764) *Satan, Sin and Death* (c. 1735) the skeletal figure of Death is holding a blood-smeared arrow. James Gillray (1757–1815), inspired by Hogarth's painting, did a satirical reworking of this with William Pitt as the devil holding a spear in a power struggle with Chancellor

Edward Thurlow and Queen Charlotte. In another Hogarth etching, *Death giving George Taylor a Cross-Buttock,* Death is fighting the boxer George Taylor (who had a booth at the Adam and Eve in Tottenham Court Road) and getting the better of him.

By the Victorian period, death was increasingly sentimentalised, and was accompanied by a wide range of mementoes of the deceased. These included locks of hair which were kept in a box or mounted in a hair brooch designed by 'hair artists'. Hair art, which became the most popular form of Victorian mourning jewellery, started as a simple way to keep the memory of a loved one, but it developed into an elaborate art form. Bracelets, rings, earrings, watch fobs and necklaces all became quite common in the later part of the Victorian period. Memorial cards commemorated recent deaths. A particular and tragic example of these is the memorial card to the Taylor children (1862) in the Victoria and Albert Museum. The three children were killed by their parents and the tragedy caused a great sense of public grief and outpouring.

Images of the Afterlife

Images of the Christian afterlife – Heaven, Purgatory and Hell – have survived from the medieval period in illuminated manuscripts, wall paintings and sculptures. From the twelfth century the doctrine of Purgatory brought a significant shift in the way people thought about death. This was reinforced through the vivid images of the torments that were experienced in that state.

The walls of medieval churches provided an ideal place for the display of Christian art and these paintings continued to be produced until the English Reformation and its associated iconoclasm wiped out so many of them. The subjects of wall paintings were mainly based on Gospel accounts and morality tales, but images of Death were often featured in themes such as The Three Living and the Three Dead, The Last Judgement and The Seven Deadly Sins. The Doom was one of the most common themes for wall paintings in the medieval parish church. It depicted the Christian belief in the judgement of souls before they entered Heaven or Hell. The purpose was to remind people of what awaited them after death and what the consequences of sin would be. These images were usually located at the east end of the chancel where they were in full view of the worshippers. On one side of the painting Heaven was depicted and on the other side Hell. Christ was placed in majesty at the top, sitting in judgement. Additional figures might include the Virgin Mary, the Twelve Apostles and angels blowing trumpets to raise the dead for judgement and alternatively welcoming those who had been chosen to enter the gates of Heaven. The unlucky ones were gleefully seized by demons to be taken down into Hell to confront the endless horrors and torments that awaited them there. None of these have survived in the City of London churches. A medieval doom painting on wood over the chancel at St Andrew's in Enfield was removed in 1779 when the church was widened and later the painting was destroyed. In St Margaret's in Barking there are beams on each side of the chancel arch showing part of a Doom painting. There are also 'Resurrection stones' carved with scenes of the Last Judgement at St Andrew in Holborn and St Mary-at-Hill.

Images of the terrors of Hell and the rewards of Heaven found expression in art throughout the following centuries. Gustave Dore (1832–1883), who produced many vivid illustrations of poverty in London in the nineteenth century in the book *London: A Pilgrimage* (1872), also drew the illustrations of Hell for a later version of *The Divine Comedy*. Edmund Spenser (1552–1599), who acknowledged his debt to his birthplace 'Merry London, my most kindly nurse', wrote the epic poem *The Faerie Queen* in which Duessa Lucifera, the head of the House of Pride, and her six advisors represent the Seven Deadly Sins.

From the Reformation of the sixteenth century, Hell presented many Protestants with a problem because whilst they rejected Purgatory, the idea of Hell as a place of eternal tortures and punishments was not consistent with their image of a forgiving and loving God. Many had to rethink this idea. The century after 1650 witnessed a range of debates concerning the issue of life after death – the journey of body and soul, the state between death and the final judgement and the nature of Heaven and Hell.

The emergence of Romanticism in the late eighteenth century challenged many contemporary perspectives of what the afterlife might hold. Romanticism placed a greater emphasis on moral passion and the role of the individual. It was a movement that found expression in romantic images particularly around the themes of love and grief, romantic suicides and melancholy settings. The old hellfire sermons and images of Hell and all that it held for sinners had struck fear into people for generations. However with Romanticism came images of a Heaven which promised reunion and in some cases even rejected the idea of punishment. William Blake (1757–1827) was a notable contributor to these ideas.

Blake had challenged orthodox ideas and believed that Satan was the hero of Milton's *Paradise Lost*. The artist John Martin (1789–1854) shared no such illusions. Although he was an artist and engraver, Martin had also been involved with schemes for the improvement of London. He published pamphlets and plans for the metropolitan water supply, sewerage and dock and railway systems some twenty-five years before those of Joseph Bazalgette. His mezzotints for an edition of Milton's *Paradise Lost*, which were exhibited at the Royal Society of British Artists in 1825, depicted a battle between light and darkness. In Martin's work, the sinners at the Last Judgement are cast down into the inferno while the good are led to a landscape of blue and gold. In another painting by Martin, *The Plains of Heaven*, the landscape is one of peaceful serenity.

William Blake also worked with a theme that was common in depictions of the apocalypse and death. *Death on a Pale Horse* was also a theme used by one of England's greatest artists, John Mallord William Turner (1775–1851). Turner was deeply affected by his father's death in 1829 and *Death on a Pale Horse* reflects a much darker shift in Turner's art as Death, a skeleton, is spreadeagled across a white steed.

The Victorian period witnessed changing perceptions and artistic representations of the afterlife. A greater emphasis was placed on the idea of peaceful reunion with one's family in Heaven, and less attention was given to Hell. The extent to which these images influenced, or struck terror into, the mass of population is uncertain. Images probably lost their ability to strike fear into people as they had done in previous times. However they began to find expression in a wider circulation of popular publications which used the combination of illustrations and melodramatic stories. Death was highly visible in Victorian culture as people were encouraged to give public expression to their grief. This was supported by an industry of sentimentality reflected in mourning dress, mementoes, song sheets, memorial cards and locks of hair. Paintings and illustrations of the Victorian deathbed, melodrama, grieving at the graveside, heroic deaths and tragedy became the stuff of many of these publications.

Examples include *The Doubt: Can These Dry Bones Live?* (1855) by Henry Alexander Bowler (1824–1903), in the Tate Britain. This painting depicts a woman leaning over the headstone of a grave in deep contemplation, possibly casting doubts on traditional beliefs about the afterlife. *Ophelia* (1851–1852) by John Everett Millais (1829–1896) portrays the tragic death of Ophelia, the beautiful young woman from Shakespeare's *Hamlet*, as she falls into a stream and drowns. *The Lady of Shallot* (1888) by J. W. Waterhouse (1849–1917) shows the romantic but doomed eponymous heroine setting off on her final voyage along the river to Camelot.

The Victoria and Albert Museum displays paintings and artefacts related to Victorian death. Typical of the genre are paintings such as Charles Green's (1840–1898) *Little Nell Awakened by the Bargeman* (1876) from Charles Dickens's *The Old Curiosity Shop* (1841). The novel tells the story of Little Nell, her grandfather and their financial ruin and subsequent escape and death. The painting shows a pathetic looking Nell sitting by a canal holding her grandfather's head as he lies dying. Joseph Swain's (1820–1909) untitled work depicts a woman standing in mourning dress by a grave. *A Young Widow* (1877) by Edward Killingworth Johnson (1825–1896) has a similarly sad theme: a young woman dressed in mourning clothes holds a wedding dress, intimating that she was a recent bride but now widowed. Deathbed scenes of children were less of a taboo subject than now and in the Victorian period they carried a great deal of sentimentality. *Little Sister's Gone to Sleep* was the title of the picture on the cover of a song sheet, for example.

The art of death over the centuries has informed us about the ways in which different societies have responded to death. The medieval period reflected contemporary fears of an impending apocalypse, punishment for our sins and the threat of pestilence. The Victorians conveyed the visual imagery of death in a diversity of forms and rituals assisted by the rise of an industrial economy and growing commercialisation.

7
Irrational Aspects

Fear of Ghosts and Premature Burial

'Irrational' is defined as 'marked by a lack of accord with reason or sound judgement.' When making assessments about the actions of people in the past the term has to be used with a degree of caution for it is all too easy to make judgements with the benefit of hindsight and our current levels of scientific knowledge. People thought and acted within the parameters of the knowledge and understanding of the world they had at the time. For all the intellectual and scientific advances over past centuries, many beliefs have persisted into the present, one example being the interest in ghosts. So-called irrational beliefs and the fears they generate have contributed at times to panics, mass hysteria and persecution. Fear has been a constant presence throughout history. Past societies feared plague, disease, pain, fire, war, flood, starvation, the night, bad harvests, the death of an infant, Purgatory, Hell and the end of the world. At the core of so many of these fears is death and the process of dying. The terror of being buried prematurely was very real for many people, some of whom went to great lengths to prevent this from happening.

The perils of the night and the attending darkness brought with them many risks. Night-time was given over to criminals, demons and moonstruck lunatics, a time when doors and windows were bolted to keep out the unknown threats which lurked in the dark. The city bells sounded curfew at nine and people began the more than symbolic ritual of locking doors and closing shutters. Nighttime contained elements that were beyond anyone's control. People had to negotiate streets that were like cramped, dark rabbit warrens with all manner of obstacles. It was not uncommon for pedestrians and others to fall over these obstacles or to be precipitated down into cellars or into rivers. There was also the risk of being attacked and robbed. Some areas had a particularly bad reputation and people travelled these streets at night at their own risk. The notorious and appropriately-nicknamed 'Cut-Throat Lane' (Pottery Lane, Kensington) was the main route into one of London's worst slums. In the 1850s a medical officer described it as 'one of the most deplorable spots, not only in Kensington, but in the whole metropolis'. Charles Dickens described it as 'a plague spot' scarcely equalled in London. Sir John Fielding described Black Boy Alley (off Chick Lane, Holborn) as 'a terror to the watchmen' because of the violent attacks by a group of young men known as the Black Boy Alley gang.

Ghosts

The fascination with the afterlife has a long history. Despite the advance of science, secularism and rationalism since the eighteenth century, there continues to be a preoccupation with ghosts. However, present-day interest is of a different nature from that which existed in pre-Reformation times where the belief was manipulated for political and religious purposes. Most people in medieval England believed in ghosts and accepted that the dead might return to haunt the living. The belief in ghosts has shifted over the past 1,000 years from one of general acceptance to one of cynicism. However there have been sporadic revivals such as the growth of spiritualism in the nineteenth century and during the First World War. London, as might be expected, has had more than its fair share of ghosts and ghost sightings.

During the medieval period, the relationship between ghosts and the living served an important function. The Catholic Church revised and rationalised the ancient belief in ghosts. It also taught that such apparitions were the souls of those trapped in Purgatory, unable to rest until they had expiated their sins.

Between 1050 and 1250 the Church underwent significant changes. In its attempt to define the faith it persecuted heretics and those it saw as non-believers through crusades and the inquisition. The twelfth and thirteenth centuries saw a renewed interest in saving the souls of people. Chronicles provide rich sources for stories concerning miracles, demons, fairies, ghosts and other worlds. Stories of the dead rising from their graves at night were told to torment the living and maintain a sense of terror and obedience. In order to allay these threats frightened parishioners asked their priests to perform exorcisms. The many tales of ghosts and the belief in them during the medieval period also served to emphasise the sanctity of the grave. By reinforcing the image of Purgatory and life after death the population could be controlled through fear.

The concept of Purgatory, a halfway stage after death between earth and Heaven, was an important development of the twelfth century. In Purgatory the soul could repent its sins through punishment and then after time it might be considered fit for Heaven. In order to shorten their stay in Purgatory, people could buy indulgences. This corrupt system came under attack, particularly by Martin Luther in the early sixteenth century. In 2002, when archaeologists excavated some 10,500 graves in a large fourteenth-century cemetery in the former Hospital of St Mary Spital in Spitalfields, they found four bodies in their coffins clutching lead papal indulgences. These individuals would have bought the indulgences as a pardon for the sins committed during their life and would have been reassured that they had purchased their ticket to the perpetual delights of Heaven.

The doctrine of Purgatory led to a significant shift in thinking about death as well as the relationship between the living and the dead. Ideas of sin and salvation were constant preoccupations of many people and Christianity based so much of its teaching on preparing men and women for death and an understanding of what followed in the afterlife. The ubiquity of graveyards in London with their associated churches was a constant reminder of the presence of death.

In the Middle Ages, people were surrounded by death with disease, plague, famine and what now seems a short life-expectancy. This climate proved conducive for the belief in Purgatory and ghosts. Although there is an almost complete absence of ghosts in the Bible, one passage from Luke (16:30) carried particular potency: 'But if someone from the dead visits them, they will repent'. The appeal to ghosts was reflected in twelfth-century London when oaths were taken on a deceased person's tomb. It was believed that the ghost residing there would avenge any injury or betrayal of a last dying wish. There are accounts of medieval ghosts reappearing to haunt the living, particularly those who had committed an offence against the deceased or otherwise alienated them. If a criminal committed an offence without any witnesses, it was believed that ghostly visitations from the victim would force the guilty party to confess.

Such was the reverence for the dead that anyone seeking to disturb their graves did so with the risk that they too would be avenged or menaced. An example of this occurred after the disturbance of the tomb of Sybil Penn. Penn was a nurse to Prince Edward, later Edward VI, in 1538. Her widower ordered that her body be removed from its original burial place in 1564 and interred alongside his. She lay in a tomb in Hampton church until 1829 when the old church was pulled down and Penn's tomb was moved to the new church. Sybil had now been disturbed twice. Stories circulated about strange noises and the sound of a woman working on a spinning wheel in the south-west wing of Hampton Court Palace. When the area was searched, a previously unknown chamber was found which contained, among various articles, a spinning wheel. Sightings of the ghost of Sybil Penn wearing a long, grey robe continued to be reported for many years. Hampton Court also has other ghosts including two of the wives of Henry VIII. Jane Seymour has been seen dressed in white holding a candle and the ghost of Catherine Howard re-enacts the moment of her arrest. This scene is accompanied by Catherine's desperate screams in her attempt to break free of her guards.

Another example of spirits coming back to avenge their dying wishes was that of Richard Cloudesley, a wealthy landowner and benefactor who had places in Islington named after him. When he died in 1517 he asked to be buried in the churchyard of Holy Trinity in Islington, but it was rumoured that he was actually buried in a nearby field, although the reason for this is unclear. An account written in 1842, *The Islington Ghost*, claimed that there was a 'wondrous commotion' whereby the earth swelled and turned 'up on every side.' The story went on to add that Richard Cloudesley 'lay buried in or near that place, and that his body being restless, on the score of some sin', signified that his spirit should be laid to rest in the chosen place. After 'certain exorcisers set to rest the unruly spirit, the earth did return to its pristine shape.' Richard's body was re-interred in the church in 1813.

Ghosts often returned as bearers of warnings or prophetic messages. The inscription on the grave of William Shakespeare (1564–1616) in the Church of Holy Trinity, Stratford-Upon-Avon, offers such a warning:

Good friend, for Jesus' sake forebeare
To digg the dust enclosed heare;
Bleste be the man that spares these stones,
And curst be he that moves my bones.

The Reformation of the sixteenth century gave voice to religious reformers who rejected the existence of Purgatory, arguing that all people went to Heaven or Hell according to their past deeds. Protestants also rejected all manifestations of communion with the dead and, along with Purgatory, the belief in ghosts also came under attack. Reformers dismissed such beliefs as the elaborate frauds of popish priests. In 1564 the Bishop of London, Edmund Grindal, claimed that the doctrine of Purgatory was 'maintained principally by feigned apparatus, visions of spirits and other like fables.' Similarly, the diarist Henry Machyn noted that when Bishop Jewel preached at the funeral for a member of the Skinners' Company in 1560 he commented 'that there was no purgatore.'

Understandably Heaven was always the preferred destination to Hell or Purgatory and it was believed that certain people got there faster than others and did so without suffering the pains of Purgatory. Amongst those fast-tracked in this way were religious martyrs.

Sources such as funeral sermons, condolence letters, printed broadsheet epitaphs and inscriptions on tombs and monuments give details about the assumed destination of the deceased. The epitaph of John Jarret, a grocer from Southwark who died in 1626, read 'to heaven he is gone, the way before, Where of Grocers there is many more.'

Despite the best attempts of Protestants to abolish 'Popish superstitions', many people continued to believe in ghosts. Accounts of sightings of the deceased coming back to haunt the living were common among all classes.

A particular example of an apparition returning to warn someone of her impending death concerned the Duchess of Mazarine. The Duchess was one of the mistresses of Charles II and also a friend of Madame de Beauclair, mistress of James II. Many years after the Duchess died, her spirit visited Madame de Beauclair who recorded that her old friend looked 'on me with her usual sweetness [and] said, "Beauclair, between the hours of twelve and one this night you will be with me."' Needless to say Beauclair died at the predicted time.

When the famous Tyburn gallows at the crossroads of Edgware Road and Oxford Street was mysteriously uprooted in 1678, there was much speculation about who or what had caused it to collapse. A partly humorous pamphlet, *The Tyburn Ghost: Or the Strange Downfall of the Gallows*, explained that the

> most probable opinion is that it was ruined by certain Evil Spirits, perhaps the Ghosts of some who had formerly suffered there; for if persons killed retain so great an Antipathy against their Murderers, that scarce a Physician dares come near his expired Patient, lest the corpse should fall-a-Bleeding ... it is reported ... that there was seen last Tuesday-evening a Spirit sitting on one of the Cross-beams with its neck awry, making a strange noise.

In 1679 it was reported that the ghost of a midwife who had lived in Holborn returned to confess to the murder of two illegitimate children. These examples are clear evidence that efforts to root out belief in ghosts had been largely unsuccessful.

In more pragmatic tones Samuel Johnson stated a hundred years later that the existence of ghosts is a 'question which after five thousand years is yet undecided.' Johnson went further by stating that the possibility of such spectres was essential to the immortality of the soul. More critical was Henry Bourne, writing in *Antiquitates Vulgares* in 1725, who commented that stories of ghosts and spirits were nothing more than the 'Fears and Fancies, and weak Brains of Men.' Reformers continued to despair of the gullible multitude who were still prepared to accept such beliefs and those beliefs were fuelled by stories of ghostly apparitions in Elizabethan and Jacobean plays as well as the popular broadsheets, periodicals and coffee houses.

The Great Plague of 1665 generated many stories of ghosts around the lanes and alleys, particularly where known plague pits lay such as those at Finsbury Fields, Shoreditch, Smithfield, Moorfields, Bishopsgate Street, Stepney, Whitechapel and Aldgate. Bank tube station is reputed to be built on the site of a plague pit and has many associated tales of ghosts haunting the area.

One later tale, unrelated to the plague, was that of Sarah Whitehead who died in 1840 and who haunts the Bank of England. She is said to appear every twenty-five years wearing a black hooded cloak. She was the sister of an employee at the Bank, Philip Whitehead, who was found guilty of forgery and subsequently hanged in 1811. She was so distressed by his death that she not only lost her reason and believed that her brother would reappear, but also that the Bank owed her a fortune. When she died she was buried at St Christopher-le-Stocks which used to be adjacent to the Bank.

In the eighteenth century, sightings of ghosts ran paradoxically alongside Enlightenment attacks on superstition. Visitors to the city, such as the French Enlightenment writer and traveller Pierre-Jean Grosley, commented on the great fear of ghosts among Londoners. In 1779 thirty-five-year-old Lord Lyttleton of Berkeley Square was visited by a woman in white, one of many women he seduced, who told him that he would die within three days. Three days later Lyttleton died, thereby causing much gossip and prompting Samuel Johnson to declare that it was the 'most extraordinary thing that has happened in my day.' In 1746 Counsellor Morgan was executed but he later returned to a Council meeting at Westminster to bring revenge on those present. It was told that the ghost of Morgan made a haunting appearance after midnight walking awkwardly and accompanied by an 'awful odour'. He then proceeded to address the meeting and the effect on those present was so great that a pamphlet reported: 'they have never been in their senses since.'

The story of the Cock Lane Ghost of 1762 has been well documented. The house at No. 20 Cock Lane in Smithfield not only attracted large crowds of Londoners but also became a national wonder. William Kent and his 'wife' Frances came to London to seek lodgings. Richard Parsons offered to rent them a room in his house in Cock Lane. Kent confided that he and Frances were not married and that he had in fact eloped with his late wife's sister. Kent loaned Parsons, an alcoholic, a large sum of money but when Parsons could not pay him back things turned nasty. Strange knockings and sounds were heard at the house, which Parsons attributed to the ghost of Kent's wife. Parsons evicted Kent and the pregnant Frances. The latter contracted smallpox three months later and died. She was placed in a sealed coffin in the crypt of St John's in Clerkenwell. The haunting at Cock Lane continued and a medium explained that this was the spirit of Frances, returning to inform the world she had been poisoned by Kent and that he should be hanged for murder. The crowds bayed for Kent's execution whilst Parsons exploited the situation by charging people to attend séances at the bedside of his 'possessed' eleven-year-old daughter, Elizabeth Parsons.

A commission, which included Samuel Johnson, was appointed to investigate the events. Johnson spent a night in St John's next to Frances's coffin in the hope of hearing tapping. When the events at Cock Lane were eventually exposed as a fraud, Parsons, his wife, several neighbours and a newspaper editor were arrested and punished. Parsons was imprisoned and condemned to stand in the pillory three times at the end of Cock Lane. Perhaps surprisingly, it is believed that the crowd treated him with compassion on these occasions.

The churchyard of Christchurch Greyfriars in Newgate is the site of an ancient burial ground where the remains of 'the she-wolf of France', Queen Isabella, wife of the English King Edward II, lay. She instigated, with her lover Roger Mortimer, the murder of the King in September 1327. Isabella died in 1358 and was buried at Greyfriars, with the heart of Edward II. Her ghost is said to move amongst the trees clutching the heart of her murdered husband. Another ghostly figure in Greyfriars is that of Lady Alice Hungerford who also murdered her spouse. In 1523 she was executed by being boiled alive. As with Isabella, her ghostly figure has been sighted in the cloisters and aisles of the monastery.

The Tower of London is a notorious site for ghostly sightings and is considered one of the most haunted buildings in Britain. Among its eminent ghosts are Anne Boleyn, Lady Jane Grey and the two boy Princes, Edward and Richard, generally believed to have been put to death there.

A frequent theme in paranormal circles is that of the 'doppelganger'. This is a ghostly duplicate of the living observer, constituting a portent of their own death. One story from the seventeenth century relates to Lady Diana Rich, the young and beautiful daughter of the Earl of Holland. She was walking in the garden of her father's house in Kensington when, to her horror, she spotted her absolute likeness. She was dead from smallpox within a month. If that was not enough, she had a sister who had the same experience shortly before she too suffered an untimely death and followed her sister to the grave.

Several theatres including the Theatre Royal in Drury Lane, the Adelphi Theatre and the Palladium have their spectral regulars, as do many pubs. The Spaniard's Inn in Hampstead dates from 1585 and is reputed to be haunted by a number of ghosts including Juan Porero who died in a duel over a woman and whose body is buried in the garden; the highwayman Dick Turpin and Jack Sheppard – the petty criminal and multiple prison escapee who was executed at Tyburn in 1724. The Grenadier in Belgravia is the assumed home of the ghost of a young guards officer who was flogged to death following the discovery that he had been cheating at a game of cards. He is particularly active around the anniversary of his death in September. The Gatehouse in Highgate dates back to 1306 and is haunted by Mother Marnes, who was murdered for her money. At the Trafalgar Tavern in Greenwich, built in 1837, a man is often seen sitting in the bar wearing Georgian dress. The Morpeth Arms in Pimlico, near the Tate Britain, was originally built in 1845 close to the Millbank Prison. A plaque records the story of a prisoner who was reputed to have tunnelled for months hoping to escape, but became trapped in the vaults beneath the pub and died. The Langham Hotel in Portland Place is haunted by the ghost of a Victorian doctor who committed suicide at the hotel after murdering his wife, and also the spirit of a German Prince who committed suicide by hanging himself from the balcony.

In the area of Tavistock Square and Gordon Square in Bloomsbury, a set of footprints are said to commemorate a tragic story from the eighteenth century. The first sighting of these imprints was recorded in 1778 in a letter from a Thomas Smith to John Warner. It concerned a duel between two brothers in 1686 over a woman and the letter commented that 'the print of their feet is near three inches in depth and ... the number of [prints] may be about 90.' In the middle of the nineteenth century, the poet Robert Southey claimed to have counted twenty-six footprints. Garlick Hill in the City of London has been the location for the sighting of a grey figure holding its hands across its chest looking toward the altar of the church of St James Garlick Hythe. The ghost, who was nicknamed Jimmy Garlick, reputedly belonged to a mummified body found in 1855 in the vaults. Amongst various people to whom the corpse is ascribed is Dick Whittington whose cat is also said to haunt the church.

In 1803 the locals in Hammersmith were frightened by reports of a 'malevolent ghost'. The white figure, which emerged from the gravestones, chased a pregnant woman who later died from shock. The spectre also frightened many other people as well as numerous animals. It was thought to be the ghost of a man who had committed suicide by cutting his throat a year previously. As the incidents continued, Francis Smith came to the belief that the ghost was someone playing a prank and he decided to wait for the joker. When he suddenly saw a figure walking towards him he shot at it with a gun but only succeeded in hitting and killing an unfortunate bricklayer, Thomas Millwood. Smith was found guilty of manslaughter and sentenced to a one-year prison sentence. A real hoaxer, James Graham, who went out wearing a white sheet, was actually arrested. Nonetheless sightings of the Hammersmith 'ghost' continued to be reported for many years after and on two occasions hoaxers were arrested.

The nineteenth century saw an upsurge of interest in activities such as spiritualism and mesmerism, and a culture that embraced death through ritual, art and literature. Such interest was reflected in the growth of societies and clubs dedicated to making contact with the dead. The Ghost Club, established in 1862, is one of the oldest existing organisations associated with psychic matters. It was formed by a group of London gentlemen with the intention of exposing fraudulent mediums, but also to investigate psychic phenomena. Its members have included the philosopher C.E.M. Joad, the biologist Julian Huxley and the novelists Algernon Blackwood and Sir Osbert Sitwell.

Although the work of people such as Emanuel Swedenborg (1688–1772) and Franz Mesmer (1734–1815) provided earlier possibilities of direct personal knowledge of the afterlife, the history of modern spiritualism dates from the mid-nineteenth century in America and developed in England from the 1850s. Spiritualist churches and 'home circles' began appearing in Britain in 1865 and the British National Association of Spiritualists (renamed in 1884 as the London Spiritualist Alliance and now known as the College of Psychic Science) was founded in London in 1873. Despite the fact that many fraudulent people were attracted to the movement, it also attracted many genuine and notable members including Sir Arthur Conan Doyle (1859–1930) and the physicist Oliver Lodge (1851–1940).

Premature Burial

The dread of being buried alive found expression in literature and burial instructions, such as those left by Lord Chesterfield in a letter to his daughter-in-law on 16 March 1769: 'All I desire for my own burial is not to be buried alive'. Perhaps the most famous story is that by Edgar Allen Poe (1809–1849), *The Premature Burial* (1844), in which the sense of absolute terror is vividly portrayed in the book: 'The unendurable oppression of the lungs – the stifling fumes of the damp earth – the clinging of the death garments ... We know nothing so agonising upon earth – we can dream of nothing half so hideous in the realms of the nethermost Hell.'

Poe's chilling story of premature burial reflected and reinforced a fear that had become pervasive among sections of society during the nineteenth century. Taphephobia – the fear of being buried alive – was mirrored in literature, medical journals, newspapers and in real-life stories. The fears were so real that anti-premature burial campaigns emerged. But what generated these fears? An important factor was the problem of actually defining death. Until at least the seventeenth century when a person died the signs of death were taken to be a cessation of the heartbeat and arterial pulsations. It was common for people not to be examined by a medical practitioner after death. Even in the nineteenth century there were doctors who were incompetent at diagnosing death. The difficulties of diagnosing death provided fuel for well-meaning alarmists who, on the scantiest of evidence, claimed that many people were being buried alive.

Jacques-Bénigne Winslow (1669–1760), the Danish anatomist, argued that the determining signs of death were too uncertain to be relied upon and that the onset of putrefaction was the only reliable indicator that an individual had died. From this conclusion he suggested that people were in imminent danger of being buried alive. He recommended a number of measures to ensure the certainty of death. For example, 'the individual's nostrils were to be irritated by introducing sternutaries, errhines, juices of onions, garlic and horseradish.' He also suggested that gums were to be rubbed with garlic, and the skin be stimulated by the use of 'whips and nettles,' limbs could be violently pulled, and the ears shocked 'by hideous shrieks and excessive noises'; warm urine might also be poured into the mouth. Failing these attempts the corpse might have the soles of the feet cut with razors and then long needles pushed under the toe-nails. Few people aping death would cope with these tests.

There were many cases of people who were believed to be dead but then discovered to be alive, fortunately before they were to be buried. John Stow recorded a case of a man executed for a felony in February 1587. He was taken to the Surgeons Hall near Cripplegate for anatomical dissection and found to be alive, although he only lived for a further three days. Anne Greene was 'executed' at Tyburn in 1740 only to recover in the anatomy theatre. Anne lived on for many years.

Judgement concerning death was often left to non-medical persons and a hasty burial was not uncommon, particularly at the time of epidemics when there was a desire to be rid of a body as quickly as possible. This was particularly so during the bubonic plague of 1665

(Left) 1. St Botolph's Church, Aldgate. Daniel Defoe, in his book *A Journal of the Plague Year*, describes a great burial pit at St Botolph's Church: *it was about forty feet in length, and about fifteen or sixteen feet broad ... they had thrown into it 1114 bodies when they were obliged to fill it up, the bodies being then come to lie within six feet of the surface.*

(Above) 2. The Cross Bones Graveyard, Redcross Way, Southwark. A nearby notice reads: 'The shrine on these gates honours up to 15,000 people' buried in this graveyard. John Stow, in his *Survey of London* in 1603, described the burial site as being appointed to single women forbidden the rites of the church so long as they continued a sinful life.

3. *The Suicide of Lord Londonderry, Viscount Castlereagh* by George Cruikshank (1822). So unpopular was Castlereagh that crowds followed his funeral procession through the London streets, cheering. Unlike other suicides who were buried at a crossroads, Castlereagh was given the pomp of a state funeral.

(Above) 4. *The Danse Macabre.* An image from medieval times and used later by artists such as Thomas Rowlandson to show death as the great equalizer.

(Left) 5. The Cenotaph in Whitehall designed by Sir Edwin Lutyens. It was first designed as a temporary wood and plaster sculpture for the Peace Day events of 19 July 1919. It proved so popular that it was recreated as a permanent work in Portland stone.

6. The tomb of King Henry III (r. 1216–1272) in Westminster Abbey. His gold effigy rests on top.

(Above) 7. The Circle of Lebanon at Highgate Cemetery contains tombs, vaults and winding paths dug into hillsides.

(Left) 8. Preserving an image of life after death. Jeremy Bentham (1748–1832) sits in University College, University of London. He willed his body to be preserved and displayed.

(Right) 9. John Evelyn (1620–1706) bemoaned the state of the air and smoke that pervaded London: 'inhabitants breathe nothing but an impure and thick mist, accompanied by a fuliginous and filthy vapour' (1661, *Fumifugium, or the Inconvenience of the Aer and the Smoak of London Dissipated*).

(Below, left) 10. The Monument. The site of a number of dramatic and well documented suicides, particularly in the nineteenth century.

(Below, right) 11. The bullet that killed Nelson. Large sections of the public flocked for information and souvenirs in relation to the death of notable figures.

12. View from the inside and the top of the Monument as depicted by *The Graphic* (1891).

13. The strange but sinister looking plague doctor.

14. A Victorian depiction of suicide. The River Thames has been the recipient of many such deaths.

15. Effigies of Knights Templar in the nave of Temple Church in High Holborn. The Church was consecrated on 10 February 1185 in a ceremony conducted by Heraclius, the Crusader Patriarch of Jerusalem.

16. The grisly Tyburn gallows which used to be situated near to where the present Marble Arch stands. Tens of thousands went to their death at Tyburn until it was removed in 1783.

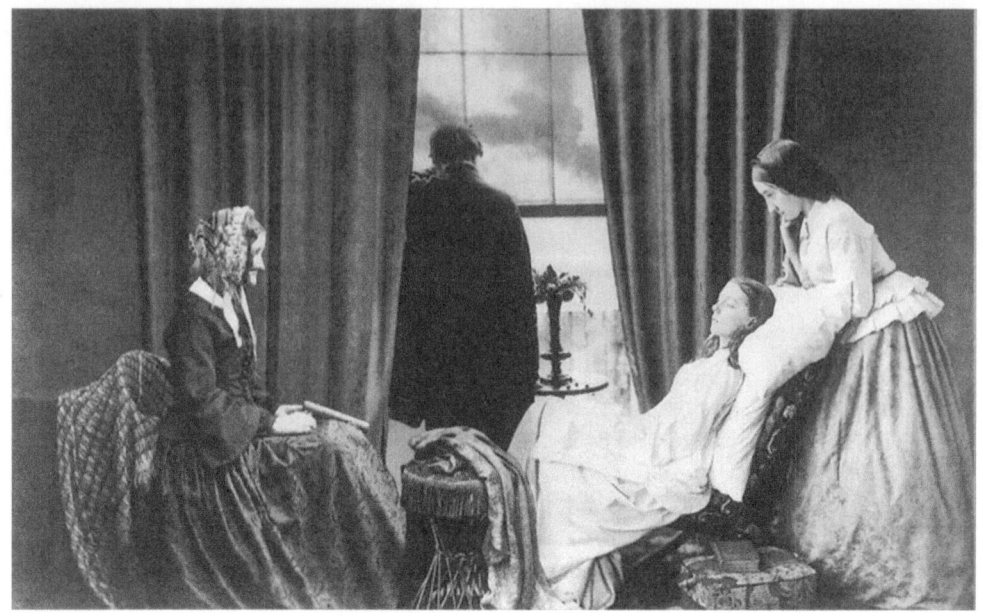

17. 'The Victorian way of death' (*H. Peach Robinson*, 'Fading Away', 1858).

18. The Duke of Wellington's funeral procession passing through Trafalgar Square in 1852.

when 68,576 deaths were recorded. This figure would certainly be much higher if unrecorded deaths were added. During the plague, a butcher in Newgate Street escaped a premature burial because the corpse bearers, either through an oversight or negligence, had not removed him from the room in which he died. During the night he recovered and came downstairs complaining that he felt cold. Doubtless his appearance gave his family quite a turn. He was more fortunate than many unlucky souls who must have been taken off in a cart to be dumped unceremoniously into one of London's plague pits. In his *Journal of the Plague Year*, Daniel Defoe records a scene which could almost be out of *Monty Python and the Holy Grail*: a cart was being taken to Mill Hill with a pile of bodies to be disposed of when the driver heard someone shouting 'Hey, where am I?' On investigating the cry, the driver found a man among the tangle of bodies who asked 'I ain't dead am I?'

A less fortunate victim was Lawrence Cawthorne, a butcher in Newgate Market, who fell ill and was quickly buried. It was when people heard muffled screams and scratching coming from the tomb in the chapel where he was buried that Cawthorne's dreadful fate was discovered. When the body was retrieved his shroud was torn to shreds, his eyes were swollen and, according to the version in *The Most Lamentable Account and Deplorable Accident which ... Befell Lawrence Cawthorne*, his brains were 'beaten out of his head.' His premature burial had stemmed from the greed of his landlady who stood to inherit Cawthorne's belongings. In her haste to despatch him she had quickly placed him in the tomb as soon as it was evident that he had fallen seriously ill. An account in *A Full and True Relation of a Maid Living in Newgate Street in London* (1680) records the tragic event of a sixteen-year-old maid who had lived in Newgate Street. She cried and screamed for four days from her burial place in a London cemetery but attempts to rescue her were sadly in vain.

In January 1729, the *London Journal* reported on the premature burial of a milk woman's daughter from Enfield. The report stated that

> some people at the funeral thought she looked fresh, and taking a looking glass, and applying it to her lips, they fancied they perceived a dew on it as from breath, but the cruel mother mock'd and reviled them, and swore she

should be buried, and so she was; but this coming to the ears of a near relation, he got the grave dug up, and the coffin open'd, when she was found with her knees drawn up, and the nosegay in her hand beaten to pieces with struggling for life. A surgeon was sent for to bleed her, but it was then too late.

A woman was nearly buried alive in the Church of St Giles Cripplegate. The case was mentioned in the 1870s by Henry Wilby, a medical writer who referred to it as an example of the possibility of premature burial. The woman fell into such a deep coma that she was believed to be dead and she was laid to rest in the church crypt. A devious sexton, who had designs on stealing her wedding ring, also inadvertently saved her life. At night he sneaked into the crypt and tried to remove her ring finger with a knife. The pain was so great that the woman screamed and caused the sexton to run away in terror. The woman managed to climb out of her coffin and stagger home. Her family must have thought they had really seen a ghost when she turned up on the doorstep. She lived for many more years and gave birth to four more children. Wilby offered this case in the genuine belief that it would alert people to the dangers of premature burial. There were so many apocryphal stories about such burials, however, that it is difficult to distinguish fact from fiction.

Fears of premature burials had been particularly rife in Germany and France and had generated many debates as well as a spate of devices for security coffins. In Britain the hysteria had not been as widespread, although by the early nineteenth century an increasing interest was aroused as literature and sensational accounts from Europe became available in English. Some of the more well-to-do sections of society started to make provisions against such a diabolical fate. One method was to delay burial and leave the deceased lying in their caskets for a period of time. The Duke of Wellington who died on 14 September 1852 was not buried until 18 November, two months after his death. Other methods of securing death and making sure that the body had no hope of reviving were particularly gruesome. Requests in wills were made to have the coffin filled with lime, or to have the head amputated or the throat cut. Elizabeth Thomas of Islington left instructions to her physician to pierce her heart with a long metal pin.

The combination of high death rates, growing morbid sensitivities, publications and the popularity of Gothic horror and ghost stories helped to fuel fears of premature burial. Elaborate methods were devised to prevent the possibility of being buried alive. A simple method of allaying premature burial anxiety was to place crowbars and shovels in the deceased's caskets, the idea being that if they revived they could dig their way out. Another device involved a pipe that went through the ground and into the casket and could be used for emergency communications. Wealthy families even hired servants to wait by the pipes and listen for calls for help. Some also had coffins fitted with special nails that, when driven, punctured capsules of poison gas. It seems that the Victorians were preoccupied not only with the ritual of death but also with the state of death.

The most popular device by far, however, was the Bateson Revival Device. It was advertised as 'a most economical, ingenious, and trustworthy mechanism, superior to any other method, and promoting peace of mind amongst the bereaved in all stations of life. A device of proven efficacy, in countless instances in this country and abroad.'

George Bateson was a nineteenth-century inventor and his device consisted of an iron bell mounted on the lid of the casket just above the head of the body. The bell was connected to a cord through the coffin that was placed in the dead person's hand in case of a last tremor of the 'deceased' which would then sound alarm. The ringing would also depend on some attentive gravedigger being sufficiently close to hear it and come to the rescue. There is no evidence or record that this device actually saved anyone's life but at least it enjoyed enough sales for many years to earn Bateson a good financial return. Despite having a genuine fear of premature death, Bateson clearly distrusted his own invention because in his will he asked to be cremated. He became so obsessed with the fear of death that it was believed he was driven mad and subsequently committed suicide in 1886 by dousing himself with linseed oil and setting himself on fire in his workshop.

In 1896 Arthur Lovell, a spiritualist and quack, founded the London Society for the Prevention of Premature Burial. Its aims were to raise people's awareness of the risks of premature burial, the scientific study of death and a commitment from the medical profession that no one would be buried alive. William Tebb and Walter Hadwen were leading members of the Society. Tebb had been a vocal opponent of vaccination which he put on a par with alcoholism, smoking and lust as among the most evil elements in society. In 1905 the Society began its journal, *The Burial Reformer*, which contained sensational stories of near-escapes from premature burials. Tebb claimed that he had found evidence of 219 cases of narrow escapes from premature burials, 149 actual instances and a dozen where people were either dissected or embalmed before they were dead. Circulation figures for *The Burial Reformer* have not been recorded but the Society managed to recruit two MPs into its ranks who attempted to push through an unsuccessful bill in 1908 to safeguard against premature burial. The Society started to decline after 1910 and in 1936 its few remaining members merged with the Council for the Disposition of the Dead.

The superstition and the fears of earlier societies had been dispelled by rationalists of a more enlightened age. However, responses to the slaughter in the First World War triggered, as Jay Winter writes in *Sites of Memory, Sites of Mourning* (1995), a revival of traditional forms of expression. The revival of interest in spiritualism during and after the war was one such expression. Soldiers claimed to see the sightings of an angelic army at Mons and the purveyors of 'psychic photography' claimed to capture the spirits of dead soldiers hovering above the living. The return of apocalyptic and biblical themes were, it seems, a response to exceptionally traumatic events.

8
Death and Disaster

Many books have been written about the disasters and catastrophes that have affected London and carried off its citizens, sometimes in huge numbers. We cannot do justice to such events within the confines of a single chapter. We will not, for example, examine the impact of the Black Death or the Great Plague on London at any length. Instead this chapter deals with events that perhaps are less well-known, that offer features of particular interest or are peculiar in some way. In some cases, these disasters led to no more than a handful of deaths.

The worst storm in its history hit Britain on 26 and 27 November 1703. Its effects in London were described by Daniel Defoe, an awed but fascinated eye-witness. Ironically, this hurricane hit London when much of it had recently been rebuilt after the devastation caused by the Great Fire. The decision had been made to employ less flammable materials in the rebuilding but it seems that much of the work was rushed and bodged. In addition, many of the new buildings were taller than their predecessors which may have channelled the wind and increased its turbulence. Massive amounts of structural damage occurred. Chimney stacks crashed into the streets or through roofs into houses, whole buildings collapsed, tiles flew in all directions, sometimes embedding themselves deeply in whatever was in the way, lead from church roofs curled up like rolls of carpet and was flung long distances and spires and pinnacles tumbled, smashing to smithereens in the streets.

Death was unpredictable and capricious in its choice of victims. A watchman going about his business in Ratcliff Highway was crushed by a falling chimney. A successful businessman died when part of his house in Hackney collapsed. Two children were fatally injured by collapsing masonry in Whitehall. There were some miraculous escapes, however. A child was killed in its cot only a few feet away from its parents' bed; they survived physically unscathed. A serving maid was injured seriously but survived to be rescued because some rafters had arrested the fall of a chimney stack. Around 8,000 people died in England, but the exact number of fatalities in London is not known. It may have been the surprisingly low figure of about twenty in the built-up area. Defoe estimated that more than twenty died on and around the River Thames, particularly in the Pool of London where vast numbers of ships were reduced to matchwood. Some houses and shops were looted and some voyeurs walked the streets to ogle at others' misfortunes, but within days it was 'business as normal' in London. This seems to have been a leitmotif of the way Londoners have coped with death.

Oliver Cromwell's head was possibly another of the victims of the 'Great Storm'. In July 1661, the bodies of Cromwell, Bradshaw and Ireton – regarded as the most culpable regicides – were exhumed, hanged at Tyburn and buried there. Their heads were parboiled and then impaled on poles on the top of Westminster Hall. The story, which may well be apocryphal, goes that Cromwell's head was still there in 1703. It apparently blew down in the storm and fell into the street where it was found by a sentry. Although time is unlikely to have been kind to the head, the sentry presumably knew what it was and decided to take it away and hide it; perhaps he thought it had some value, or less likely, that he might find a use for it some time. When he died, his wife sold it to a collector of curios and its subsequent fate and exact whereabouts constituted a conundrum for many years. The current consensus is that it is interred in the wall of Sidney Sussex College in Cambridge.

The River Thames used to freeze over with some frequency in the days when it was wider and more sluggish, partly because its flow was impeded by the piers of Old London Bridge. When they could, Londoners in huge number used to venture onto the ice where innumerable 'Frost Fairs' were held on the frozen river. Everyday activities took on a new and novel aspect when they could be carried on from the middle of the river. In 1564, for example, a football match was played on the ice. In 1608 booths for business and pleasure were set up, and in 1683 a row of shops was erected which included a printing press enjoying a ready sale for novelty items produced on the river. The last great Frost Fair was in the winter of 1813–14. For sixteen continuous days a solid mass of ice blocked the Thames from Blackfriars to London Bridge. Sheep were roasted in mid-stream and sold in slices promoted as 'Lapland Mutton'. The thaw arrived unexpectedly and huge pieces of ice broke away carrying stalls, swings, traders and revellers with them. Many of them drowned.

Risks are inherent in going into frozen water and over the centuries, a considerable toll has been taken in the lives of the foolhardy, the stupid or the simply unlucky. Cold snaps also took a regular, if less spectacular, toll of London's poorer and more vulnerable citizenry who starved when food supplies of fish and grain stopped because ships were unable to use the river. Others simply froze to death when supplies of seacoal were interrupted. Many employers temporarily shut their businesses and laid their workers off. This caused enormous privation and led to illness, starvation and death.

Over the centuries, Old London Bridge was the scene of large numbers of fatalities. Fire was a constant hazard. In either 1212 or 1213, the records being unclear, a fire broke out in Southwark. Londoners have always been keen on free entertainment and when the southern portion of the bridge caught fire, sizeable crowds came onto the northern or City end of the bridge anticipating a conflagration that they would be able to tell their grandchildren about. They approached as near as they dared when to their horror the buildings at their end also ignited, possibly because of sparks. Caught between a flaming Scylla and an equally fiery Charybdis, many panicked and squeezed into the openings between the houses, leaping into the river or attempting to climb into the boats which rushed to their assistance. Some of the boats were simply overwhelmed by the numbers and capsized. Many of their occupants and those who had dived into the river were swept to their death in the fierce currents. The number of fatalities is not known but is likely to have run into several hundreds.

In 1450, during Cade's Rebellion, London Bridge was at the centre of desperate hand-to-hand fighting during which the insurgents, who were mostly from Kent, attempted to capture the bridge in order to gain access to the City. The defenders controlled a drawbridge which was part of the structure and so the rebels set fire to the houses on the bridge in an attempt to force the defenders to retreat. Unfortunately, many of the occupants were in the houses sheltering from the fighting. Substantial numbers were either immolated or drowned when they leapt off the bridge.

In 1632 a maidservant had an accident with a bucket of hot ashes in one of the houses at the northern end of the bridge. The bridge burnt merrily away for a couple of days although fortunately on this occasion there seems to have been little loss of life.

The piers of Old London Bridge were protected by large timber starlings, or cutwaters. These had the effect of channelling the current through the arches of the bridge with considerable force and making the passage of the bridge not unlike the shooting of a weir. Great skill was required by the Thames watermen to navigate these openings successfully, particularly when the tide was turning. Circumspect passengers, and they included Cardinal Wolsey and Doctor Johnson, were content to disembark on one side of the bridge and resume their journey on the other. The watermen, of course, had little option but to shoot the bridge and over the years large numbers of them paid the ultimate price. When he was Secretary of the Navy in the seventeenth century, Samuel Pepys did not want to be seen to be a sissy and on his journeys to and from Westminster and Greenwich he always shot the bridge, but never without his heart in his mouth. Hazards like white water attract hotheads and there were many occasions on which men, mostly young and sometimes the worse for drink, ordered the watermen to shoot the bridge. Passengers and watermen often died as a consequence of this foolhardiness.

In 1641 Queen Henrietta Maria's barge was passing under London Bridge when it hit an obstruction and capsized. All on board were saved with one exception. This was Anne Kirke who was Woman of the Bedchamber to the Queen. Anne seems to have been liked by all who knew her and her death was commemorated in verse. The prestigious position she held also meant that she was one of the very few people who died shooting Old London Bridge who also had her likeness reproduced in a portrait.

In 1689 John Temple committed suicide under the bridge. He owed the important public posts he held to nepotism. There was, of course, nothing unusual about this but being of a sensitive nature he had become seriously depressed after badly fouling up one after another of the various duties he was entrusted with. He ordered the waterman to shoot the bridge and when the boat reached the roaring cataract he jumped overboard and immediately sank out of sight. This is not surprising because he had filled his pockets with stones.

Not all of those who died at Old London Bridge necessarily drowned. In 1762 records tell of a man who was crossing when he was killed by a brickbat accidentally dislodged from a house on the bridge that was being demolished. The carriageway across the bridge was narrow before all the houses and other buildings were removed and in 1758 a woman and her child were crushed to death by passing traffic. Apparently this was by no means the first time that fatalities of this sort had occurred. The building of the replacement for Old London Bridge was started in 1824 and completed behind schedule in 1831. Forty men either drowned or were killed some other way during its construction.

The winter of 1866-7 was exceptionally cold. Once again, appalling hardship including starvation was experienced by many and looting and bread riots broke out in the most deprived areas of London's East End and Dockland. Others saw the extreme weather conditions as a chance for fun and games: thousands headed to London's parks to skate on their lakes and ponds. On 15 January 1867, despite warnings posted in Regent's Park telling people not to go on the ice, hundreds ignored them. With a sudden loud crack, the ice broke and many of them were precipitated into the water. There was little that attendants or the horrified onlookers could do because the lake was deep at that time. Forty drowned or died from the cold.

The Savoy Palace was a huge mansion originally built in the thirteenth century close to the Strand and constantly updated and improved until it became a hospital for the poor in 1505. It suffered many vicissitudes until the site was cleared around 1820. All that now remains is the Savoy Chapel. The Palace belonged to the widely hated John of Gaunt, Duke of Lancaster (1340–99) and was attacked by Wat Tyler's supporters during the Peasants' Revolt in 1381. Many of its valuables were destroyed or thrown into the Thames, but random looting was not allowed. Thirty-two men who eagerly helped themselves to the Duke's wine were trapped in the cellars and left to die of starvation as a punishment.

In 1780 London was racked by the Gordon Riots. They lasted about a week and the ostensible cause was a protest against measures that Parliament was taking towards partial emancipation of the Catholic population. As can happen with riots that occur over such a long period, many who took part had either forgotten what the riots were about, or in some cases neither knew nor cared anyway. For some, rioting was little more than an excuse to embark on an orgy of destruction and looting, for others it was a form of entertainment. Among the places that were attacked and set on fire was Langdale's Distillery in Holborn. Some rioters broached the casks and simply drank themselves into permanent oblivion with their mouths at the bungholes. Others lay in the gutters and lapped up the gin as it coursed down the nearby streets, in some cases consuming so much that they never woke up. More horrible was the fate experienced by those who drank themselves into near-insensibility in the gutters but were still conscious enough to experience the agonies of immolation when they were overwhelmed by streams of burning gin.

Brewing was a highly competitive industry in London in the early nineteenth century. Companies vied with each other to build and operate ever-larger vats for the storage of beer. Size definitely counted as far as brewery prestige was concerned. One enormous container was 60 feet in diameter, 23 feet high and had a capacity of 10,000 barrels of beer. Before it came into use a banquet for 200 guests was held inside it. In 1814 a similar giant vessel at Meux's Brewery in St Giles, just off the Tottenham Court Road, burst and a tsunami of porter knocked down the brewery walls, demolished a number of nearby houses and caused the death of eight people by drowning, injury, inhaling poisonous fumes or terminal intoxication.

Scandalously, the company was not required to pay compensation to the relations of the bereaved or those whose property was damaged, but it successfully petitioned Parliament for a refund on the duty it had already paid on what it claimed were 7,664 lost barrels of porter. It received 18s 11d per barrel. Independent experts reckoned that about 3,500 barrels had actually been lost.

In November 1802, three men ambushed and robbed a well-to-do merchant on Hounslow Heath. He died from injuries sustained in what was evidently a particularly ferocious attack. There was no clue as to the identity of the attackers until about four years later when a convicted thief called Benjamin Hanfield was awaiting transportation. Believing that he was dying, he confessed to his part in the murder and named his accomplices. They were Owen Haggerty and John Holloway who were both found guilty and sentenced to be hanged outside Newgate Prison on 23 February 1807. Fascinated by the brutality of the murder and the time it had taken to solve it, an unusually large crowd of about 40,000 turned out. From 1783 the street named Old Bailey, adjacent to Newgate, had become the major place of execution in London. Theoretically, crowd control was easier here than at the previous location at Tyburn, close to Hyde Park. However, the southern end of Old Bailey tapered towards Ludgate and seriously constricted the movement of the crowd in that area. Such was the density of the crowd that panic broke out as some attempted to fight their way out of the press. A pie-man bent over to retrieve the pies that had been knocked to the floor. He fell and disappeared in a melee of flailing feet. Like skittles, others fell and many never rose again. A baby made a miraculous escape when its mother handed it to her neighbour as she lost her footing and went down, only to be crushed to death. The baby was passed to safety over the heads of the crowd. Twenty-eight people died and about seventy received serious injuries. An enterprising local publican was quickly on the scene moving among the dead and the dying and gathering up scarves, gloves and other minor items of clothing which he placed in a hand barrow. There was always a buoyant demand for second-hand clothes in London.

Caroline was undoubtedly one of England's most rumbustious Queens. She was also one of the most popular for a wide variety of reasons. Her husband, who after waiting an inordinately long time to become King George IV, was, on the other hand, one of the most widely loathed and scorned. Caroline was German and when she died in 1821 it was arranged that her hearse would be taken through the West End before heading east for Harwich and the Continent. The London crowd turned out in huge numbers to wish the dead Queen well, and to display their contempt for the King. The mood was ugly and the forces of law were limited. They consisted of a Bow Street foot patrol and a company of Life Guards. Although the Bow Street patrols can clearly be identified as the predecessors of the Metropolitan Police a few years later, they were ill-equipped to deal with large and angry crowds. They were not uniformed, their only weapons were wooden staves and their training and discipline were poor. The Life Guards were of course regular mounted soldiers in a crack regiment and should have been highly trained and disciplined.

The mood of the crowd grew uglier and uglier, and some spectators started to pelt the patrolmen with mud and then with stones. Injuries were inflicted. Ironically it was not members of the Bow Street patrol that provoked what became a riot. While a magistrate stood by impotently, the Life Guards fired warning volleys over the heads of the crowd. This only caused greater resentment and as the crowd surged forward, the soldiers began to lay about them with the flats of their swords. When a Life Guard was knocked from his horse by a man wielding a flagpole, his companions panicked as the crowd surrounded them and fired shots indiscriminately into the crowd, causing two fatalities. The incompetence and the impotence displayed by the forces of law and order on this occasion added substance to the demand that was gradually building up for the creation of a permanent, uniformed, trained and professional police force.

London in the nineteenth century was the busiest seaport in the world. The Pool of London extended eastwards from London Bridge as far as Wapping on the north bank of the Thames and the Surrey Docks on the south bank. The range of goods that occupied the holds of these ships was baffling in its extent and variety. By 1860 many enclosed docks had been built, starting with the West India Docks in 1802 and 1806, the London Docks in 1805 and East India Docks in 1806. Much of the cargo that arrived in the ocean-going ships was transferred to lighters and brought upstream to wharves just below London Bridge before being stored in massive riverside warehouses. Many of these were located in Tooley Street on the Southwark side of the river. The cargo they contained included such commodities as sugar and spirits and were potentially highly flammable. The buildings in which the goods were housed were multi-storey buildings with wooden floors and features such as hoist ports, stairwells and chutes which could act as conduits for air to feed the flames if a fire broke out. Their complicated internal layout provided problems for fire-fighters. The owners of these premises preferred to pay insurance rather than to install expensive fire precautions. The scene was set for the greatest conflagration in London since the Great Fire, and one that would not be equalled until the Blitz.

One summer's evening in June 1861 a fire broke out in Scovell's warehouse, which contained a potentially volatile mix of such items as sugar, rice, saltpetre, tallow, jute and cotton. It had been a hot day and, fatally as it turned out, workers had understandably opened every door and window they could in order to allow in what little circulating air there was. It was a Saturday night with only a skeleton staff on the premises. Scovell's was quickly ablaze and it was soon evident that it could not be saved. With frightening speed the fire spread through the close-packed complex of warehouses and factory premises, some of which contained other combustible substances such as paint and oil. Men from various fire brigades attended but there was little they could do as the fire spread hungrily and it had to be left to go out of its own accord. Vast numbers of sightseers made their way to any vantage points from which they could enjoy this bonanza of free visual entertainment. Perhaps surprisingly only two fire-fighters were killed. One of them was James Braidwood who was London's first overall fire chief. He had been trying to get some semblance of order out of the chaos that passed for fire regulations and fire-fighting in London at that time. The Tooley Street fire was evidence of how urgent the job was and how much still had to be done. Other fatalities were among the kind of people always drawn to the scene of disasters. Many barrels of liquor had fallen from the burning buildings into the Thames. A number of opportunists, oblivious to the dangers, had obtained boats and were attempting to heave some of these casks aboard when they were caught in the treacherous currents and swept downstream into a great pool of blazing tallow. There was no escape.

The issue of Irish nationalism was a running ulcer in the body of British politics for the best part of two centuries. There were periods of relative inactivity and others when it forced itself to the top of the political agenda. Such a time was 1867. Two leading Fenians, Burke and Casey, had been arrested and placed in the House of Detention in Clerkenwell, but their comrades decided to free them. They laid their plans with some care. While Burke and Casey were taking their exercise in the prison yard, the others were to place a wagon filled with explosives against the outside of the prison wall. When the wagon was detonated, a large hole would be made in the wall through which Burke and Casey would escape. The date for the escape attempt was to be 13 December 1867. Unfortunately for the Fenians, the prison governor had received a warning that there might be an 'incident' and he had cancelled the open-air exercise for the prisoners that day. The conspirators did not know this and went ahead. The explosion was spectacular and the hole they blew in the prison wall was 60 feet wide but while it did not enable their comrades to escape, it did bring down a terrace of working-class dwellings nearby, killing twelve people and injuring 120 others. Six suspects were arrested. Five of them were acquitted, the other, Michael Barratt, being convicted of murder as it was believed that he had triggered the explosion. Barratt had the dubious distinction of being the last man to be judicially hanged in public. This was outside Newgate Prison on 26 May 1868.

Mass murder and unintentional cannibalism make a powerful and intriguing duo of elements for devotees of the murkier aspects of human behaviour. They come together in one of London's most enduring legends – that of Sweeney Todd. So many melodramas have been penned around the theme that it is hard to distinguish fact from fiction. The fundamentals are these: in the 1780s, a barber with premises in Fleet Street would invite selected customers to sit in a particular seat in his shop. When the barber activated a hidden device, the chair tipped up and precipitated its occupant into the cellar below. Usually the victim broke his neck, but the barber could finish him off with a cutthroat razor if necessary. The bodies, so the story goes, were then manhandled along an underground passage to a cellar belonging to the diabolical barber's equally devilish accomplice, a female pastry cook and pie-maker in Bell Yard. The couple then dismembered and chopped up their victims and used the fleshy parts as the main ingredient in mutton pies whose tastiness was such that they enjoyed great popularity with those members of the legal fraternity who had chambers nearby and others who came from miles around. The number of those murdered and disposed of in this fashion has been estimated to be between 30 and 160.

This gruesome phantasmagoria has provided novelists, dramatists, poets and film-makers with a wealth of material but many of them probably do not realise that beneath the melodrama there is almost certainly a substantial residue of fact. There was indeed a barber's shop, possibly at No. 186 Fleet Street, very close to the church of St Dunstan's-in-the-West. This church had extensive cellars and passages radiating in various directions. Fleet Street was the semi-respectable façade, as it were, of a notorious criminal rookery or 'Alsatia' and these passages were probably used by local thieves and others to escape from the scene of their crimes. Bell Yard, where the egregious pie-maker had her premises, still exists, but in 1780 it consisted of a jumble of down-at-heel dwellings and shops. The pie shop was probably at the north end of Bell Yard, close to Carey Street. A character with the name Sweeney Todd seems to have been hanged outside Newgate Prison in 1802 and was buried, as was the practice, within the precincts of the prison. He had apparently been an unrepentant villain of the darkest hue. It may be the same man who was a barber, renting premises in Fleet Street, and who is recorded as having been arrested on unspecified 'serious charges'. Subsequent excavations during building work in this area of Fleet Street have unearthed large numbers of human bones. Such gory caches are by no means uncommon and do not by themselves constitute absolute proof that Sweeney Todd and his no less awful pie-making accomplice practised their fiendish activities in this locality.

Sweeney Todd, the demon barber of Fleet Street, is a bogeyman deeply etched into the popular culture of London. Like Jack the Ripper, the very mention of his name evokes frissons of terror. If he did indeed exist, he was almost certainly responsible for far more premature deaths than the Whitechapel Murderer. He even made his way into Cockney rhyming slang, in which Sweeney Todd or 'The Sweeney' refers to the Flying Squad.

Smithfield is a district of London with blood on its hands, a place of mass death. Trading in live and dead sheep, pigs and cattle took place there for 500 years or more and, remarkably, the London Central Meat Market continues to function to this day. At Smithfield in 1381, Wat Tyler was stabbed by the perfidious Lord Mayor of London, William Walworth, as he parleyed with the King on behalf of his peasant followers. Shortly afterwards, he was beheaded close by. Many political prisoners, possibly including the Scottish patriot William Wallace, were executed at Smithfield but the district's most infamous associations are probably with the many men and women who died there rather than abjure their religious beliefs. In many cases, of course, these unfortunates were regarded as heretics. The crimes for which they were called upon to answer, were, in effect, political.

The first Smithfield martyrs were Lollards, supporters of John Wycliffe (1324–84) whose heterodox views led to their persecution, especially during the reign of Henry IV (1399–1413). Those accused of heresy were given the opportunity to recant and, if they did not, they were burnt at the stake. Lollard trials and burnings continued sporadically through the fifteenth and into the sixteenth century. In 1494 Joan Broughton died at Smithfield, the first female Lollard to die for her beliefs. She was over eighty years of age.

Those in power have always believed, quite wrongly, that they can expunge ideas simply by destroying the people who voice them. So it was with Henry VIII (r. 1509–47) who destroyed those who denied his position as Supreme Head of the Church. One such was John Forest, although he had already infuriated the King. He was one of Catherine of Aragon's chaplains and had loyally supported her over the matter of the divorce from the King. He was consigned to Smithfield where he was roasted alive in a metal cage. Henry was ready to have Catholics and Protestants alike executed for heresy, but when his daughter Mary came to the throne in 1553, a wave of terror was unleashed against those bold enough or stupid enough to stand up for their Protestant beliefs. The first Protestant to die at Smithfield during Anne's reign was John Rogers, the vicar of St Sepulchre without Newgate. He was burnt at the stake on 4

February 1555 in front of a large crowd which included his wife and their eleven children, one a baby at the breast.

In June 1558, seven Protestants were burnt at Smithfield, an unusually large number to be burnt at one time. They were among twenty people who had been arrested for attending a clandestine Protestant service but they refused to attend Mass, that being the price for their pardon. A large, sympathetic crowd turned out to watch them die and were warned that any of them showing support for the condemned prisoners would be severely punished. The threat notwithstanding, the crowd gave vent to its accumulated rage and there was little that the authorities dared to do.

An estimated 283 Protestants were burnt during Mary's bleak reign, fifty-six of them at Smithfield. Those hoping for the fresh wind of ecumenicalism and tolerance to course through English Christianity with the arrival on the throne of Elizabeth, were in for a severe disappointment. Now it was the turn of Catholics to suffer persecution and many were immolated at Tyburn, often after having suffered on the rack – a fiendish torture device which underwent various technical refinements and enjoyed great popularity, although not with its victims, at this time. Given the numbers that died at Smithfield, it is not surprising that many people over the years have attested to the ghostly smell of burning flesh and the sound of anguished, terrified screams drifting across West Smithfield, and especially around the gateway into the churchyard of St Bartholomew the Great. The place has 'atmosphere', as they would say.

9
Pestilence and Public Health

London has always been dirty, but most of time it was also stinking and pestilential. Epidemics, pandemics and stench were not the monopoly of London; other English towns were foetid and disease-ridden. London, however, has always provoked the superlatives. Its enormous size relative to all other towns and cities meant that it was quite simply the filthiest, most noxious and most effective breeding ground for disease in the Kingdom. The diseases were often fatal. In 1831, the death rate in London stood at 25.2 per thousand. This compared with 22.5 for England as a whole. The diseases which ravaged the capital only began to be tackled effectively in the second half of the nineteenth century.

London's history could be viewed as the history of its water supplies. London stood on a large river into which many tributaries flowed. Wells and springs provided access to a huge water table trapped by the clays and gravels of the Thames Basin. Such names as Camberwell, Clerkenwell and Sadler's Wells are reminders of their existence. The Romans chose to build a city on the site for many reasons, one of which was that there seemed to be an abundance of fresh water.

As London grew, so demand for water increased. As the ague-ridden marshes on the south bank were drained, watercourses built over and the wells and springs dried up, efforts had to be made to find water elsewhere. As late as the nineteenth century, men eked out a frugal living by walking the streets with a yoke over their shoulders from which hung open-topped barrels of water, often drawn from nearby wells. They touted for custom and added their shouts to the general cacophony that was such a feature of the streets of London. The lucky ones found custom with the owners of taverns and eating-places who placed regular orders for fresh, cool and clean water to accompany the meals they provided.

In about 1238 a pipe-line was built from the manor of Marylebone in open country about three miles west of the City. It conveyed water from the stream known as the Tyburn to the Great Conduit in Cheapside. This was close to St Paul's and was erected specially for the purpose. It was a huge lead cistern reinforced with stone and at first the water was freely available to all. Other conduits were added over the centuries to help to feed London's ever-growing demand for water. Pipes were sometimes of stone or clay but more often they were made from hollowed-out pieces of elm. Over short distances, for the purpose of connecting into the premises of domestic and industrial consumers, the pipes were often made of lead. Even in those days, much water was lost through leakages.

The most obvious source of water remained the Thames. John Stow in his monumental *Survey of London* explained how water was conveyed through lead pipes straight into peoples' houses from a pumping device located under an arch of London Bridge. This clever device involved a waterwheel and came into use in 1582, not being decommissioned until 1822. The Thames water was of course filthy and full of disease-bearing organisms.

The first major scheme to tap into water supplies that were distant from London was the well-known project developed by Sir Hugh Myddelton, completed in 1613. This brought clean water from springs and streams in Hertfordshire to a reservoir at New River Head in the Islington district just north of the City. For a substantial fee of at least 5s per annum, the householder could be connected to the mains, which were made of wood, by a lead pipe called a 'quill'. Since the supplies to individual houses only operated a few days a week, it was advisable to install a storage tank in the cellar, probably of lead. Wooden pipes absorbed pollutants, even from this relatively clean source. Lead of course contains various toxins. Constant exposure to these toxins over long periods could be fatal.

During the rebuilding of London after the Great Fire of 1666, owners of new houses were given the opportunity of being supplied with water from either the New River Water Company or the London Bridge Waterworks. This gave them the choice of water that was relatively pure, or water that was close-to-hand but likely to be polluted and to look, smell and taste foul. They often chose the latter because it was considerably cheaper.

The quality of its water supplies deteriorated as the population of London and its environs grew. The Thames and the various tributaries that flowed into it in the vicinity of London became progressively filthier. These streams were used as convenient receptacles for every sort of refuse – animal, vegetable or mineral. If this ordure was tipped into the street, it stank and got in the way. Throwing it into the nearest watercourse meant that there was some chance that it would be washed away from the immediate vicinity. Perhaps the most notorious of the tributaries was the Fleet which became a festering open sewer, flowing – perhaps we should say oozing – through the western fringes of the City in an area densely occupied by housing and industrial premises. Like virtually all of the streams that made their way into the Thames in the area we now think of as central London, the Fleet was eventually covered over. Only then did these streams cease to be quite so filthy and germ-ridden. Just how awful the ordure and other pollutants that were contained in these streams could be was shown in 1846 when gases produced by the material in the Fleet caused it to explode and a tsunami of excrement coursed down its shallow valley and demolished three Poor Law workhouses in Clerkenwell, drowning some of their occupants.

Lining the banks of streams like the Fleet were knackers' yards, tanneries, glue factories, slaughterhouses, tar-works and other working premises. These not only emitted their own offensive smells but deposited their effluents and refuse in the nearest convenient stream. These tributaries took on a colour compounded of all the noxious substances they received and also deposited a repulsive, stinking, viscous slime along their courses. This was visible at low tide both in the tributaries and in the Thames itself around the outflows. In hot, humid weather the stench given off by the water and the mud was simply indescribable. In wet weather, with heavier flows of water, the smell from this repulsive detritus would be somewhat diminished.

Jonathan Swift (1667–1745) gives a sense of the disgusting nature of the City's open water-courses in his 'Description of a City Shower' (1711):

> Now from all parts the swelling kennels* flow,
> And bear their trophies with them as they go:
> Filth of all hues and odours seem to tell
> What street they sail'd from, by their sight and smell ...
> Drown'd puppies, stinking sprats, all drench'd in mud,
> Dead cats and turnip-tops, come tumbling down the flood.

Kennels are drains or gutters.

As late as the second half of the nineteenth century, the various private companies that supplied water to London's citizens did so largely through wooden pipes and, using the excuse that those pipes could not stand up to constant pressure, seriously restricted the times at which water was available from standpipes. Their subscribers were therefore tempted to draw water from alternative sources at other times, which were often polluted and occasionally lethal.

Waste disposal has always posed formidable problems for Londoners. In the fourteenth century it became illegal to discharge sewage into watercourses and cesspits were provided as receptacles for this purpose. However, Londoners ignored official decrees and continued to throw human excrement and all sorts of other waste matter into the nearest convenient stream, simply because it was easy to do so. If it flowed away it became someone else's problem.

The state of the cesspits and the frequency (or otherwise) with which they were emptied provided a topic for Londoners to carp and gripe about. Men called 'rakers' or 'gong-fermors' emptied the cesspits. This job carried little status but was comparatively well paid because of its intrinsically unpleasant nature and the anti-social working-hours – it was normally performed at night. Perhaps it also attracted an element of danger money: in 1326 the unfortunate 'Richard the

Raker' fell into a cesspit and was described somewhat unsympathetically as having drowned 'monstrously in his own excrement'. Samuel Pepys had cause for grievance with the inadequacies of his neighbour's cesspit when he wrote grumpily in his diary on 20 October 1660: 'Going down to my cellar ... I put my feet into a great heap of turds by which I find that Mr Turner's house of office is full and comes into my cellar.'

Before the nineteenth century there was no modern germ theory of disease. Londoners, however, had worked out empirically that there was a connection between dirt, unpleasant smells and various kinds of illness. The agent that most people thought was responsible for transmitting illness was 'miasma' (something smelly and poisonous in the air or in water). Even before the invention of powerful microscopes and the knowledge this brought of minute disease-bearing organisms, the feeling developed in the 1820s that the use of water from the Thames was undesirable and that alternative sources needed to be found. A Parliamentary Select Committee was set up at the end of the 1820s and the distinguished civil engineer Thomas Telford (1757–1834) was asked to make suggestions for finding new supplies of clean water for the metropolis. He laboured in vain as there was no action on his recommendations.

The private companies supplying water to London had a vested interest in attempting to staunch growing public concerns about the dubious quality of, and the dangers posed by, the existing water supplies. Their spin-doctors got to work. According to one 'expert', there was 'probably not a spring, with the exception of Malvern, and one or two more, which is so pure as Thames water'. For sheer mendacious effrontery such an official statement would take some beating – even today.

The Thames continued to be the major source of London's water supplies. Some improvement in its cleanliness seems to have been effected by a process of filtering the water through beds of sand before it was piped to the consumers. As late as 1816 salmon were still taken in the river in some numbers but evidence that the Thames was getting progressively dirtier is suggested by the fact that the last record of a salmon being caught was in 1833. Salmon do not like badly-polluted water.

By the 1840s serious concerns were being expressed about many of the social effects of the twin processes of industrialisation and urbanisation, not only in London but throughout Britain. It was evident that a heavy human price was being paid in terms of the blighted environment, the poor and overcrowded housing, the epidemic diseases, the hazardous working conditions and the short and miserable lives of much of the urban industrial workforce. The prevailing philosophy of laissez-faire argued that it was not the job of governments to intervene extensively in the economic and social life of the nation. 'Market forces' should be allowed the greatest possible freedom. Although laissez-faire policies were never applied absolutely, the concept obviously did not sit easily with the idea that the government should accept any responsibility for the health of the nation. The largely untrammelled pursuit of wealth-production and private profit was clearly having dire social and environmental consequences.

The horrors that the Industrial Revolution brought could not be entirely ignored by those in power. The issue of public health forced itself onto the political agenda. What was known as the 'Sanitary Movement' developed in the 1840s and owed much to the tireless efforts of Sir Edwin Chadwick (1800–1890). Chadwick was a bumptious busybody who had played a key role in the highly unpopular reforms of the Poor Law in 1834. His experience with the Poor Law had convinced him that the distress accompanying the emergence of an industrial society had considerable financial and human costs both of which could be reduced by the development of preventative public health measures.

In 1842 Chadwick produced a voluminous and far-reaching report on the sanitary conditions of the working classes. It shocked the nation. In it Chadwick demonstrated the close connection between unsanitary living conditions and endemic/epidemic disease. He showed how disease carried away breadwinners and forced their families into what is now called the 'dependency culture', having to be paid for out of the Poor Rates. In Bethnal Green in the East End, the average age of death among labourers was an appalling sixteen years. For the better-off in London, it was forty-five. Chadwick argued that misery and despair among the industrial working class led to crime, drunkenness and immoral behaviour which also had damaging financial implications. Finally, Chadwick urged reforms to tackle the appalling state of affairs he had identified in the sphere of public health.

Chadwick was widely disliked not only personally but because of the mare's nest of neglect and vested interests that his report highlighted. He was extremely persistent and his report highlighted many deficiencies in London's drainage and sewage systems which he believed were responsible for much preventable death. These systems were the responsibility of the kind of self-perpetuating, unco-ordinated and inefficient cliques that he hated so much. The man has to be given credit for placing the issue of public health at the forefront of the political agenda and his efforts were at least partly responsible for the passing of the keynote Public Health Act of 1848. This Act created a breach in the dam of self-serving interest, complacency, indifference, obfuscation, ignorance and dislike of state intervention behind which effective ways of dealing with avoidable death had been hidden for too long.

Further widespread legislative action was to follow over the next decades, the effect of which was a cleaner, healthier environment as responsibility was assumed by the agencies of national and local government. Combined with great advances in scientific knowledge and in surgery and clinical practice the scene was set for dramatic reductions in preventable death in London and throughout the United Kingdom. Meanwhile London was in danger of being overwhelmed by a flood of human excrement. Action was needed, and quickly!

How often is it that an invention which unquestionably brought great benefits to mankind over time has had disastrous consequences in the short term? Such was the impact of the flushing water-closet.

Various flushing devices had been made from the sixteenth century onwards but it was probably the ingenious Joseph Bramah (1748–1814) who invented, manufactured and marketed the first popular flushing water-closet. These devices were eagerly bought up by the well-to-do as much because they were fashion items as for their ostensible practical purpose. By 1800 Bramah was producing hundreds of flushing water-closets each year. A crisis was about to occur!

The problem was that flushing closets used huge quantities of water compared with cesspools and pits. Not only did those houses fitted with water-closets now require far more water but the greatly enlarged discharge that resulted put a huge burden on the already inadequate drains, sewers and cesspits, one which they were frequently unable to deal with. Much of this water eventually made its way into the Thames, still a major source of London's water, but not before it had sometimes flowed through sources of contamination such as burial grounds.

In 1801 the population of London was nearly 1 million. By 1861 the population had increased about fourfold but both the amount of water used and the quantity of liquid waste had increased out of all proportion. This put large numbers of Londoners, more or less irrespective of class, at risk of disease or death from waterborne infection. Many people took their water supplies from a tap shared by several families or they scooped water by the bucketful out of the nearest river. It was all too common for such sources to contain dangerous, sometimes lethal, invisible disease-bearing organisms.

The archetype of potentially-lethal diseases that are transmitted in contaminated water is cholera. This arrived in England for the first time in 1831 and spread across the country with terrifying speed. It is an acute intestinal disease caused by the bacterium *Vibrio cholerae* which is ingested through polluted water. Its most obvious symptom is chronic diarrhoea bringing on severe dehydration, agonising muscular cramps and culminating in the worst cases with circulatory collapse before death. Cholera outbreaks in 1831–2, 1848–9, 1853–4 and 1866 killed more than 36,000 Londoners. Most of the victims would have suffered such agonies that death must have provided welcome relief.

Officialdom and the medical world were virtually powerless; society at large panicky and confused. 'Conspiracy-theorists' argued that the scare around cholera had been created deliberately by the government to divert attention away from the ferment of debate and unrest around the Reform Bill. Some people thought that doctors and druggists were growing rich as a result of the extra work that the cholera entailed and that they had a vested interest in keeping the disease prevalent as long as possible. In reality the medical profession could do little to reduce mortality rates.

There was widespread fear of entering hospital. This was because the Anatomy Act of 1832 permitted the use of the bodies of paupers for medical dissection. Rumours circulated that indigent cholera victims would be hospitalised compulsorily then murdered and sold to the anatomists. Rapid burials were used by the authorities as a measure intended to slow the spread of the disease. This offended the working-class tradition of accompanying the send-off of the deceased with good old-fashioned junketing. Funerals traditionally took place on Sundays so that friends and relatives did not have to take time off work. Now the official requirement that funerals must take place on other days, as soon as possible after death, prevented some mourners from taking part. This was strongly resented. Rapid interments raised fears about premature burial too. Opium and laudanum were often used to treat cholera victims and they could produce a state of coma difficult to distinguish from death itself. No one wanted to wake up inside a coffin!

The apparently random manner in which cholera struck, killing all classes and ages but with equal unpredictability allowing some to survive, led many people to question basic religious assumptions. What kind of a God permitted the deaths of the supposedly innocent? Assurances that the innocent died to assuage the sins of those still alive cut little ice with the bereaved. It was cold comfort to be assured that those who had died would find their rewards in the hereafter. Repentance was put forward as the surest way of avoiding the fatal consequences of cholera but it was noted that many of those who had tried to shrive their sins still died from the scourge. Some self-righteous individuals claimed that cholera was the reward for the 'sin' of drunkenness. Certainly prolonged alcohol abuse can damage chemicals in the stomach which act as a barrier to infection. The malnutrition so common among London's poor would have had much the same effect.

The cholera visitation of 1832 came and went and few lessons were learnt. The next, and more serious pandemic was in 1848. Now it is a pleasure to introduce one of London's rather unsung heroes. In 1849 John Snow, a general practitioner in Soho, published a paper called *On the mode of communication of cholera*. In this he produced a cogent argument to the effect that whatever caused cholera was transmitted via contaminated water and was not 'something in the air' or a harmful smell or 'miasma', as most people believed. Snow drew a map identifying where 500 cholera deaths had occurred in Soho during a ten-day period in September 1854. Those who had succumbed were concentrated in houses in which the water supply was drawn from the Broad Street pump. Snow believed that this water had been contaminated by seepage from a leaking cesspool or drain. He had the handle of the pump removed. Local residents had to draw their supplies from elsewhere. The incidence of cholera in the district fell immediately.

Snow had made an effective case but he was a somewhat retiring man unable to take on doubters very forcefully. In 1866 another outbreak followed killing 6,000 in London alone and it was left to Robert Koch, a German researcher, about twenty years later to establish conclusively that cholera was transmitted in water containing a dangerous micro-organism and that it thrived in dirty and unsanitary conditions.

Typhoid fever is caused by a member of the Salmonella family, *Salmonella typhi*. Typhoid is marked by prolonged bouts of diarrhoea – or occasionally, strangely enough, by constipation – severe abdominal pain, raging fever, excruciating headaches and exhaustion. Complications which may be fatal include pneumonia, intestinal perforation, haemorrhaging and coma. In the nineteenth century mortality rates were between 10 and 20 per cent. Typhoid killed nearly 1,500 Londoners every year from 1850 to 1870.

In technical terms, typhoid fever is described as faecal-orally spread. This simply means that the causative organism moves from the gut of the infected individual into the mouth of its next victim. This can happen when water supplies are polluted with faecal matter. The bacteria can also travel from person to person via the unwashed hands of someone, for example, preparing food for others. Flies are effective carriers of typhoid, landing first on faecal material and then on food or someone's face. Typhoid is typically a disease of poor sanitation. Its enemies are effective sewers, clean water and attention to personal hygiene. London at this time provided typhoid with the optimum conditions for its spread.

The disease was probably regarded as a regrettable but inevitable concomitant of life in the capital. Then two events occurred which focussed attention on typhoid as never before. In 1859 Prince Albert died of typhoid and a year earlier London had been subjected to the 'Great Stink'. An unusual combination of prolonged hot weather with low rainfall and a severely reduced flow of water in the Thames created a river which was virtually an almost stagnant open sewer. Disraeli called it 'a Stygian pool'. The stench emitted was appalling, even by London's standards. Those who believed that diseases were transmitted by miasmas in the air gloomily predicted massive mortality. To general amazement death rates proved to be no higher than usual. In this situation, those doctors and researchers groping towards the alternative explanation that the disease was somehow contained in sewage-contaminated water found that their views became more widely accepted. It was a couple of decades later that the causative organism of typhoid was isolated and identified.

However it was clear that urgent action was required to improve London's sewage and drainage systems. Some minor piecemeal measures were taken through the 1840s but the landmark development was the establishment of the Metropolitan Board of Works in 1855. This will forever be associated with the name of Sir Joseph Bazalgette (1819–91) who was appointed as its chief engineer. He built a system of intercepting sewers to remove London's sewage and excess rainwater. On both sides of the Thames these conducted the sewage to tidal outfalls and processing plants well to the east of the then built-up area of London. This remarkable system has withstood the test of time and London's subsequent massive growth. In 1866 there was a serious outbreak of cholera in the East End in parts not yet connected to the new sewer system. About 90 per cent of the Londoners who died in this outbreak of cholera were from this area. This at last convinced even some of the most hard-bitten doubters that the disease was waterborne. Significantly there were no further outbreaks of cholera or typhoid in London. Bazalgette also embanked much of the Thames in central London. This helped to increase the flow in the river. In conjunction with improvements in purifying what continued to be the capital's major source of water, this meant that no more 'Great Stinks' were experienced and the river was a great deal cleaner. This had beneficial effects on the health of those living in the metropolis and reduced preventable deaths.

Typhus was endemic and epidemic in Britain in the early nineteenth century. It was 'the poor man's disease', the product of squalor, poor sanitation, dirt, overcrowding and verminous living conditions. In 1837–8 an outbreak in London wiped out more than 6,000 people.

Typhus is caused by the organism *Rickettsia prowazeki* and is spread by the human body louse. This creature defecates on the victim's skin whereupon its infected faeces enter the body by being scratched or rubbed into the itching bite it has made. Typhus produced intense, prolonged fever ending, for 50 per cent or more of the victims, with fatal heart or brain complications.

Pediculus humanus – the human body louse – is a small but hungry wingless insect which has a particular liking for dark, badly-ventilated buildings of which there were many thousands in Victorian London. The prisons of the eighteenth and nineteenth centuries provided especially propitious conditions for the spread of typhus. In May 1750 the courtroom in the Old Bailey was busy working its way through an unusually large number of cases. Those waiting to be called spent their nights in the notoriously stinking, dirty and pestilential precincts of the adjacent Newgate Prison. During the day they were confined in a small, packed and unhygienic enclosure called the Bail Dock just outside the courtroom. An outbreak of 'gaol fever' or typhus in the prison then spread with frightening rapidity via the Bail Dock into the courtroom and it resulted in the deaths of two judges, the Lord Mayor and more than forty court officials, barristers and jurymen.

It mattered little to the authorities that much larger numbers of prisoners housed in Newgate had died from 'gaol fever' or other contagious conditions over the years. In modern parlance, that 'went with the territory'. It was the path that these people had chosen and they had to take the consequences. The Lord Chief Justice sent an urgent message recommending that in the future Newgate and the Old Bailey should be regularly 'cleansed and washed with vinegar' and those prisoners who had been in Newgate beforehand should also be scrubbed with vinegar. This was not out of solicitude for the prisoners but from concern for the well-being of the legal and other personnel of the court. To this day on certain ceremonial occasions, judges hearing cases at the Old Bailey carry nosegays of sweet-smelling flowers. These symbolically commemorate the 'miasmas' or evil smells that prisoners brought with them into the court and the necessity of having something sweet-smelling close to hand to ward off the harmful emanations.

Tuberculosis is caused by *Mycobacterium tuberculosis* which was discovered in 1882. In its pulmonary variation (*phthisis*), it was the most widespread and persistently deadly disease of the nineteenth century. It was commonly known as 'consumption'. London's overcrowded and filthy surroundings provided ideal conditions for its spread. The disease thrived in the under-nourished and semi-debilitated bodies of the poor and the unventilated and squalid surroundings in which they lived. It was the London which Dickens described so vividly in *Oliver Twist*:

> a maze of close, narrow and muddy streets ... windows broken and patched ... rooms so small, so filthy ... wooden chambers thrusting themselves out above the mud, and threatening to fall in – as some have done; dirt-besmeared walls and decaying foundations; every repulsive lineament of poverty, every loathsome indication of filth, rot and garbage.

Two types of tuberculosis, human and bovine, can infect humans. The latter is contracted by drinking infected milk from tubercular cows, by no means uncommon before pasteurisation, while the former occurs by inhaling the bacilli when someone nearby sneezes, coughs or spits. Tuberculosis was often the cause of death, one of the facts of life. The London poor were resigned to it.

Infant and child mortality were rife in the poorer parts of London in the eighteenth and nineteenth centuries. About 20 per cent of the children of the very poor died before their first year. A further 20 per cent of those who survived infancy died before they were fifteen. Some were carried away by the variety of illnesses which thrived in the loathsome squalor of some of London's worst districts. Children were severely at risk from bronchitis, pneumonia and typhus. Common infectious diseases of childhood such as scarlet fever, measles and whooping cough were more severe given the debilitated condition of so many children. It was common for complications to prove fatal. For example, death from measles was often the result of secondary broncho-pneumonia. The diet of the poor was seriously deficient in protein, fat and most of the essential vitamins. It is hardly surprising that many of them had little resistance to what we now regard as minor childhood ailments.

Others died as the result of deliberate infanticide or by neglect and ignorance. For parents in dire circumstances, children were often regarded as little more than a nuisance, an extra greedy mouth to be fed until such time as they could be sent out to earn a wage and contribute to the family income. Thirty-three women in London were hanged for infanticide between 1580 and 1709. In most cases these were youngish unmarried women who could not support the child or who wished to destroy the evidence of the 'immoral' act for which they would be severely stigmatised. The cases were miserable and sordid. Elizabeth Harwood drifted in and out of paid employment. She went out under cover of darkness to a field at Twickenham, gave birth and promptly drowned the baby in a stream. She was hanged at Tyburn in 1739. Sarah Allen lost her job when she became pregnant and, full of despair and bereft of hope, strangled her hapless infant. She died at Tyburn in 1737. These tragic acts were not those of evil women. They were the product of desperation and sheer hopelessness engendered by the dirt, disease and low quality of life of so many of London's poor.

Dirt was in the air. London was a place with a bewildering diversity of industries, most of them small-scale. Their production processes mostly required fuel. Householders required heating. Before the thirteenth century, domestic and industrial consumers of fuel in London used timber supplies but early in that century what came to be known as 'seacoal' began its long association with the capital. It was called seacoal because it arrived in London having nearly all been shipped by sea down the East Coast from ports in Northumberland and Durham.

Burning coal gave off a distinctive and often unpleasant smell, contributing to the existing bouquet of varied aromas that suffused London. It also created atmospheric pollution. In an age when the miasmic theory of disease reigned supreme, it is hardly surprising that the smell, the smoke and the fallout from coal were believed to be responsible for many of the diseases, some of them deadly, which were a constant feature of London life.

It seems that the pollution from coal burning was serious enough to warrant official investigations in the 1280s and official decrees that the use of seacoal should be banned. Londoners, displaying their usual casual attitude to such pronouncements, happily continued burning coal. Such action was not, however, without its dangers. One such miscreant was identified and then hanged, drawn and quartered in 1307. Others were certainly fined. Coal continued to be used in London, especially as shortages forced up the price of wood for fuel, and by the end of the reign of Queen Elizabeth I in 1603 more than 50,000 tons of coal was being consumed annually in the capital. With the development of effective means of allowing smoke to escape, coal was now being used widely as a domestic fuel.

Concerns were frequently being expressed about the effect that the increasing use of coal was having on the quality of London's air and on the health of its inhabitants. Densely-populated and industrially-active urban locations generate a great deal of heat which raises the air temperature in their vicinity. Where coal is burnt, minute particles of partially-combusted coal are released. Some are deposited close by and in certain conditions others may stay in suspension, trapping heat rising from the ground. In that sense the use of coal as fuel starts to have effects on the climate.

In 1620 James I commented on the harmful effect that he believed coal smoke was having on the fabric of St Paul's Cathedral. Other influential figures who expressed concerns about the use of coal were the diarist John Evelyn (1620–1706), the largely unloved Archbishop Laud (1573–1645) and the maverick scientist Sir Kenelm Digby (1603–65). Digby's researches had convinced him that poisonous elements in coal smoke were causing the seemingly large number of lung disorders among London's citizenry. Sometimes these were fatal. Evelyn described London as cloaked in:

> such a cloud of sea-coal, as if there be resemblance of hell upon earth, it is in this volcano in a foggy day: this pestilent smoak, which corrodes the very iron, and spoils all the moveables, leaving a soot on all things it lights: and so fatally seizing on the lungs of the inhabitants, that cough and consumption spare no man.

At the end of the eighteenth century about a million tons of coal was being brought into London annually. This was evidence of growing wealth and advancing technology but there was a heavy price to pay in terms of air pollution. The size of the built-up area of London did not increase in proportion to the rise in its population so not only the extent but also the density of coal-burning and its unpleasant side-effects increased. A repulsive patina of soot cast its pall over streets, buildings and washing and over people, their clothes and their possessions. The use of umbrellas from the late eighteenth century was not simply to keep out the rain. They also gave protection against the unburnt carbon particles that fell with it.

Satirical cartoonists and writers found a source of humour in London's murky atmosphere. In the 1840s Dr Reid, who was in charge of ventilation at the Houses of Parliament, conducted an experiment. He put up a large veil on the roof to check the fallout of dust and soot and claimed in a single day to have captured 200,000 visible particles of soot. It is likely that by the nineteenth century many Londoners had become inured to air pollution, or in the case of literary figures like Charles Dickens or Sir Arthur Conan Doyle, for example, to have even been comforted by its enveloping presence and they made much use of it to add atmosphere to their stories. Most Londoners would not have romanticised it however. They would simply have moaned, shrugged their shoulders and got on with the job of living or in some cases dying from its results.

Dickens used London's fogs and murk in order to create a mysterious and threatening atmosphere. For example, in *Bleak House* (1853) he wrote: 'Fog everywhere. Fog up the river, where it flows among green meadows, fog down on the river, where it rolls defiled among the tiers of shipping ... Fog in the eyes and throats of ancient Greenwich pensioners, wheezing by the firesides of their wards.' In *Our Mutual Friend* (1865) he comments that: 'the whole metropolis was a heap of vapour charged with the muffled sound of wheels and enfolding a gigantic catarrh.'

In the *Bruce Partington Plans* (1908), a Sherlock Holmes story by Sir Arthur Conan Doyle, the narrator Dr Watson writes: 'In the third week of November, in the year 1895, a dense yellow fog settled down upon London. From the Monday to the Thursday I doubt whether it was ever possible from our windows in Baker Street to see the loom of the opposite houses.'

Visitors from overseas certainly commented on London's murk, not necessarily disparagingly. Sarah Duncan, a Canadian visitor in 1891 said: 'It was no special odour or collection of odours that could be distinguished – it was a rather abstract smell – and yet it gave a kind of solidity and nutriment to the air and made you feel as if your lungs digested it. There was comfort and support and satisfaction in that smell.' Other transatlantic visitors however were less impressed with the poor visibility which blotted out church steeples and with the sooty grime that seemed to be all-pervading. They hated the way it got up the nose and stung the eyes.

London was indeed often murky. Often it was foggy – and what fogs! Those of the nineteenth century were by common agreement more frequent, thick, impenetrable and acrid than those of earlier times. No wonder people often referred to London as 'the smoke'. Just one specific early example will suffice. On 10 January 1812, a day without wind, London was plunged into darkness for several hours. The lamps in the shops were lit but the street lights were not and there were many accidents in the darkened streets involving vehicles and pedestrians.

Gustav Dore (1832–1883) captured the atmosphere effectively in many of his evocative drawings. Generally November seems to have been the worst month for persistent, choking and clinging fogs. On some days in January it scarcely got light all day with pollution blotting out the sun although it was relatively clear at ground level. Dickens described smoke as 'the London ivy' because of the way in which it wreathed itself around every building and clung to every dwelling. In *Bleak House* he gives an evocative description: 'Smoke lowering down from chimney pots, making a soft black drizzle, with flakes of soot in it as big as full-grown snowflakes – gone into mourning, one might imagine, for the death of the sun.'

There was a human price to pay for the fog and other forms of aerial pollution. On one occasion a group of seven people drowned after accidentally walking into the Thames. During a fog that lasted for six days in December 1873, fifteen people drowned in the London Docks. Two men groping their way home after work fell into the

Regent's Canal and drowned. There was increased mortality from disease during times of fog. While mortality always rose in winter, it is known that during the 1873 fog there were 700 more deaths than would normally be expected at that time of the year. Many of these were the victims of heart and lung problems. In the winter of 1886 the prolonged foggy conditions produced mortality rates equal to those of the worst cholera years. There were 11,213 deaths from bronchitis and another 480 from emphysema and asthma. The health authorities listed nausea, vomiting, bronchial and respiratory complaints, poor digestion and lack of appetite and general feelings of malaise as results of the smoke and fog with which London was so often suffused.

There was sporadic legislation to control smoke emissions in the period 1875 to 1914. That these acts were not very successful is strongly suggested by the fact that in 1912 it is estimated that over 76,000 tons of soot fell on the County of London each year.

The streets of London contained all manner of hazards to health. For much of the year in early Victorian times the streets were smelly, filthy, muddy rivulets, largely uncleaned. Parts of built-up London, in say 1850, would strike us today as a seemingly incongruous mixture of the urban and the rustic. Housing, even sometimes that of the clearly affluent, was frequently cheek-by-jowl with slum property, industrial premises, stables, pig-sties and slaughterhouses. Sheep and cows jostled for space in the streets with horse traffic. Pigs and chickens avoided death by inches as they moved about, foraging through the filth that lay everywhere. Semi-feral dogs scavenged in large numbers, excreting at will. The horse was the prime mover of mid-Victorian London. In 1830 it was estimated that horses deposited several hundred thousands of tons of their droppings on the streets of London and this figure grew as the century progressed.

In 1873 London had 1,500 privately-run slaughterhouses; by 1897 there were still 500. It is no wonder that the streets in parts of London resembled a country town on market day. In 1876 no fewer than 349,435 cows and bulls, 1,659,324 sheep and 14,394 pigs were brought to the meat-markets of London. As these were herded through the streets they added to the general cacophony and traffic chaos as well, of course, as dropping their dung at random and adding to the cornucopia of smells that was such a feature of London life. In wet weather the streets and pavements were awash with huge quantities of muddy ordure, much of it excreted by animals. During prolonged hot, dry spells this filth dried out and turned to dust. It blew into clothing, noses, eyes and mouths. It came in through open doors and windows and settled everywhere. These conditions bred prodigious numbers of flies. Many of these would land on food having just walked over dog and horse droppings in the street. Fatal disease spread. For Londoners, it was part of life.

10
Commemoration and Memory

London has long been the centre of national commemoration. Public monuments, state funerals, plaques, statues and locations dedicated to the deceased have been the means through which this commemoration has taken place. While the famous, as would be expected, have had a greater visibility in commemoration there are considerable numbers of plaques and even some statues to the lesser known. This chapter will be organised around two particular themes: state and other 'notable' funerals and public monuments. However it will start with the history of the obituary, a familiar but rather neglected aspect of commemoration.

The obituary has a long history. The origins of the obituary are somewhat obscure but it has been traced back in newspapers and journals in the English-language press to 1625. The lawyer Richard Smyth recorded a selection of deaths in London between 1627 and 1674 which included the plague year of 1666. Among the obituaries is one of the sexton of Cripplegate parish but most of the deaths recorded are those of the social elite, including the Earl of Bedford (1641), Henry, Duke of Gloucester (1660) and Mary, Princess of Orange (1660). He also noted a number of suicides such as that of Mr Ravenscroft, a cheesemonger, who threw himself into a pond near Islington in 1649.

The obituary developed during the eighteenth century and became more detailed and at times even displayed a literary flourish in the nineteenth century. Many institutions recorded obituaries of their members. The Royal Society first published obituaries of its Fellows in 1830, in *Proceedings of the Royal Society of London*. Prior to this, obituaries were read at the Anniversary meeting, often by the President himself, and were printed in the record of that meeting. John Thadeus Delane was the first editor of the *Times* (editor 1841–1877) who took an interest in the obituary, recognising that the death of certain people warranted more than just a brief notice. In the twentieth century with the help of a number of reforming newspaper editors, the obituary became not just a brief biography of the deceased but also an art form in its own right. Benjamin Franklin (1706–1790) made the comment, 'I wake up every morning at nine and grab for the morning paper. Then I look at the obituary page. If my name is not on it, I get up.'

Notable Funerals

Large-scale funerals through London have provided one of the most visible displays of the ceremony and theatre of death and this has been evident by the huge crowds that have turned out to watch many of them. State ceremonies from the earliest period to the present served not only as displays of political power but also as tests of loyalty to the monarch and state. However it was not only heads of state and monarchs that guaranteed large crowds. People turned out to pay respect to those that were deemed to be popular heroes or personalities, sometimes in contradiction to the attitude of the authorities. There have been so many state and other notable funerals and interments in London that it is impossible to do justice to a fraction of them here. Those chosen were unusually large, had various unusual features or evoked unexpected responses in those who viewed them.

The first King to be buried in London after the Norman Conquest was Henry III (1216–72) who was placed in the splendid tomb at Westminster Abbey erected by his son Edward I. Despite a magnificent funeral he was temporarily buried in the old grave of Edward the

Confessor (1003–66) to whom he was particularly devoted. Nineteen years later he was moved to his own tomb. The last monarch to be buried in London was George II (1727–60) whose service was described as a 'disorderly and poorly attended affair'. All subsequent monarchs have been buried at Windsor.

Funerals for monarchs have tended to be elaborate and costly affairs. Henry V (1387–1422) had a great funeral procession from Dover to St Paul's Cathedral. Four horses drew the chariot into the nave as far as the choir screen. In recognition of his role as a great warrior King the inscription on the ledge of the tomb platform translates as, 'Henry V, hammer of the Gauls, lies here'. When the tomb of Edward I (1239–1307) was opened in 1774 his body was found nearly intact, wrapped in a waxed linen cloth and wearing royal robes of red and gold with a crimson mantle. He had a gilt crown on his head and carried a sceptre surmounted by a dove and oak leaves in enamels.

The Tudors spared no expense on ceremony. Henry VIII's funeral was magnificent. His huge coffin was covered with palls of blue velvet and a cloth of gold. On top of the coffin was a wax effigy robed in crimson velvet and a crown full of precious stones. The effigy was clad in jewelled bracelets and gloves adorned with rings. The funeral of Elizabeth I, who died on 24 March 1603, was described by the chronicler John Stow: 'there was such a generall sighing and groning, and weeping, and the like hath not beene seene or knowne in the memorie of man.' A total of £11,305 was spent on this event. The funeral of her successor, James I (1566–1625), cost almost five times more with a funeral address which lasted two hours. This stands in stark contrast to his son Charles I (1600–49) who was quickly whisked away after his execution to be buried at Windsor rather than Westminster Abbey.

Although Queen Mary II's funeral in 1695, at a cost of £50,000, was an expansive and grand affair with a lavish procession to Westminster Abbey, royal funerals from the Restoration and throughout the eighteenth century were generally less grand. Factors contributing to this included a decline in the power and significance of the monarch, growing political stability and changes in the organisation and administration of state funerals. After the funeral of George II all subsequent burials took place at Windsor, which lessened the opportunity for public participation. A break with tradition came in 1843 when Prince Augustus Frederick, Duke of Sussex (1773–1843), the sixth son of George III and favourite uncle of Queen Victoria, requested to be buried at Kensal Green cemetery. Charles II (1630–85) was buried at Westminster Abbey but contemporaries criticised the funeral ceremonies as mean and scanty. Charles had died as a Catholic and this was widely resented at the time.

The account of George II's funeral on 13 November 1760 by Horace Walpole (1717–97) described the procession with its line 'of footguards, every seventh man bearing a torch, the horse-guards lining the outside, their officers with drawn sabres and crape sashes, on horseback, the drums muffled, the fifes, bells tolling and minute guns, all this was very solemn'. Walpole also gave a vivid portrait of those in mourning:

> The real serious part was the figure of the Duke of Cumberland ... attending the funeral of a father, how little reason soever he had to love him, could not be pleasant. His leg extremely bad, yet forced to stand upon it near two hours, his face bloated and distorted with his late paralytic stroke ... This grave scene was fully contrasted by the burlesque Duke of Newcastle – he fell into a fit of crying the moment he came into the chapel and flung himself back in a stall, the Archbishop hovering over him with a smelling bottle – but in two minutes his curiosity got the better of his hypocrisy and he ran about the chapel with his glass to spy who was or was not there, spying with one hand and mopping his eyes with the other.

Even this did not descend into the sort of farce that was displayed in some of the early nineteenth-century royal ceremonies. Despite the outpouring of genuine sympathy at the death of Princess Charlotte, daughter of the Prince Regent in 1817, undertakers were drunk at the funeral. Worse was that of George IV's funeral. So disgusted with the chattering and laughing during the service was *The Times* that it thundered that it had never seen 'so motley, so rude, so ill managed a body of persons'. However it did not particularly rue the passing of George, when it commented in July 1830 that 'there never was an individual less lamented by his fellow creatures than this deceased King.'

Responses to funerals often depended on how well-liked the person had been during his or her life. The funerals of Henry VIII, Elizabeth I and George III appear to have indicated that they were genuinely popular. Royal funerals, from the seventeenth century until the early nineteenth century, generally took place at night which considerably enhanced the drama of the occasion. The most popular royal funerals in this period, in the sense that they evoked a genuine outpouring of grief as opposed to one of appropriate solemnity, were those of Mary II in 1694 after her unexpected death at the age of thirty, Princess Charlotte who died in childbirth in 1817 and Queen Caroline, George IV's estranged wife. Prince Albert's funeral in 1861, although a private affair, inspired a substantial collective sense of grief.

However large-scale funerals were not just the preserve of monarchs. Those of Nelson and Wellington in the nineteenth century far surpassed any royal funeral ceremony. Crowds also responded to funerals that were not always sanctioned and organised by the state. Funerals of popular figures could take on the sense of majesty reserved for heads of state. Similarly the crowd were quick to express their hostility towards those who were rich and powerful but also unpopular.

George Villiers, the Duke of Buckingham (1592–1628), was, next to King James I, the most powerful and one of the richest men in the country. He was adviser and favourite to the King and reputedly his lover. Buckingham was also widely and deeply despised and hated. When John Felton assassinated him in Portsmouth there was almost national rejoicing. Arrangements were made to conduct Buckingham's funeral at night to avoid any potential hostility. At his funeral at Westminster Abbey on 23 August 1628, soldiers had to form an armed guard to protect the coffin from the jubilant crowds who had turned out in their thousands to cheer his funeral procession. The drums were beaten particularly loudly in order to drown out the cheers and jeers of the crowd. His assassin, Felton, who was executed at Tyburn, became a national hero and gained great sympathy. Despite his infamous reputation London still bears Buckingham's name in some of the streets near Charing Cross such as Buckingham Street, George Court, Duke Street, and Villiers Street.

During the first Civil War (1642–6) state funerals were conducted in Westminster Abbey to notable Parliamentarians such as John Pym (1643), Robert Devereux, the third Earl of Essex (1646) and Oliver Cromwell (1658). Pym was given a state funeral but after the Restoration in 1660 his body was exhumed and reburied in a communal grave with other leading Parliamentarians in St Margaret's churchyard, Westminster. Essex was buried with great pomp but within a month of the funeral his grave was vandalised. Cromwell was given all the ceremony befitting a head of state but his body was dug up in January 1661 and ritually decapitated at Tyburn.

Despite these grand organised political ceremonies the people were quick to show their respects to those who had been condemned by the authorities. This was particularly the case with the Leveller Robert Lockyer. The Levellers were radicals mainly within the Parliamentary army who campaigned for an extension of the vote and religious toleration. Lockyer had been executed in St Paul's churchyard in 1649 for demanding higher pay for his men, an action that was deemed to be mutinous. Thousands turned out for his funeral. In defiance of the authorities the horse and hearse were draped in black, an honour reserved for officers, and more than 4,000 supporters followed the cortege from Smithfield, many wearing the black and green colours of the Levellers. Wisely the State did not intervene, particularly given the presence of hundreds of partisan soldiers at the funeral.

A deeply-hated figure was thief-taker Jonathan Wild (1683–1725). Not only was he jeered and pelted along the whole route from Newgate to Tyburn but he was buried late at night in secret. However it was not a well kept secret because his grave was opened within a few days and his body was taken away. The *Daily Journal* reported on the discovery of the 'remains of [a] dissected body' in St Margaret's Parish. Even stranger was the donation of a skeleton, reputedly that of Wild, in 1847 to the Royal College of Surgeons by a Dr Frederick Fowler. Whether it was Wild or not, the skeleton can still be seen in the College in the Hunterian Collection in Lincoln's Inn Fields.

The responses to Wild's death stood in stark contrast to those at the death of popular London hero, thief and multiple escapologist Jack Sheppard (1702–24). Thousands of people thronged the near three-mile route between Newgate Prison and the Tyburn gallows to see him as he proceeded to his execution. When he was executed, the crowd, fearing that the hearse was going to take his body to the anatomists, flung stones and anything they could get their hands on at the driver. Poor Jack's body was torn and dragged by those trying to protect it. He was eventually buried in the churchyard of St Martin-in-the-Fields but only after further riots. Sheppard's reputation was sustained through innumerable broadsheets and ballads and effectively established him in the folklore of celebrated Londoners.

Many occupations, trades and organisations in London have provided their own rituals and regalia for their deceased members. The Livery Companies of the City of London are a notable example of this. There are 107 livery companies today. Their origins go back many centuries with about two-thirds of them pre-dating 1600. They developed as fraternities and guilds (or mysteries) that flourished throughout Europe for many centuries and were responsible for the regulation of their trades. Funerals were particularly important occasions for the companies and were generally attended by all their members. The coffin of the deceased member would be covered by a sumptuous pall or 'herse-cloth' and the company arms. City companies had their own herse-cloths, some of which still survive such as those of the Fishmongers, Saddlers, Pewterers, Brewers, Girdlers and Merchant Taylors. Robert Garslang, a grocer of London, in 1460 ordered a new marble stone to be placed over his body with the name and arms of his company 'to have me in special memory'. William Turke, a fishmonger, asked that a stone be provided 'remembering my name and the names of my sad wife and daughter Joan, to have out souls prayed for'. In addition to having their own rituals, the City Livery Companies also provided resources for state funerals. At Nelson's funeral eleven of the barges were owned by the Livery Companies bearing their own individual colourful banners.

The nineteenth century witnessed a series of grand funerals such as those of Lord Nelson (1806), Princess Charlotte (1817), the Duke of Wellington (1852), the Prince Consort (1861) and Queen Victoria (1901). They were further commemorated by services in churches throughout Britain. These deaths stimulated an awareness of national community and a sense of shared grief. They also shared – in their scale, commemoration and popular response – continuity with twentieth-century funerals such as those of Winston Churchill and Princess Diana.

Following Lord Nelson's death on his flagship HMS *Victory* on 21 October 1805 at the Battle of Trafalgar, he was taken back to England for one of the most colourful funerals ever provided for a commoner. His coffin was carried from Greenwich to Whitehall Stairs 'in one of the greatest Aquatic Processions that ever was beheld on the River Thames'. So huge were the crowds that turned out to mourn him that the front of the procession had reached St Paul's Cathedral before the end of the procession had left the Admiralty. The organisation had been fraught with tension about who should take part. It was only pressure from the press that forced the organisers to allow the sailors of the HMS *Victory* to attend while the two loves of his life, Emma Hamilton and Horatia, his daughter, were barred.

For three days from 4 January 1806 Nelson's body lay in state in Greenwich Hospital's Painted Hall. It is estimated that nearly 100,000 people visited the Hall to pay their last respects. The coffin, which was surrounded with trophies including captured French and Spanish flags, was transported by the King's Barge up the Thames to Whitehall Steps on 8 January, followed by a two-mile procession of boats, and from there taken to the Admiralty in Whitehall. The following day his funeral took place with thousands of people lining the streets on the bright January day. *The Times* of 10 January 1806 gave details of the procession which 'at half-past ten [in the morning] ... commenced from the Admiralty'. It included royalty, nobles, ministers, high-ranking military officers and at least 10,000 soldiers. The service, which commenced at 1 p.m., ended at 6 p.m. when Nelson's gold-encrusted coffin was lowered into an ornate tomb in the crypt beneath the dome of St Paul's. It had been one of the most spectacular and lavish funerals London had ever seen.

Nelson's funeral was a hard act to follow. However on the 18 November 1852 such a funeral took place which the *Illustrated London News* of 20 November 1852 wrote 'surpassed in significant grandeur any similar tribute to greatness ever offered in the world'. The funeral was that of the illustrious soldier and statesman, Arthur Wellesley, the 1st Duke of Wellington (1769–1852). Twice Tory Prime Minister from January 1828 to November 1830 and again from 17 November to

9 December 1834, his funeral was attended by more than 1 million people, many of whom had arrived in London on the railways and had spent the previous night sleeping in the streets in order that they could witness the event. The burial took place in St Paul's Cathedral which was illuminated with 6,000 new gas lights. It was the first large-scale service of its kind to take place under the Dome of the Cathedral.

Preparations had meant that St Paul's was closed for nearly six weeks whilst extra seating could be installed to accommodate the 13,000 guests attending. The start of the burial service was delayed by almost an hour on account of the late arrival of the coffin. Certainly the pomp and ceremony was exceptional. The *Illustrated London News* eulogised on 'the greatest hero of our age' adding that the popular respect was one of 'solemnity and a grandeur never before seen in our time and in all probability, not to be surpassed in the obsequies of any other hero heretofore to be born'. The poet Dante Gabriel Rossetti, reflecting on the nation's response, wrote 'Multitude, Hold your breath in reverent mood' whilst the poet laureate, Alfred Tennyson (1809–92), in his 'Ode on the Death of the Duke of Wellington' opened with:

Bury the Great Duke
With an empire's lamentation,
Let us bury the Great Duke
To the noise of the mourning of a mighty nation,
Mourning when their leaders fall,
Warriors carry the warrior's pall,
And sorrow darkens hamlet and hall.

In more realistic tones the *Spectator* of 20 November remarked that the 'sentiment was overlaid by the timber, the estimates and the plans; the thing was done so handsomely that the material was in excess of the spiritual'. Wellington's funeral came shortly after the very successful Great Exhibition and at the outbreak of the Crimean War. The historical context for Wellington's funeral was important and, as John Wolffe (*Great Deaths*) stated, it epitomised the 'Victorian celebration of death' and was 'more of a show of pageantry and less of an expression of genuine mourning'.

After the Duke of Wellington, the funerals of prominent people were inevitably something of an anti-climax. There were warm and favourable responses to the funerals of politicians such as Disraeli in 1881 and Gladstone in 1898 and national heroes including David Livingstone and General Gordon (despite the absence of his body). There were factors from the mid-nineteenth century which contributed to a definite increasing sense of collective mourning and awareness. The monarchy was recovering from the disreputable excesses associated with the reigns of George IV and William IV, the apparent detachment of royalty from politics and an increase in the circulation of newspapers and publications that emphasised the role of Empire through stories of exploration, bravery and military heroics.

The turn of the century marked the end of the Victorian era. On 22 January 1901 Queen Victoria died at Osborne House. The response to her death, aided by the improvements in communications, was unprecedented. The Queen had requested that the event should be simple and with as little 'pomp as possible'. These wishes were ignored. Her coffin was conveyed by train to Victoria Station and then transferred to a gun-carriage drawn by eight horses. It then proceeded through the centre of London to Paddington Station to be taken to Windsor. Despite some criticisms of the expense, there was genuine and widespread mourning and the feeling that her death marked a watershed in the history of Britain and the Empire. The responses to the death in 1910 of her son, the playboy King Edward VII, were less favourable, although excuses were made for his raffish lifestyle and aloofness from the life of his subjects.

Four years later the massive slaughter and brutality associated with the First World War evoked a wave of commemorations, both public and private, in the form of public funeral ceremonies and the proliferation of monuments after the war. Many of those who had fallen were never brought home and were buried in mass graveyards in foreign fields. One hero, whose body was returned, was John Travers Cornwell. John, or 'Jack' as he was known, was born in Leyton in January 1900 and was given a funeral to rank with that of any monarch. Jack gave up his job as a delivery boy with the Brooke Bond Tea Company in October of 1915 and enlisted in the Royal Navy. On 16 June 1916 he was sailing on HMS *Chester* to join the battle fleet at Scapa Flow when the ship met a scouting group of four German destroyers. In the battle that followed, thirty-four men were killed and forty-two wounded on the *Chester* and young Jack Cornwell was the only member of his gun crew left alive. He kept to his post but after the battle was taken to Grimsby Hospital where his condition deteriorated and he died. A matron at the hospital said that his last words were, 'Give my love to my Mother, I know she is on her way here'. He was then buried in a war grave at Scartho Road Cemetery, Grimsby. His bravery was acknowledged in despatches: 'He ... remained standing alone at a most exposed post, quietly awaiting orders till the end of the action, with the gun crew dead and wounded all around him'. His death, which was widely reported in the newspapers, clearly touched thousands of people and eventually his mother gave in to public demand and agreed for his body to be exhumed and taken to London for re-burial with full military honours. His funeral procession formed up at East Ham Town Hall with a gun carriage bearing his coffin and the band of the Naval Volunteer Reserve led a huge group of servicemen with thousands of mourners in attendance. The whole route was lined by throngs of those affected by the story and wanting to witness the spectacle. After receiving a posthumous Victoria Cross more recognition was given to Jack: Jack Cornwell Cottage Homes for disabled and invalided sailors were provided, three naval scholarships were awarded for deserving boys and on 21 September a John Cornwell Day was pronounced in all elementary schools.

Memory is sustained through memorials, large-scale commemorations and also by oral accounts. Many memories eventually fade but some are revived through anniversaries such as the bicentenary celebration of the Battle of Trafalgar in 2005, which also served the purpose of stimulating a wide interest in the event and in Nelson. After the First World War almost every town and village erected memorials to the war dead accompanied by an annual Remembrance Day in November as a way of showing respect and sustaining memories of the fallen. Deaths in the Second World War, genocide and the nuclear bomb continued the need to remember. This has been done not only through memorials but also visits to historic sites such as the battlefields of the Western Front.

Monuments

It was not until the late thirteenth century that the practice of inscribing gravestones began. Before then individual memorial stones or monuments were virtually restricted to the wealthy and the social elite who would be laid to rest within churches and cathedrals. The vast majority of the population who died in England were buried in the local churchyard but medieval grave-markers have often sunk into the ground and wooden markers have long since perished.

London was an important centre for the production as well as the display of monuments. The tomb of Richard II was made in 1396–9 by London masons Henry Yevele and Stephen Lote, and coppersmiths Nicholas Broker and Godfrey Prest cast the gilt bronze effigies. From the sixteenth century monuments were made and transported all over Britain from workshops in Southwark, St Martin's, St Giles and the City. Many of the masons and tomb sculptors originated in the Netherlands and Belgium and had come to London as refugees during the sixteenth and seventeenth centuries.

Why the number of memorials increased in this period is difficult to explain. Clare Gittings suggests in *Death in England* (1999) that the increasing emphasis on commemoration from the seventeenth century might be seen as one sign of a developing unease about mortality and an attempt to avoid oblivion. Paradoxically during the Civil War of the mid-seventeenth century there was also a great deal of damage to monuments such as those in Westminster Abbey, Queen Henrietta Maria's chapel in Somerset House and Archbishop Laud's chapel at Lambeth Palace. Monuments also suffered huge amounts of damage in the nineteenth century as a result of the enthusiastic but often misguided restoration of church interiors.

One of the most important forms of memorial in Britain is the headstone. This became a common feature from the late seventeenth century. Graves were marked by single pieces of stone set into the earth. On some graves there were matching footstones. Imagery and inscriptions were initially very limited, often bearing little more than a skull and crossbones. These are among the many funerary memorials from the eighteenth century which have survived.

Public monuments before the sixteenth century are very rare. Statues of every monarch since Elizabeth I can be found across London with the exception of the uncrowned Edward VIII. A statue of Queen Elizabeth I stands at St Dunstan-in-the-West on Fleet Street (1586) – the stone figure originally stood at Ludgate. Hubert Le Sueur's equestrian statue of Charles I (1600–49), which dates from the early 1630s and has been on the present site since 1675, can be seen at Charing Cross. Memorials to monarchs and royalty continued to be erected over the next two centuries. A few of these include those to King Edward VI (1537–53) who has two statues (1737 and 1681) in the north wing of St Thomas' Hospital Lambeth in recognition of his re-founding of the hospital; Charles II (1630–85) whose statue has stood since 1692 in the Figure Court of the Royal Hospital in Chelsea and James II (1633–1701) outside the National Gallery. The Duke of York Column is a monument to Prince Frederick, the 'Grand Old' Duke of York (1763–1827), second eldest son of King George III, and is located between the two terraces of Carlton House Terrace near the Mall. Charlotte (1744–1818), Queen to George III, is represented at Somerset House on the Strand (1780) and Queen Square (1780). Predictably there are many memorials to Queen Victoria (1819–1901) including those in Regent's Park (1869), Caxton Hall (1902) and Temple Gardens on Victoria Embankment (1902). The well-known landmark to her husband Prince Albert (1819–61) is the Albert Memorial opposite the Albert Hall, built from 1864–76. The subjects of statues are not always easily recognisable. How many people give a second glance to that of George I on the spire of St George's Church in Bloomsbury or Edward VII standing outside Tooting Broadway underground station?

One of the most famous landmarks in the City, dating from 1671–76 is the Monument (commemorating the Great Fire of 1666) designed by Robert Hooke and Sir Christopher Wren. London also commemorates 600 non-royals through public monuments. The eighteenth-century growth in public statues and monuments were often the work of the leading architects and sculptors of the day. An early example of a non-royal subject was the statue by the Flemish sculptor Peter Scheemakers (1691–1781) of Thomas Guy, at his foundation of Guy's Hospital in Southwark in 1734. Monuments to civic and military figures were erected during the eighteenth and nineteenth centuries, particularly in parks and squares. These include monuments to Lord Nelson (1758–1805), Sir Charles Napier (1782–1853) and General Havelock (1795–1857), all in Trafalgar Square. The pioneer of anti-smallpox treatment, Edward Jenner (1749–1823), has a statue in Kensington Gardens; politicians Charles James Fox (1749–1806) in Bloomsbury Square and Lord George Frederick Cavendish Bentinck in Cavendish Square in Marylebone (1802–48); and the writer Oscar Wilde (1853–1900) near St Martin-in-the-Fields. The rise of the public park from the 1820s created another location for the placing of monuments such as that of Lord Holland, Henry Vassall-Fox, 3rd Baron Holland (1773–1840) in Holland Park by G.F. Watts and Edgar Boehm (1872).

Some statues have been entirely removed from their sites such as the one to the 'Butcher of Culloden', Prince William, Duke of Cumberland (1721–65). He was the second son of George II and his statue originally stood in Cavendish Square from 1770. Made of lead, it was removed in 1868 to leave an empty plinth but no one quite knows why. Statues have proved controversial such as the one to Oliver Cromwell (1599–1658) outside the Houses of Parliament. Cromwell's role in the Civil War and as Lord Protector had proved to be a matter of controversy since the Restoration. In 1894, the Liberal Prime Minister, Lord Rosebery, proposed that Parliament set up a statue of Oliver Cromwell at Westminster, to mark the 300th anniversary of his birth in 1599. Cromwell's reputation by the nineteenth century was being revised by people such as Thomas Carlyle and Rosebery who were great admirers. Nonetheless such a proposal was bound to meet fierce opposition from MPs and Rosebery personally paid for the statue to be made. In order to keep the unveiling low key for fear of public opposition there was no ceremony at the unveiling at the early hour of 7.30 a.m. on the morning of 14 November 1899.

Memorials and public statues appeared in large numbers in Britain's towns and cities during the Victorian period. Some represent little more than vain attempts to remember those who never did anything memorable, but they also included those recognised as having contributed to the common good. Prison reformer Elizabeth Fry (1780–1845) has a medallion (1874) over the entrance to Wormwood Scrubs and the philanthropist and promoter of Sunday Schools,

Robert Raikes (1736–1811), has a bronze figure (1880) on Victoria Embankment Gardens; nurse Edith Cavell's (1865–1915) statue stands opposite the National Portrait Gallery in Trafalgar Square. Many actors have had commemorations erected to their memory, such as Sarah Siddons (1755–1831), whose marble statue (erected in 1897) stands at Paddington Green, and Sir Henry Irving (1838–1905), whose statue can be found near the National Portrait Gallery.

Statues or busts of engineers and scientists include Joseph Bazalgette (1819–91), the civil engineer who changed London by masterminding the creation of an effective sewerage system throughout the city in the mid-1850s. His statue is next to Hungerford Bridge, on the Embankment. Isambard Kingdom Brunel (1805–59) is commemorated on Victoria Embankment and Temple Place (1877); gardener, designer, writer and creator of the Crystal Palace Sir Joseph Paxton (1803–65) at Crystal Palace in South London (1869); engineer Robert Stephenson (1803–59) at Euston Station (1871) and Sir Isaac Newton (1642–1727), mathematician and physicist, at Leicester Square (1874).

Commemorations to famous writers include Charles Dickens (1812–70) at the Prudential Assurance Building in High Holborn. This marks the site of where he lived between 1834 and 1837. A bust of Dickens was placed there in 1907. Londoner John Milton (1608–74) was given long overdue recognition in 1882 with the erection of his statue on Victoria Embankment opposite Blackfriars Bridge. There are a number of memorials to William Shakespeare (1564–1616) including those on Victoria Embankment (1882), in Leicester Square (1874) and a bust (1895) in the Churchyard of St Mary the Virgin, Aldermanbury outside the Guildhall. A bronze monument (1884) to William Tyndale (1494–1536), translator of the English Bible, is in Victoria Embankment Gardens. Artists and architects include William Hogarth (1697–1764), who is marked by a stone bust (1875) in Leicester Square, and architect Inigo Jones (1573–1652) whose statue (1729) is at Chiswick House.

Honouring 'great men' and great deeds was a mainstay of the Empire and explorers and military 'heroes' certainly fitted this category. Captain James Cook (1728–79) is commemorated (1914) in the Mall, a bronze statue (1866) to arctic explorer Sir John Franklin (1786–1847) stands at Waterloo Place whilst the burial place of David

Livingstone (1813–73) lies in Westminster Abbey. Robert Clive 'of India' (1725–74), who is credited for establishing the military supremacy of the East India Company and regarded as a key figure in the establishment of British India, has a bronze figure (1912) in uniform at King Charles Street near St James Park.

Politicians and statesmen are well represented. A statue to Richard Cobden (1804–65), manufacturer and liberal statesman, is in Camden High Street (1868); Henry Fawcett (1833–84), Liberal MP and supporter of votes for women, has a memorial (1886) on Victoria Embankment erected by 'his grateful countrywomen'; a statue (1905) to Prime Minister W.E. Gladstone (1809–98) is on the Strand; William Huskisson (1770–1830) MP, best known for being the first person to be killed by a train, has a stone statue in Pimlico Gardens (1915) and the servant of Henry VIII, Sir Thomas More (1478–1535), was recognised with a stone figure (1882) on the Victoria Embankment. The Duke of Wellington (1769–1852) is the only person to have two equestrian statues in London, one at Hyde Park Corner and the other at the Royal Exchange (1844).

War Memorials

War memorials have a long history although until recent times they commemorated battles and great victories rather than the war dead. Most of the memorials erected before the Boer War (1899–1901) were to individuals, usually officers, or to regiments. For example, St Nicholas's Church in Deptford has a memorial to a death in the conflict with Spain (1584–1604). Westminster Abbey commemorates individuals who lost their lives in the War of the Austrian Succession (1739–48); Third Anglo-Dutch War (1672–4); American Revolutionary War (1775–83) and the French Revolutionary War (1793–1802). The Crimean War Memorial in Waterloo Place, St James, unveiled in 1859, commemorates the 2,162 officers and men of the Brigade of Guards who fell in those hostilities. The memorial was cast in bronze from cannons captured at Sebastopol but it was removed in 1914 as the plaque states: 'The Guards' Memorial was pulled down in the year of our lord 1914 and was re-erected 30 feet north in order to permit the erection of the Florence Nightingale and Sidney Herbert statues.'

Although the first outdoor war memorials were built in the aftermath of the Crimean War, examples are rare. Monuments to the fallen of the Boer Wars are slightly more common. They include the statue by Adrian Jones on the Mall which commemorates the Royal Marines in both the Boer War and the Boxer Rebellion in China (1900); the Boer War memorial located on the south wall at the west end of the Great Hall of the Guildhall was erected in 1907 and the Boer War memorial (1906) in Highbury Fields, Islington, by Sir Edgar Bertram Mackennal (1863–1931) which commemorates Islington residents who died in that war.

The great age of memorial building was in the aftermath of the First World War. The impact of the Great War on Britain was huge and resulted in a wave of public commemoration. Attitudes towards war in general changed from commemorating military triumph to commemorating those who had lost their lives during these conflicts. As such, monuments became an established part of sustaining the collective memory of the sacrifice made by the many servicemen and women and the bereavement of those they left behind. Jay Winter's book, *Sites of Memory, Sites of Mourning* (1995), demonstrates how war memorials helped the bereaved to recover from their loss and gave mutual help to communities in mourning. The UK National Inventory of War Memorials has compiled a comprehensive record of war memorials in the UK and the Channel Islands listing around 56,000 memorials with more to be added which will bring the figure to around 70,000 in total. There are hundreds of war memorials across London in places as diverse as railway stations, churches, cemeteries and pubs. The most famous of all is the Whitehall Cenotaph.

The London Cenotaph, designed by Sir Edwin Lutyens (1869–1944), was intended to be a temporary structure initially made from plaster and erected in 1919 as part of celebrations for the Allied Victory Parade. The popularity of the monument and the event saw demands to make the Cenotaph permanent. The *Times* newspaper on 21 July 1919 described it as follows:

> Simple, grave and beautiful in design, it has been universally recognised as a just and fitting memorial of those who have made the greatest sacrifice; and

the flowers which have daily been laid upon it since the [Peace Day] march show the strength of its appeal to the imagination.

Although the *Times* wanted it moved from its site in Whitehall, Lutyens felt that 'no other site would give this pertinence' and after some deliberation the Cabinet decided that it should be re-erected as a permanent memorial, and that it should remain in Whitehall. The permanent structure was unveiled on 11 November 1920 by King George V, on the same day as the funeral in Westminster Abbey of the Unknown Soldier (the tomb of the soldier killed during the war is in Westminster Abbey). These would become shrines to the fallen in all wars and the focus of national ceremonies on Armistice Day and Remembrance Sunday.

The poppy and the two minute silence would become the defining symbols. The latter was prompted by a letter to the *London Evening News* on 8 May 1919 by an Australian journalist, Edward George Honey, who proposed a respectful silence to remember those who had given their lives. The idea was brought to the attention of King George V who issued a proclamation on 7 November 1919 calling for a two minute silence. The significance of the poppy was the result of the poem *In Flanders Fields* written in 1915 by the Canadian surgeon John McCrae who died in 1918.

Some cemeteries commemorate individuals whose bodies were returned such as sixteen-year-old John Travers Cornwell VC in Manor Park Cemetery. Cornwell is also commemorated on a collective memorial at St Botolph-without-Bishopsgate along with the officers and men of the Honourable Artillery Company. Some companies gave recognition to their employees who died in the war such as the Prudential Assurance War Memorial in Holborn, which displays three panels bearing the names of 794 former employees who lost their lives.

Many railway stations have memorials dedicated to their employees who died during the Great War. Out of 186,475 railway workers from the railway companies of Great Britain and Ireland who served under arms during the First World War, 18,957 were killed in action or died of wounds received on active service. Many of these memorials were erected three or four years after the war. At Liverpool Street Station the *Great Eastern Railway Magazine* for 22 June commented on the unveiling ceremony by Field Marshal Sir Henry Wilson. 'A silent audience filled the hall, the sorrowing friends of those brave men whose names are writ upon the flag-draped scrolls'. Wilson stated that 'On this tablet are placed the names of 1,200 or 1,400 of your comrades who, doing what they thought was right, paid the penalty'. He then closed his speech with a reading from Rudyard Kipling's poem *Recessional*:

> The tumult and the shouting dies;
> The Captains and the Kings depart;
> Still stands thine ancient sacrifice,
> An humble and a contrite heart.
> Lord God of Hosts, be with us yet,
> Lest we forget – lest we forget!

After the ceremony Wilson returned through London from Liverpool Street Station and was assassinated by IRA gunmen. A memorial tablet was erected to him beside the Liverpool Street war memorial. There are eleven panels of names at Liverpool Street and also a circular bronze portrait of Charles Fryatt who was Captain of the Great Eastern Railway Company's steamer *Brussels*. Fryatt helped to evacuate many allied troops from France in defiance of attacks from German U-Boats. In June 1916 he was captured and he was shot the following month.

At Paddington Goods Station in 1921 a Roll of Honour was unveiled during a service attended by all grades of staff of the Great Western Railway. Some 6,000 people gathered for the moving spectacle, many holding bunches of flowers that were to be laid at the foot of the memorial. At the unveiling Viscount Churchill, Chairman of the Great Western Railway, said: 'members of the Great Western Railway Company – no fewer than 2,524 of them – gave their lives so heroically for their country's sake'. At Euston Station 3,719 employees were remembered by a 45ft high obelisk which bears the inscription: 'In grateful memory of 3,719 men of the London & North Western Railway Company who, for their Country, Justice and Freedom, served and died in the Great War, 1914–1919. This monument was raised by their comrades and the company as a lasting memorial to their devotion'. The main pedestrian entrance arch at Waterloo Station contains a tablet commemorating 547 employees of the London and South Western Railway who made the ultimate sacrifice.

Attitudes to death changed between 1850 and 1918. The factors contributing to this change were a decline in religious beliefs and a substantial fall in the death rate. The impact and the trauma of the First World War accelerated these changes and the Victorian culture of mourning proved inadequate in dealing with the reality of mass death in foreign fields.

11

Curious Memorials and Monuments

'London is Stranger than Fiction' was the title of an eccentric and rather engaging series of drawings with brief descriptive information that appeared in *The Evening News* in the years just after the Second World War. In these features the artist Peter Jackson regaled readers with a mass of eclectic information about London's past which included mention of the death mask of a murderer which had grown whiskers and was housed in Scotland Yard's Black Museum and the tombstone in Bunhill Fields Cemetery covering the remains of Mary Page who died 11 March 1728. On it was the curious inscription: 'In 67 months she was tapped 66 times, had taken away 240 gallons of water without ever repining at her case or ever fearing the operation'.

Two other gems from Jackson's pen include the information that in the north aisle of Westminster Abbey a stone slab stands close to the burial place of Ben Jonson (1572–1637) inscribed with the words 'O Rare Ben Johnson'. Apart from the misspelling, the real curiosity here was that Jonson was so poor when he died that he could not afford the normal space for a grave and was therefore buried in an upright position. Second was the case of Catherine of Valois, wife of Henry V, who died in 1437 and was buried in the Lady Chapel of Westminster

Abbey. During later building work her body was removed and put on public view in an open-topped wooden box. Among those who went to see her was Samuel Pepys who recorded the experience in his diary: 'I had the upper part of her body in my hands, and I did kiss her mouth, reflecting upon it that I did kiss a Queene, and that this was my birthday, thirty-six years old, that I did kiss a Queene.'

It is to celebrate and be in accord with the spirit of Jackson's idiosyncratic evocation of oddities and curiosities that this chapter concerns itself with a selection of notable or unusual memorials of death in London. Many of these are to be found within churches, others are wholly secular. Those featured here are but a tiny percentage of London's memorials and monuments. Generally speaking, they are among the less well known or less visited of such items.

Going back to Ben Jonson, briefly. The story is told that Jonson believed that his stature as a poet merited his burial with the other worthies in Poet's Corner and he had a chat with the Dean of the Abbey about the details. When he explained that he was financially embarrassed and could not make the financial outlay for a tomb designed to house his cadaver in the normal horizontal position, the Dean assured him that this did not have to be a problem. So it was that Jonson was indeed buried vertically. The poor man, literally, could not afford an appropriate inscription and the grammatical solecism that appears on the slab is the result of an admirer of his called Jack Young passing by and asking who it was that was being interred. Distressed by his hero's indigence, Young immediately offered the sum of eighteen pence to have an appropriate statement carved on the stone. Unfortunately the mason involved was a little slapdash and the slab that can be seen to this day is the result.

Thomas Hardy (1840–1928) was very much a man of Dorset. Much of his poetry and fiction is thoroughly imbued with his love of rural England and his concern about the changes that were being wrought in it during his lifetime. It is not surprising that he let it be known that he wished to be buried beside his first wife in the rural churchyard at Stinsford in Dorset. Stinsford features in some of his novels as 'Mellstock'. No sooner had he died than the powers-that-be, those who always know best, decided that his literary merit was such that he deserved a place in Westminster Abbey. In the event, he was cremated and his ashes were placed in the south transept where they remain to this day. With a gesture towards Hardy's wishes, it was decided that his heart should be buried at Stinsford. There is a persistent story that the heart never actually made it into the cosy confines of his wife's grave. Apparently the heart was placed in a biscuit tin to await the burial ceremony. It is said that his sister absent-mindedly left the lid open and that the family cat consumed it.

In Poet's Corner in Westminster Abbey is a tablet commemorating the life of Thomas Parr. His life story was written by 'The Water Poet' John Taylor (c. 1578–1653). He gave this work a rather verbose title: *The Old, Old, Very Old Man or the Age and Long Life of Thomas Parr of Winnington in the Parish of Alderbury; in the County of Salop who was born in the Reign of King Edward IV in 1483. He lived 152 years nine months and odd days and departed this Life at Westminster the 15 November 1635 and is now buried in the Abbey.*

Despite this biography not having the catchiest of titles, Taylor tells the story with a wealth of fascinating if not always strictly verifiable detail. Taylor claimed that 'Old Parr', as he was understandably known, was 'discovered' living in the West Midlands by the Earl of Arundel who described him, somewhat ungraciously, as 'a remarkable piece of antiquity'. He immediately resolved to bring him to London and have him exhibited. He was placed on a horse-drawn litter and apparently was accompanied by his daughter-in-law. His arrival in London caused a great stir as crowds flocked to see this living prodigy and he was presented, among many others, to Charles I. Sadly the grand old man died after a couple of months, it being generally thought that London's smoky atmosphere finished him off, contrasting as it must have with the pure air of Shropshire. The question clearly arises as to how long he might have lived had he stayed at home!

It is said that Parr married for the first time at the age of eighty. Aged 105, he did penance, clad in a white sheet, at Alderbury Church for what was described as 'unchaste behaviour' with one Katherine Milton. We do not know how old she was at the time. Perhaps she was a mere flibbertigibbet of eighty or so years. When Parr was 112 his wife died. Finding the life of a widower uncongenial, he married again, aged 122. His supposed age at death has always provoked controversy and his alleged sexual activity as a centenarian has, not surprisingly, led to much salacious tittle-tattle. He was examined after his death by William Harvey, the medical man famed for establishing the circulation of the blood. Harvey found Old Parr to be in exceptionally good condition for someone of his age, except for the fact that he was by then, of course, dead. Legends continued to accumulate around Old Parr. It was generally assumed that longevity ran in the family. It is said that he had a son who reached 113, a grandson who lived to be 109, a great-grandson who slipped his cable at 124 and a great-granddaughter who rather let the side down by dying at a mere 103. There is not a shred of evidence for any of this.

There are at least three other alleged centenarians commemorated in various burial places in London. The graveyard of the Royal Hospital in Chelsea contains the grave of William Hiseland. He died aged 112 in 1732. He fought at Edgehill in 1642 in the army of King Charles, in Ireland for William III and under the Duke of Marlborough for Queen Anne. St Paul's in Covent Garden contains the remains of the comic actor Charles Macklin who, according to his memorial in the church, died aged 107 but whose coffin plate states that he was a mere ninety-seven years of age. On the exterior of the Savoy Chapel in the Strand a plaque commemorates one Thomas Britton who died in 1839 at the age of 101. In 1901 Elizabeth Hanbury died at Richmond-on-Thames and *The Times* newspaper gave her age as 108 years and 144 days. We can have more confidence in the truth of this memorial than the earlier ones.

All Saints is Fulham's parish church. It stands close to the north end of Putney Bridge. The tower dates from 1440 but the rest of the church was rebuilt in the early 1880s in the Perpendicular style. It contains a number of memorials transferred from the previous church. Probably the most interesting is the Lady Margaret Legh monument. This was erected in 1605 and is one of the earliest funerary carvings depicting a seated effigy. She sits, carved in fine detail, left hand to her chest, right arm cradling a chrysom baby on whom she concentrates her petrified but clearly loving attention. To her left is another chrysom child while the sculpture also contains an hourglass, symbolic of the inexorable passing of time. A baby who died before its mother had been churched was termed 'a chrysom child'. He or she would be shrouded in a white linen garment presented to them by the priest when he anointed them with the holy oil at their baptism. This garment was criss-crossed with diagonal strips of linen. In 1552 this practice was banned. Another notable monument is to Viscount Mordaunt. He was an avid Royalist who died in 1676 and he is portrayed, slightly ludicrously, dressed in a Roman toga and carrying a baton, such portrayal being fashionable at the time. Ten Bishops of London lie in the churchyard and an eleventh is buried within the precincts of the church.

In the past, every schoolchild in England was taught that Henry I (r. 1100–35) never smiled again after he was told that his only legitimate son, William, had been drowned in a storm at sea while returning to England from Normandy. The King had a favourite Court Jester called Rahere. Try as he might, Rahere completely failed to restore as much as a flicker of fun to the bereaved King's countenance. The pall of gloom that hung over the court clearly affected even the previously blithe Rahere who decided to devote himself to the serious business of firstly becoming a monk and then undertaking a pilgrimage to Rome. Rahere caught malaria while abroad and, chastened by the experience and thankful to have made a recovery, he vowed to return to London and start a hospital for the poor. This is the origin of Bart's Hospital. The present wonderfully atmospheric Church of St Bartholomew the Great in Smithfield is basically the chancel, the only major surviving part of a great Augustinian priory founded by Rahere. He became the first prior and he has not strayed far because when he died in 1143 he was buried within the precincts. He lies close to the magnificent tomb-chest on which he is portrayed recumbent in the habit of his order. Overlooking Rahere's tomb is a delightful oriel window. This was added in 1515 by the then prior and was used to keep watch over the gifts in cash and kind submitted at Rahere's tomb. Clearly even in the sixteenth century there were thieves about for whom nothing was sacred. Jester-turned-prior is a bit like poacher-turned-gamekeeper.

St Andrew Undershaft in Leadenhall Street, EC3, contains a hanging memorial to Alice Byng who died in 1616. She wears a ruff and kneels at a *prie-dieu* or prayer desk. What is odd about this memorial is that Alice had three husbands, not we are assured all at the same time, and they were all stationers. Why the predilection for stationers? In the same church is a monument in marble and alabaster to John Stow (1525–1605). He is shown, as in life, bald-headed and sitting writing at a table. A zealous historian, he is probably best-known for his *Survey of London* which was published in 1598. An inscription assures us that 'He exercised the most careful accuracy in searching ancient monuments, English annals and records of the City of London ... he wrote excellently'. Every year around the anniversary of his death on 5 April, the Lord Mayor of the City accompanied by Sheriffs and other big-wigs attends a ceremony in the church when the quill pen in the effigy's hand, supplied by the Stationers' Company, is renewed and a copy of his book is presented to the writer adjudged to have written the best essay on London history in the previous year.

St Helen's in Bishopsgate with St Martin Outwich has a wealth of high-quality Elizabethan and Jacobean monuments. An oddity is that to Sir Julius Caesar Adelmar who died in 1636. His name itself qualifies as something of a curio but his memorial is unusual in that it consists of a tomb-chest without a human effigy. Instead it is adorned by the representation of a legal deed with its seal broken off symbolising that he has paid the debt of Nature.

St Peter upon Cornhill, EC3, is an ancient religious site but the present church dates from 1682 when its rebuilding was completed after it had been destroyed in the Great Fire of London. It only has one monument of note. This is on the south wall of the chancel and is a circular memorial showing the heads of seven cherubs. These are a reference to the seven children of James Woodmason. They all died in 1782 in a fire in their house in Leadenhall Street when their parents had left them for a few hours to go to a ball at St James's Palace on the occasion of the Queen's Birthday. Several other people died in the conflagration and in fact more people died in this one house fire than in the entire Great Fire of London.

Even those who are not enamoured of the concept of monarchy cannot but be touched by the tragedy of Lady Jane Grey, the reluctant uncrowned Queen of England. She was the cat's-paw of ambitious and unscrupulous men and paid the price for being a threat to the other main claimant, Mary Tudor. Jane was beheaded in the Tower of London early in 1554 and her father was likewise dealt with on nearby Tower Hill a few days later. He was executed for treason and it was the practice, when the axe had done its gory work, for the executioner to hold the head up to show everyone watching that the victim was definitely dead. The head survived. The Grey family had a mansion close to the Tower and it was buried there in the private chapel. Both house and chapel were eventually demolished and the Church of the Holy Trinity in the Minories was built on the site. In 1852 the head was rediscovered in a remarkably good state of preservation given the time and the traumas it had experienced. When Holy Trinity closed in 1899 the head was transferred to St Botolph's in Aldgate. It was not on open display but, if the visitor asked politely, it could be viewed in its airtight glass container. Unfortunately for those with a liking for the macabre, about thirty years ago, the head was reburied with due reverence under a paving stone by the entrance to the church. Father and daughter finally lie in eternal rest a few hundred yards from each other.

In the somewhat grimy surroundings of Clerkenwell Road stands St Peter's Italian Church, built in the 1860s and once the centrepiece of London's main Italian community based around nearby Saffron Hill. By the 1930s this community numbered about 11,000 and was well established, being associated particularly with the catering industry, not least in the manufacture and sale of ice cream. The Italians had largely avoided the surge of anti-immigrant feeling which culminated in the 1905 Aliens Act and which had been particularly directed at Jews from Russia and Poland. They were, however, hit hard in June 1940 when Mussolini declared war on Britain. Not only did they have to put up with violent attacks and destruction of their property by mobs of 'patriots' but because they were now considered as enemy aliens, large numbers of men and youths were interned on the Isle of Man. Worse was to follow. On 1 July 1940 the former luxury-liner *Arandora Star* left Liverpool bound for Canada. The passengers were internees. They consisted of 712 Italians and 478 Germans, many of them from London. Most of them died when the *Arandora Star* was torpedoed by a German submarine. This example of the appalling stupidity and tragic waste of war is remembered in a plaque near the main entrance to St Peter's Church which can be seen from the street. Although this example is somewhat out of the book's time frame, it was felt that the poignancy of the memorial warrants its inclusion.

Charles Macklin (1699–1797), previously mentioned, was a distinguished actor-manager who deserves a memorial for longevity but actually gained one for being aggressive. He was notorious for his fiery temper and he frequently got into fights during one of which he killed his opponent. He escaped the death penalty on the grounds of self-defence but was traumatised by the trial and before his death ordered a memorial showing a skull being pierced by a knife. This is a wall tablet which can be seen on the wall of St Paul's Church in Covent Garden.

Very easy to miss in Cloak Lane, EC4, parallel to Cannon Street, is an incised stone memorial to the dead who were formerly interred nearby in the churchyard of St John the Baptist. When a section of the District Railway was built in the early 1870s, it was deemed necessary to remove the human remains buried nearby to be reverentially interred elsewhere and to commemorate the event with a suitable reminder in stone.

The Church of St Peter ad Vincula can be found within the precincts of the Tower of London. Many people who were executed nearby on Tower Green lie buried there including Anne Boleyn, Catherine Howard, Lady Jane Grey, the Earl of Strafford and the Duke of Monmouth, but as curious a memorial as any is that to the lesser-known Captain Valentine Pine. He was a seventeenth-century soldier of fortune who died in 1677. His epitaph is notable for containing his name in acrostic, albeit using some poetic licence. It starts thus:

> Vndaunted hero, whose aspiring mind,
> As being not willing here to be confin'd,
> Like birds in cage, in narrow trunk of clay,
> Entertain'd Death, and with it soared away.

In the church of St Dunstan-in-the-West in Fleet Street, EC4, is a memorial to Hobson Judkin, 'The Honest Lawyer'. He died on 30 June 1812. A tablet explains that his friends got together to erect the monument, 'as a token of gratitude and respect for his honest and friendly conduct to them through Life.' It goes on to urge anyone reading the tablet to model their conduct on that of Judkin. Can it be that he was the first and last 'Honest Lawyer'?

St Edmund the King in Lombard Street, EC3, contains an inconspicuous wooden tablet commemorating the Reverend Geoffrey Anketell Studdert Kennedy (1883–1929). An Anglican priest, he wrote poetry in his spare time. He was an army chaplain on the Western Front during the First World War and in 1917 he won the Military Cross for a number of forays into No Man's Land helping the wounded while under heavy enemy fire. He was the rector of St Edmund's from 1921 to 1929. Popular with the 'other ranks', he attracted the nickname 'Woodbine Willie' during the war because of his pragmatic habit of gaining the confidence of the troops by dispensing Woodbine cigarettes along with spiritual succour. The nickname was an affectionate one but Kennedy was heartily sick of it after the war because it stuck to him. His experiences led him to Christian socialism and pacifism and he wrote several poems about his wartime experiences. One of them includes the line: 'Waste of glory, Waste of God – war!'

At the busy traffic intersection where Shoreditch High Street, Kingsland Road, Hackney Road and Old Street meet is the Church of St Leonard's in Shoreditch. A memorial on the north wall remembers the life and work of Dr James Parkinson (1755–1824) who lived locally and used the church for worship. Parkinson was the first medical man to analyse and describe the distressing shaking palsy eponymously known as Parkinson's Disease. More eye-catching is the memorial to Elizabeth Benson who died in 1710. This shows two realistic skeletons energetically pulling at the branches of an uprooted tree – symbolic of the Tree of Life – from which hangs a shroud containing a Latin inscription.

In the churchyard of St John-at-Hackney in Mare Street, E8 you can find a fairly ordinary table tomb, below which are the remains of one of England's saddest eccentrics. This was James 'Mad' Lucas who died and was buried here in 1874. He became a rich recluse obsessed with a fear of physical attack. He was devoted to his mother and when she died, he embalmed her himself and placed her remains in a glass coffin in the substantial family home at Great Wymondley near Hitchin. Nothing would persuade him to surrender the body for burial and eventually police had to break in and take her away. This experience clearly unhinged Lucas. He then built strong barricades inside his house, armed himself and employed bodyguards to deter unwanted strangers. He slowly took on the appearance of a hermit and never washed, combed his hair or cut his nails. He had a soft spot for tramps, however, perhaps because he looked like one himself, and he kept sweets for the local children who came to the house, as long as they didn't mock him. His fame spread and he had many visitors, including Charles Dickens, and gave short shrift to those whose bona fides he doubted. He died from a stroke. He is recalled in the name of the village pub at Great Wymondley – The Hermit of Redcoats.

Sir Nicholas Crisp was an ardent Royalist who, before he died in 1666, expressed the wish that his heart might be buried at the feet of his hero, Charles I. His wishes were largely ignored because his heart was placed in an urn close to his own memorial in the church of St Paul in Hammersmith, his body being buried in the churchyard. Crisp made provision for his heart to be removed from the urn once a year and refreshed with a glass of wine. This ritual was scrupulously observed until the middle of the eighteenth century when the urn was sealed up.

St John's Wood Church, NW8 contains a number of memorials. Perhaps the most interesting person commemorated is John Farquhar who died in 1826. Having made a fortune as a dealer in arms and munitions to the East India Company and as a speculator, he bought Fonthill Abbey in Wiltshire. This extraordinary building was the brainchild of the fabulously wealthy but extremely eccentric William Beckford. Highly educated but a shy and complex man of reclusive nature, he resolved to spend a substantial part of his fortune building a replica of a medieval abbey with a great octagonal tower 300 feet high. No sooner was this enormous structure complete than it fell down. Displaying the innate optimism of the true eccentric, Beckford immediately set to work rebuilding it but the job was only just completed when the kitchens collapsed bringing down substantial parts of the abbey's fabric with them. Undeterred, Beckford embarked on a second rebuilding but by now even his financial resources were so strained that he was forced to sell Fonthill. Although Farquhar had presumably heard the phrase 'buyer beware', he eagerly bought the place lock, stock and barrel only for it to collapse once more not long after he had moved in. Farquhar was no mean eccentric himself. When Beckford met him for the first time he immediately dubbed him 'Old Filthyman' because, despite his wealth, he lived in appalling filth and squalor and looked like a tramp severely down on his luck.

In St Luke's in Charlton Village, SE7, is a monument commemorating Spencer Perceval who, as Prime Minister, was assassinated in the lobby of the House of Commons in 1812. It would have been but cold comfort to him had he known that he was assassinated by mistake. He had a premonition of death the night before he died and, clearly shaken, he poured out his fears to his family who urged him not to attend the House that day. He agreed but a message arrived requiring his attendance at a crucial vote. When he arrived at the House, lurking in the lobby was John Bellingham who nursed a strong sense of grievance against Lord Leveson Gower, a former ambassador to Russia. Bellingham blamed him for not making sufficient effort to secure his release from a Russian prison. Bellingham shot Spencer Perceval at close range, either because he mistook him for Gower or because he was in such a state of distress. Bellingham was hanged for the crime just one week later outside Newgate Prison. Spencer Perceval's last words were accurate but under the circumstances curiously formal, even a trifle pedantic. They were, 'Oh I am murdered!'

St Mary's in Rotherhithe, SE16 shows one of London's most singular monuments. On the north wall is a plaque to Prince Lee Boo. He was a prince on an island in the Pacific Ocean who, despite apparently belonging to a nation of cannibals, displayed great kindness to shipwrecked British sailors in 1783. Out of heartfelt gratitude, they invited him to return home with them. He agreed, but no sooner had he arrived on Albion's shores than he died of smallpox aged just twenty.

Memorials, placed within a church in remembrance of an individual, cast fascinating light on the fashions, fads, foibles and mores of the times they date from, or more specifically of that section of society that could afford what were sometimes very elaborate and expensive commemorative items. They vary from large florid canopied monuments to simple wall tablets but they nearly always recall the 'great and the good' or those who aspired to be such and had the necessary resources to pay for them. When these people died, they clearly felt the need to be remembered in this way. For all that, they did not achieve immortality.

It is only to be expected that the ecclesiastical buildings of London, because of the role the capital has played in the life of the nation, are uniquely rich and diverse in the monuments and memorials to the dead that they contain. Buildings at the heart of places like Westminster Abbey and St Paul's Cathedral contain a bewildering profusion of such items, but humbler churches also contain items that shed considerable light on the attitudes to death of our forefathers as well as a mass of primary evidence for the historian of fashion, armour, culture and manners. It should be noted however that the erection of memorials did not always follow on the death of those they commemorate. On occasion, monuments were prepared years or even decades before death while others were commissioned after death and completed so much later that the armour or costume might be of a significantly later style. It is also worth remembering that a monument or memorial is not always placed close to the remains of the deceased. Chest and table tombs, whether inside the church or in the burial ground outside, do not contain human remains, which are interred below ground.

The first time we come across death being specifically portrayed is in the fifteenth century with carved corpses or cadavers complete with burial shrouds. Early examples often show an effigy of the deceased as he was in life surrounded by all the evidence of his worldly achievements. Another effigy, lower down, depicts a corpse in the state that we all can expect, that is, cadaverously wrapped in a shroud and without earthly possessions. To emphasise the contrast between the living and the dead, the corpse is often shown highly decayed and with its skin stretched tightly over the underlying skeleton. Less gruesome to modern eyes was the portrayal of salvation on medieval monuments. This often took the form of a small carving on a tomb-chest of the soul of the deceased being carried up to Heaven by angels in something looking much like a napkin. Skeletons continued to appear but are somewhat less gruesome than earlier ones and by the seventeenth century tend to be superseded by corpses in shrouds symbolising resurrection and immortality. A good example of this genre is the well-known memorial to the poet and cleric John Donne in St Paul's Cathedral. This is dated 1631 and shows Donne standing upright in his shroud. In fact he is almost teetering on top of the urn and looks positively ghoul-like as well as slightly ridiculous.

It is said that Donne had a portrait of himself made which Stone, the sculptor, used as his inspiration. This monument started a fashion. Contemporary alternatives included the depiction of the act of resurrection itself where the corpse of the deceased clad in its shroud emerges from its coffin or from a ground full of bones. Sometimes a corpse was depicted in a recumbent position dressed in its grave apparel and awaiting the Last Trump, often symbolised by a cherub hovering above and blowing a trumpet.

Hatchments make an appearance from around the 1620s. These are diamond-shaped panels usually with a wood frame and painted on canvas or wood. They display the heraldic achievement of the deceased but, as if in code, the background indicates additional information about the marital status of the deceased. The hatchment of a married man who predeceased his wife, the most common hatchment, will display his arms on the dexter side (the left to the observer) on a black background impaling hers against a white background on the sinister side. Hatchments were carried in procession to the church for the funeral service. They might then be removed and displayed as evidence of bereavement and mourning on the house of the deceased, usually over the main door. Otherwise they remained in a prominent position within the church. Hatchments are uncommon in London's churches. St Edmund the King in Lombard Street, EC3 contains two, that on the east wall of the chancel relating to Princess Charlotte, the only daughter of the obese gentleman who was Prince Regent for so many years and who went on to become King George IV. St James's in Garlickhythe, EC4 shows two hatchments on the south wall. St Luke's in Charlton Village, SE7 and St Mary Magdalene in Bermondsey, SE16 contain one each.

Many impressive and large sculptured stone effigies and other memorials survive in London's churches but in medieval times it was the practice only to bury those who could afford it inside the church. Their memorials could eventually cause problems of overcrowding even though those with the means to have such memorials were only a small percentage of society as a whole. One possible solution was to incise stone slabs with details of the deceased and let them into the floor. These tended to become worn by passing feet over the years so the idea of metal memorials developed, sometimes as part of larger stone ones or sometimes on their own, let into pavements and other flat surfaces.

London had a number of workshops where these brasses were made and it was the custom for those wishing to be remembered in this way, if they were really rich, to commission them during their own lifetime and they might be very fine examples of craftsmanship. Those whose pockets were not quite so deep could choose a standardised 'off-the-peg' design but have it embellished with bespoke detail. Between the mid-fifteenth and the early sixteenth century there was a short-lived vogue for brasses depicting the deceased as a skeleton or as a horribly emaciated body in its funerary shroud. Sometimes worms were shown eating away at the bodily remains. The use of memorial brasses largely died out in the sixteenth century although the Victorian period saw something of a revival in their popularity.

Brasses have always been vulnerable to wear and tear, to theft or in the sixteenth and seventeenth century in particular, to the actions of the iconoclasts who ripped them up as evidence of the Catholic imagery they so hated. London is not particularly rich in memorial brasses but a visit to the following places in central London will reward the eager searcher: in the City, All Hallows by the Tower; St-Dunstan-in-the-West; and St Helen in Bishopsgate. Westminster Abbey, as might be expected, contains a rich seam. The Savoy Chapel has a brass commemorating two bishops who died of bubonic plague in 1522.

A distinct oddity among London's memorials is to be found in the church of St Mary Aldermary, EC4. On the north wall of the chancel is a completely blank monument with an urn and swag, apparently dating from the early eighteenth century. The story is that this was placed on the wall by a dutiful and grieving widow. Her grief was short-lived because she married a second husband with almost indecent haste whereupon she lost interest in composing a suitable epitaph for the memorial to her first one!

One of London's most enduring oddities is the preserved figure of Jeremy Bentham (1748–1832) which is housed in a glass cabinet in the cloisters of University College in Bloomsbury, one of the constituents of what became the University of London. Bentham was a polymath with an extremely wide range of publications to his name and the advocate of various radical causes which gained him respect in some circles and a reputation for eccentricity or even perversity in others. He lent his support to the establishment of an institution for those who were barred from higher education because they were not members of the Church of England – he believed in religious tolerance and the benefits of universal education. He died shortly after the College was opened, having decided that he wanted to remain in it forever, but not before he had had himself publicly dissected. So there he is, ensconced in his cupboard, his favourite walking stick in his hand. It is not surprising that he looks so lifelike. These are actually his embalmed remains with the exception of his head which is a replica in wax. The original is said to have been used as a football. Even the clothes he is dressed in are some of those he wore when alive. Once a year, the mummified Bentham used to enjoy a little excursion. He was carefully carried the short distance to the College's AGM where he was placed so as to be able to keep an avuncular eye on proceedings. Doubtless, had he been able, he would have declaimed about how much better they did things in his time. Bentham was distinctly odd. He kept a cat called the Reverend Sir John Langbourne and fed it exclusively on macaroni.

In Aberdeen Place, NW8 just off Maida Vale stands an imposing pub with the intriguing and unique name of Crocker's Folly. Inside it is a splendid and opulent riot of marble, deeply-moulded plasterwork and highly polished woodwork. The pub dates from the 1890s when it was simply called The Crown. It was built by a local publican and venture capitalist called Frank Crocker. He knew that the Great Central Railway was being built down to London from the West Riding of Yorkshire and the East Midlands and that it was planning to build a terminus station somewhere in what is now the postal district of London, NW8. Fortune favours the bold, or so the proverb goes. Acting quickly, Crocker built a plush and well-appointed hotel to refresh, feed and accommodate the well-to-do and discerning travellers he was sure would come to London via the Great Central. Imagine his dismay when he learnt that the terminus was going to be built about a mile away! The poor man was so distressed that it is said he committed suicide by hanging or, more spectacularly, by throwing himself from the building's highest gable. The Crown was now a railway hotel without a railway and it had to adjust to a lesser role as an overly grandiose pub for the local community. With typically irreverent Cockney wit, it became known as Crocker's Folly, testimony in material form either to the foolishness of greed or to the perverse and arbitrary nature of the cock-up factor. It soldiered on through the decades, fading gradually and at best shabby-genteel, until it was bought by a brewery which spent a large amount of money restoring it to its late-Victorian grandeur. On its reopening it was given as its official name the informal nickname by which it had been known for eighty years. Actually it is unlikely that Crocker did plummet to his death from its roof, but for all that it remains a memorial to a bold entrepreneur whose venture brought him nothing but heartache and premature death. This historic pub is currently (March 2007) closed and boarded up.

In Bishopsgate, EC2 stands Dirty Dick's pub. The original Dirty Dick is supposed to have died in 1814 and to have been a well-educated and dandified young man called Nathaniel Bentley. Seemingly with the world at his feet, he was arranging a grand banquet to celebrate his forthcoming marriage when he received news that his bride-to-be had died. Totally bereft, he shut up the dining room and never entered it again, allowing its contents to rot or simply gather dust. He became a miser and recluse who lived surrounded by squalor and paid little attention to his own cleanliness or that of his surroundings. It is extremely unlikely that the pub stands on the site of Bentley's miseries and it seems that some of the contents of his house in Leadenhall Street were brought to Bishopsgate to furnish what in effect was an early version of a theme pub. At one time the place was festooned with all manner of curious items such as mummified cats and ancient tuneless violins, everything liberally covered in dust and cobwebs. It is possible that the story of Dirty Dick provided Charles Dickens with his inspiration for the abandoned wedding feast hidden away in a locked-up room in *Great Expectations*. The pub has now been substantially cleaned up but the name lives on as a memorial to the tragedy that was Nathaniel Bentley's life.

When you think about it, an extremely curious idea is that of a shrine to someone who never existed. Sherlock Holmes is an enduring fictional character. There are many theories as to whom Sir Arthur Conan Doyle (1859–1930) had in mind when he created Holmes with his rapier-like intellect, unremitting dispassionate logic, scientific approach to evidence, brilliant deductive powers, generally misanthropic nature and his intolerance of those who thought less quickly than himself. Holmes is all the more winsome as a character because he manifestly had his weaknesses – he could be appallingly untidy, he played the violin badly, he was moody and impatient and he had recourse to narcotics when things were not going well or when he was bored. He will forever be associated with his lodgings at No.221b Baker Street and a tableau of these rooms and of items associated with his stories was put together and displayed at the Festival of Britain in 1951. This collection was owned by a London brewery and the decision was taken to use the material to refurnish and provide a theme for a pub previously known as the Northumberland Arms but then renamed The Sherlock Holmes. It is in Northumberland Street, WC1 and devotees of the Sherlock Holmes genre flock there from all parts of the world to pay homage to the master sleuth.

In Devons Road in Bow, E3 is a pub with the unique name of The Widow's Son, although it is usually referred to as The Bun House. The story goes that the pub was run by a widow assisted by her only son but he eventually had to go off to the Napoleonic wars. He promised that he would be back by Easter and she promised to have a hot cross bun – his favourite – ready for him. He was presumably killed in action because he never came back but his mother kept her side of the bargain. Every year until she died she hung up a hot cross bun for him over the bar and the tradition has lasted to this day, a memorial to the power of maternal love or to the futility and waste of war.

What is the impulse behind the apparent human need to create monuments and memorials? Lewis Mumford in *The Culture of Cities* (1938) takes up the issue and explains it in terms of a vain desire, particularly on the part of the rich and powerful, to seek what he aptly describes as a 'petrified immortality'. He goes on to say: 'they write their boasts upon tombstones; they incorporate their deeds in obelisks, they place their hopes of remembrance in solid stones'.

Every monument, statue, headstone and mausoleum has

a purpose – it is intended to be seen and to convey some sort of message to the viewer. When originally erected it is likely to have been deliberately sited in a position relevant to its subject. In Trafalgar Square stands an equestrian statue of Charles I. This was erected after the Restoration, specifically at the place where some of the regicides had been executed and within sight of Whitehall where the King himself had been executed. It is, incidentally, England's earliest free-standing public statue. Some monuments have been moved which can mean that they lose part of their purpose by being extracted from their original context. Paradoxically, on being moved, a monument may gain a new and more relevant context. In the grounds of what is now the Imperial War Museum in Lambeth stands a structure simply known as 'the obelisk'. This was originally erected in nearby St George's Circus in 1771 to commemorate the life and works of a former President of Bethlehem Hospital, otherwise known as 'Bedlam'. This hospital had previously been located in Moorfields but was moved to a new site in Lambeth. The obelisk was then re-sited in the hospital grounds in a new and appropriate context only later to lose that context when the hospital was transferred again and the buildings adapted for use as a museum.

The eighteenth century saw the erection in Westminster Abbey of a host of monuments to national leaders and this left little space for the commemoration of the heroes of the wars against revolutionary and Napoleonic France which therefore tend to be found in St Paul's Cathedral. The creation of the Thames Embankment from 1868 provided a prime site for the display of statues of another crop of later national heroes.

Monuments to Prince Albert proliferated after his death in 1861. The national memorial is of course that erected in Kensington Gardens and designed by a leading exponent of the Gothic, Sir George Gilbert Scott, with some reference to the Eleanor Crosses of the late thirteenth century. Albert was well intentioned, earnest, pompous and humourless. It is a sumptuous memorial to a man who engendered grudging respect but little affection from many in the world of industry, science and commerce for his wholehearted support for such projects as the Great Exhibition. Britain's traditional landed ruling class and most political leaders disliked him for the hold he had over the Queen. He was deplored by many simply because he was German.

The grandiloquent Albert Memorial and the numerous other statues to his memory elsewhere indicate that the erection of a public statue is not necessarily an indication that the person represented was held in high regard by the public as a whole. Monumental statues, particularly those erected in the Victorian age, were used to glorify the concepts of royalty, hierarchical authority and continuity, thereby countering growing radical demands for greater social and economic equality. Thus in the Mall close to Buckingham Palace stands the Victoria Memorial, unveiled in 1911. This expensive and elaborate memorial to Victoria constitutes a complex allegory. Around the base are four bronze lions symbolising Power. They are embraced by bronze figures representing Peace, Progress, Manufacture and Agriculture. The marble base is designed as a symbol of British naval power. Above the cascade basins are pairs of figures representing Painting and Architecture, Shipbuilding and War. Going upwards can be seen figures of Truth, Justice and Motherhood and then the Queen herself. The structure is topped by Courage, Constancy and the Winged Victory in magnificent gilded form. The meaning of such allegories must have been lost on the majority of the country's citizens who would have been unable to find any relationship between such concepts which were largely metaphysical, and their own real and frequently very harsh everyday experience of life.

The heyday of the erection of public statues in London was the nineteenth century. It was an age of hero-worship. Honoured in this way were royalty, leading politicians and statesmen, senior military and naval men, some men of letters, a few scientists and a smattering of men from other fields of achievement. With the exception of Queen Victoria, there were very few women.

It is interesting to note some of the statuary monuments that were *not* built. Protracted and sometimes acrimonious debates took place about the nature of, and location for, a national memorial to Nelson. A committee of eminent men chaired by the Duke of Wellington was kept busy pondering over the relative virtues of no fewer than 120 designs and forty actual models. Any number of columns, obelisks and other structures were submitted for consideration, most of which featured Nelson but some managed to dispense with any actual representation of the great man himself. One such was a trident, 89ft high, described rather unkindly as looking like a 'large toasting fork'. Another proposal was for a statue of a languid-looking Nelson atop a plinth from which he gazed down on a collection of naked nymphs apparently engaged in playing water polo. One submission would have had Nelson teetering precariously on top of a globe 30ft in diameter. These three would have been located in Trafalgar Square, as would have a British Naval Museum in the shape of a Gothic cenotaph. This was intended to honour Nelson's memory and to act as a repository for a collection of items glorifying Britain's naval achievements. It was the intention that once a year on Trafalgar Day a powerful beacon would flash out from its spire.

A proposal to commemorate victory at Waterloo and to honour the 'Iron Duke', Wellington himself, nearly twenty-five years before he actually died was put forward in 1828. This was an elaborate and ponderous structure to be located at Hyde Park Corner in such a way as to oblige all vehicular traffic arriving in London from the west to pass through it. Fortunately the plans to proceed with what even then would have constituted an enormous obstruction to traffic, were not proceeded with. A triumphal arch, similarly dedicated, across the New Road (now Marylebone Road) near the northern end of Portland Place, was planned for 1820. Perhaps we should be grateful that we were spared a huge bronze statue of Nelson that might have risen out of the middle of the Thames between Waterloo and Westminster bridges or the enormous effigy of Sir Robert Peel on splayed metal stilts that it was proposed should stand in the Thames, acting like some monstrous sentinel, close to either Westminster or Vauxhall Bridges.

It is almost exclusively the so-called 'great and good' whose lives and works are commemorated in statuary. Sadly many of these images in bronze or stone are of people who most definitely had feet of clay. In front of the National Gallery stands a representation of King James II (r. 1685–88). A fanatical womaniser and unusually arrogant, even for royalty, James was loathed by most of his subjects and was once described as having all the faults of his father but even less sense.

In Old Palace Yard by the Houses of Parliament stands a magnificent equestrian statue of Richard I by the prolific sculptor, Baron Marochetti. It was unveiled in 1860 and epitomises the concept of medieval male chivalry. In fact it encapsulates in bronze the enduring power of myths. No other English King has spent so small a part of his reign in this country as Richard. He was an active homosexual and received many warnings from senior clerics about what were described as his 'unnatural vices'. He may have been brave but he was also greedy, violent, ruthless and cruel. He personally supervised the massacre of 2,700 prisoners after the fall of Acre during the Third Crusade. The motive for the prominent role he played in the Crusade was more to do with plunder and adventure than with the publicly-stated aims of restoring various sacred places to Christian control. Romantic stories of him dining on venison with Robin Hood and his Merry Men in Sherwood Forest or eventually being found by his faithful troubadour, Blondel, after he had sung for his supper outside just about every major castle in Europe, should not be given serious credence.

Few monarchs have been as little enamoured with their realm and their subjects as George I. It can be stated unequivocally that the feeling was mutual. Nevertheless, a few years after his death in 1727, a gilded equestrian statue to his memory was erected in Leicester Square. By the 1860s, Leicester Square and its surroundings had fallen on hard times. In 1851 an enormous globe had been set up there and the statue of George had been buried. In 1861 someone decided it was time to exhume the statue. It had not benefited by its time below ground. The whole thing was badly tarnished and the King had lost his arms and legs although his horse had not suffered quite so much, lacking just one leg. The statue was put on display propped up with sticks. In 1866 it was given a coat of whitewash and shortly afterwards a nocturnal reveller gave the horse black polka dots and donkey-like ears. Not content with that, he then added a dunce's cap to the King's head and gave him a broomstick as a lance. Soon afterwards, official-dom moved. The figure of the King disappeared and the horse was sold to a scrap merchant.

George IV ruled only from 1820–1830. A vast literature has been written about 'Prinny'. A rapacious sexual predator in his younger years, he grew obese and unhealthy in middle age. He was widely regarded as a dissolute fop, unpopular enough in 1817 to have his carriage stoned by the London mob while he was travelling in it. A lack of any real virtues or admirable qualities did not prevent a statue to his memory being erected in 1836 in the Battlebridge district at the junction of what are now York Way and the Euston, Pentonville and Gray's Inn Roads. It had an octagonal base decorated with Doric columns and figures representing the four patron saints of Britain. Atop the 60ft high base was a statue of George. This structure was widely ridiculed at the time and had only been in place for six years when the figure of the King was removed. The base was successively a police station, a camera obscura and a beer shop and before being demolished in 1845 it had become a major obstruction to traffic. This now largely-forgotten building went on, of course, to give the name 'King's Cross' to the adjacent station opened by the Great Northern Railway in 1852 and consequently to the surrounding district. Even many dyed-in-the-wool Londoners don't know how Kings Cross got its name.

In 1734 a statue in memory of Thomas Guy (1644–1724) was erected in front of the eponymous hospital. Guy is a good example of a flawed hero. His initial fortune came from the illegal importation of bibles from Holland and then the production and distribution of good-quality, cheap bibles. Later on he made a financial killing from the short-lived speculative boom known as the South Sea Bubble while many others had their fingers burnt. No sooner did he have money than he gave it away to good causes. He was MP for Tamworth, the town frequently benefiting from his generosity, but he abandoned the place when the voters failed to return him to Parliament. He then threatened to demolish the Town Hall he had just built for them. It was his munificence that led to the founding of Guy's Hospital. In spite of his wealth and the fact that he gave so much of it away, he was exceptionally parsimonious in his private life. For example, he was too mean to buy a table cloth, preferring to eat his meals off old newspapers on the counter of the shop he owned.

The statues of London are indicative of male-dominated societies. There is a marked paucity of women remembered in this way. It is refreshing to be able to end this chapter with a mention of the bronze statue of Emmeline Pankhurst (1858–1928) which stands in a public garden close to the Palace of Westminster. She was perhaps the most prominent of the militant fighters for women's political emancipation known as the Suffragettes. An activist to the core, she raised funds, recruited, organised, led marches and demonstrations and was at the forefront of the movement's direct-action tactics such as window-smashing and arson. She displayed enormous courage by going on hunger strike almost to the point of death no fewer than twelve times, her health being permanently damaged as a result. Men either reviled or patronised her. Although women had got the vote by the time she died, her friends and associates had an enormous struggle to gain acceptance for the idea that she should be commemorated in the form of a public statue. They argued that she deserved a site in Downing Street but the male Establishment recoiled in horror from the idea that someone they considered a virago should have a statue in such a prominent place. In a moment of indiscretion which he probably went on to regret, Prime Minister Baldwin agreed to unveil the statue in Victoria Tower Gardens where, as is the way with so many statues, it goes largely unnoticed.

No consideration of how London has commemorated its dead should omit the Watts Memorial of Heroic Deeds. It is located in Postman's Park, a tiny public garden on the site of the former churchyard of St Botolph in Aldersgate, close to the Museum of London. The memorial was the brainchild of the eminent Victorian artist George Frederic Watts (1817–1904) who, in 1887, proposed the idea of marking Queen Victoria's Jubilee of 1887 with a tribute to examples of previously unsung heroism in everyday life. Meeting with little response, Watts decided to do something himself and he designed what might best be described as a loggia, a long open gallery with a tiled roof along the wall of which were placed tablets remembering ordinary people whose bravery had led to the loss of their own lives. Over the years fifty-three such tablets were erected. Most of them come from the Doulton factory and consist of decorative glazed tiles. An example refers to the bravery of Walter Peart and Harry Dean. They were the driver and fireman of a Great Western Railway express heading for Paddington on 18 July 1898. Near Ealing a connecting rod worked loose and one end punctured the boiler. There was a blowback from the firebox and both men were severely burnt. In spite of their awful injuries they brought the train safely to a stand, thereby possibly averting a major disaster. They died from their injuries the next day. Elizabeth Boxall of Bethnal Green was just seventeen when in 1888 she was kicked and fatally injured by a horse while attempting to save a child from being run over. Harold Rickets, a constable in the Metropolitan Police, was on holiday at Teignmouth in Devon in 1916. He died attempting to rescue a boy who had got out of his depth in the sea. Edward Morris was a boy of ten who drowned in the Grand Junction Canal in 1897 while attempting to save his friend who had got into difficulties.

Somehow there is something infinitely poignant about these plaques, shyly hidden away and largely unnoticed. They are a threnody to the innate goodness, honour and courage of ordinary people. They convey much more to the authors of this work than the prominent, often ostentatious statues, images and other memorials to the so-called 'great and good', of which London has so many. Those famous enough to be captured for posterity in a statue or similar memorial were often, although not exclusively, male and born into wealth and privilege. Some were people of merit with great achievements to their names, others were not. Worth and celebrity are not always compatible bedfellows.

12
People and their Pains

In the Medieval and Early Modern periods death struck in many ways, some of which were common pains and illnesses that are mainly treatable today. Some diseases were deadly, others merely debilitating and disfiguring, but without an adequate understanding of hygiene or germs the medical profession lacked the ability to treat many of the most basic problems. From the eleventh to the fourteenth centuries, apart from plague and famine, information concerning death from disease is difficult to draw conclusions from. Illnesses were often defined in terms of fevers. Physicians did list symptoms such as 'when my hearing fails, when my tongue curls back, my lips blacken, my mouth gapes, my heart trembles, my feet go stiff'. The causes of death were defined as natural or unnatural and accidental death or murder. Such definitions were left to the coroners who were appointed from 1194.

Fourteenth-century burials in St Mary Graces Abbey (founded in 1349 and suppressed in 1539), east of Tower Hill, reveal cases of leprosy, syphilis, tuberculosis, accidental trauma and degenerative joint diseases which was consistent with findings in other medieval graveyards. In the Augustinian Priory of St Mary Merton cases of surgical intervention were found including a trepanation and an individual with a leather hernia strap.

Life expectancy was affected by high infant death rates as well as premature deaths. Nearly 40 per cent of deaths in London between 1700 and 1750, and about a third thereafter, were of children under two years of age. In 1662 the demographer John Graunt estimated that of every hundred live children born in London, thirty-six died in their first six years and twenty-four in their first ten years. More than 100 years later Doctor Michael Underwood, one of the most advanced writers on the diseases of children in the eighteenth century, commented on the terrible mortality rate of London children under five years of age during the 1790s:

> The average of births annually, within the bills of mortality, for ten successive years, as taken a few years ago (*c.* 1790), was 16,238; out of which were buried under five years of age 10,145, and from amongst these 7,987 were under two years. So that almost two thirds of the children born in London and its environs, become lost to society, and more than three fourths of these die under two years of age. This proves how hazardous a period that of infancy is, in this country; and I am sorry there is so much reason to be persuaded that the want of air, exercise, and a proper diet, has added unnecessarily to its dangers.

The presence of death was common. Children lost their mothers, often in childbirth, and mothers frequently lost their babies. Epidemics could wipe out several children in a family within days. Death struck quickly and symptoms such as a fever which started in the morning could mean death by the evening.

Those who survived beyond childhood had to confront the challenges of pain, illness, fire, poverty, poor diets, epidemics and food shortages. Seeking medical treatment could be costly as well as dangerous. Much information regarding the causes of death is contained in the London Bills of Mortality, which were first compiled in the sixteenth century by the Parish Clerk's Company of London. In 1629 they became much more detailed, showing cause of death, and by the early eighteenth century the ages at which Londoners died were also included. Annual digests were issued for 130 London parishes and others adjoining, arranged under various diseases and accident headings. Throughout the seventeenth and eighteenth centuries the major causes of death were from illnesses and diseases such as consumption (tuberculosis), fever, smallpox, cold, 'dropsie' (abnormal swelling often caused by kidney or heart disease), convulsion, 'childbed', 'bloody flux' (dysentery involving a discharge of blood) and 'teeth' (death of an infant when teething). These accounted for a third of all deaths. 'Convulsions' was a convenient term for a number of diseases among children including measles, scarlet fever, diphtheria and whooping cough, as well the early stages of smallpox.

'Chrisoms' was also a category for child death. In his *Mortality of the Metropolis, 1629–1831* (1832) Doctor John Marshall (1783–1841) comments that, 'chrisom is a Greek word for ointment used to soften the first garment of infants at their birth'. He then adds that this custom was first used out of kindness but was

> converted into a superstitious practice by the priests of both the Greek and Roman Churches. The custom appears to have been to use the anointed, or Chrisom cloth for one month after the birth of a child and if the child died within that month it was stated to have died of Chrisom.

Continuing his swipe at its religious associations he states that 'this ridiculous custom ... declined in the Metropolis from 1629–1726.'

Although the plague accounted for some 56,000 deaths in London in 1665, London's population had grown and the proportion of deaths resulting from the plague was less than it had been in 1563. However, other illnesses took their toll. In the seventeenth century, apart from old age, infant mortality, stillborn births and the plague, the following accounted for a substantial number of deaths each year: 'Rising of the Lights' (inflammation of the liver or alternatively, croup); 'Surfet' or surfeit (vomiting from over-eating or gluttony); thrush, and sore mouth; measles; jaundice (condition caused by blockage of intestines); 'Livergrown' (possibly rickets); 'Impostume' (abscess); 'Kil'd by several accidents'; ague (intermittent fever); 'Colick, Stone or Strangury' (convulsive pain in the abdomen or bowels); worms; 'Tissick' (cough); drowned; 'Purples, and spotted Feaver' (purples, a rash due to spontaneous bleeding into the skin); 'Pleurisie, and Spleen'; palsy (paralysis or difficulty with muscle control); 'breakbone fever' (mosquito-borne disease caused by a virus); 'King's Evil' or 'Evil' (scrofula, tuberculosis of neck and lymph glands); sores and ulcers; 'Apoplexy, & planet struck' (sudden severe affliction or paralysis); 'Mortification' (gangrene) and cancer.

Mortality from a combination of the ordinary, the unusual and the exotic also accounted for yearly death rates in the bills over the years. Amongst these were 'bitten by mad dog'; excessive drinking; executed; 'frighted or affrighted' (frightened to death – probably a stress-induced heart attack or stroke); canker (severe, destructive, eroding ulcer of the cheek and lip); murdered; frozen; 'Made away themselves' or suicide; French Pox (syphilis); gout; grief; 'Horseshoe head, water on the head'; 'Tympany' (swelling or tumour); lethargy; 'Quinsie or quinsy' (inflammation of the tonsils, often leading to an abscess); 'St Anthony's fire' (skin disease producing a reddening of the skin); worms; 'Cut of the Stone' (death from surgical removal of a bladder stone); scurvy and itch; 'Jawfaln' (locked jaw, possibly tetanus); 'Wolf' (malignant tumour); dead in the street; starved; piles; 'Meagrom' (severe headache); childbed (death of mother from infection following childbirth); rheumatism; 'Lunatick'; suffocated; bedridden; 'Black vomit' (vomiting old black blood due to ulcers or yellow fever); 'Gathering' (collection of pus); rickets (disease of skeletal system mainly due to Vitamin D deficiency); bladder in the throat (diphtheria); commotion (concussion, a violent shaking); eel thing (Erysipelas, a superficial bacterial skin infection); grocer's itch (skin disease caused by mites in sugar or flour); milk leg (thrombophlebitis); Bronze John (Yellow fever).

People were vulnerable to infection and contamination. Cesspits and mounds of human and animal waste polluted the streets. Sources of water became polluted with waste and excrement. One of the major sources of water for Londoners was popularly known as 'pissing conduit'. John Stow (1525–1605), writing about pollution in the waterways, commented on the origins of the name 'Houndsditch' which he claimed takes its name from 'when the same lay open, much filth ... especially dead Dogges were there layd or cast.' In Tobias Smollett's (1721–71) novel *The Expedition of Humphrey Clinker* the central character, Matt Bramble, comments on all manner of defilement in the Thames and adds that:

> Human excrement is the least offensive part of the concrete, which is composed of all the drugs, minerals and poisons, used in mechanics and

manufacture, enriched with the putrefying carcases of beasts and men; and mixed with the scourings of all the wash-tubs, kennels, and common sewers, within the bills of mortality.

Water-related diseases fell into a number of categories. When the water was drunk the diseases included cholera, typhoid, infectious hepatitis, diarrhoea and dysentery. When used for washing it could lead to intestinal tract infections and skin and eye diseases such as scabies or trachoma. Parasitic worms or other insects often caused other types of diseases. These include malaria or ague, sleeping sickness, river blindness and yellow fever. Deaths from 'ague and fever', transmitted by mosquitoes breeding in marshland and stagnant water in ditches, was among the highest causes of mortality prior to the eighteenth century.

St Giles was probably London's most notorious rookery and contained a large population of impoverished Irish people. The area, with its intense network of alleys and yards, was rife with poverty, filth, crime, overcrowding and disease. Both contemporary unofficial visitors and the reports of select committees described the area. One example: 'In St Giles one feels asphyxiated by the stench: there is no air to breathe nor daylight to find one's way out.' Little wonder that St Giles became subject to a massive slum clearance scheme during the 1840s when the need to improve central London's road system was used as an excuse to demolish most of the St Giles and Seven Dials districts. Not only did this break up and disperse the criminal fraternity that lurked in this sinister quarter but the creation of New Oxford Street carving a swathe through it in 1847 allowed the ingress of light and fresh air and did much to improve the local mortality figures.

The unhealthiest season was autumn although changes were observed in the seasonality of burials from the eighteenth century. The pattern of excess summer mortality gave way to a winter peak of the kind associated with respiratory conditions and typhus. London was regularly hit by sweating sickness. The most serious episode was in 1556–59 when a deadly mixture of the epidemic with typhus and influenza caused many deaths including those of eleven of the City's aldermen. The warm months of June, July and August were ripe for flies, lice and infections to exposed food. Tapeworms were frequently transmitted from undercooked beef and pork and could be passed into the brain and be responsible for epileptic fits. People's clothing was often infested with fleas and lice. Flies gorged themselves on the vast quantities of excrement, both from people and animals, which lay around everywhere and then passed on the germs that they picked up onto food being prepared for human consumption. Predictably the poor fared worse and were always more vulnerable. Their ragged clothing became a depository for the vermin and filth. The noxious ordure which was so much a part of London life was always worsened by rain. The poor, along with dogs, cats and other roaming livestock, were blamed for being carriers of disease and infections. William Buchan in *Domestic Medicine* (1785) raged: 'If dirty people cannot be removed as a common nuisance they ought at least to be avoided as infectious'.

John Noorthouck in *The New History of London* (1773) wrote: 'Another disadvantage attending great cities, is the foulness of the air occasioned by uncleanliness, smoke, the perspiration and breath of the inhabitants, and the putrid steams from drains, kennels, and common shores.' John Evelyn, the diarist mentioned elsewhere, complained that 'Coughs and Consumptions rage more in this City than in the whole Earth.' The lack of penetration of the sun's rays contributed to a deficiency of Vitamin D, essential for the absorption of calcium. This was a cause of rickets with which children of all classes were affected.

Smallpox became one of the most feared and most contagious diseases. The effects were awful. Smallpox has been one of the biggest killer diseases in history. It is a highly-contagious disease and easily transmitted from one person to another. The symptoms of the disease were a high fever, chills or rigors, prostration and nausea, and vomiting was also common. A rash developed on the face or in the mouth and then spread to the rest of the body. The rash developed into blister-like pustules which left scars or visible 'pockmarks'.

London experienced periodic smallpox epidemics, outbreaks of what was known as 'the speckled monster', throughout the seventeenth, eighteenth and nineteenth centuries. By 1668 more than 3,000 deaths were recorded and this figure remained consistent throughout the eighteenth century, rising to more than 6,000 by the 1830s in densely-populated London. The fatality rate varied between 20 and 60 per cent and was highest among children under five years of age.

A private charity hospital for smallpox sufferers was set up in 1746 but it was ill-suited to the numbers needing treatment. The creation of the Metropolitan Asylums Board in 1867 led to the first official smallpox hospitals in London. Each served a particular area such as the North-West (based in Hampstead), the East and North-East (Homerton), the South and South-West (Stockwell), the West (Fulham) and the South-East (Deptford). The great smallpox epidemic of 1871 created extra demands and the ship *Dreadnought* had to be used to house some of those affected. Further demands were made when another epidemic hit the country in 1881. Other floating hospitals were brought into use such as the *Atlas, Endymion* and the twin-hulled paddle-steamer *Castalia*. *Atlas* took nearly 1,000 patients of whom 120 died. The ships were berthed at Long Reach, an isolated stretch of the Thames 17 miles downstream from London Bridge.

John Graunt reflected on the increases in death from particular diseases between 1634 and 1660:

> That the Rickets is a new disease, both as to name and thing; that from fourteen dying thereof, Anno 1634, it hath gradually encreased to above five hundred Anno 1660. That there is another new Disease appearing; as A Stopping of the Stomach, which hath encreased in twenty years, from six, to near three hundred. That the Rising of the lights (supposed in most Cases to be the Fits of the Mother) have also encreased in thirty years, from forty four, to two hundred and fourty nine.

He concluded that as 'Rickets, stopping of the Stomach, and rising of the Lights, have all increased together, and in some kinde of correspondent proportions; it seems to me, that they depend one upon another.'

Stomach disorders resulting from infected food were commonplace and dysentery could kill within hours or days. Unbalanced diets also led to surfeit, a result of overeating. Robert Greene, the English dramatist and writer, fell sick and later died after eating 'a surfeit of pickle herringe and Rennish wine'. It is more likely that Green's death may have been the result of his reaction to the food rather than taking too much of it. Drinking large quantities of alcohol often led to gout. The physician Sir Thomas Sydenham wrote: 'The gout most commonly seizes such old men as have liv'd the best part of their lives tenderly and delicately, allowing themselves freely banquets, wine, and other spirituous liquors'. William Harvey, the discoverer of the circulation of the blood, was worn down by repeated attacks of gout and died in London in June 1657. Later in his life James Gillray (1757–1815), the great satirist, started drinking heavily and as a result suffered from gout. His famous etching *Gout* struck a cord with fellow sufferers. The writer Wilkie Collins (1824–89), who lived for most of his life in Marylebone, dictated much of his well-known book *The Moonstone* because he was bedridden from gout and in extraordinary pain. He took heavy doses of laudanum for his ailment.

The pox was widespread in London and, with its ability to disfigure and impoverish, it was considered a social disgrace. Syphilis, which was one of the deadliest of all venereal diseases, spread rapidly throughout Europe in the fifteenth century. Elizabethans had many names for this foul malady: lues venera, the Spanish sickness, the pox, the foul disease and the French Pox. French Pox became a convenient term among the populace and political propagandists, as it was easy and convenient to blame the spread of the disease on foreigners. In the absence of antibiotics the effects of syphilis would be dreadful: raging fever ('burnt blood'), severe aches, blindness, full body pustules, meningitis, insanity and leaking heart valves. William Clowes (1544–1604), an Elizabethan surgeon, reported in 1585 that the victims of syphilis were so numerous that the London hospitals had no room for them. He claimed to have treated more than 1,000 patients suffering with French Pox. So alarmed were the city authorities by the extent of sexual vice in London that they issued a proclamation against 'the Stynkynge and Horrible Synne of Lecherie'. Clowes was clear as to where the blame lay for the spread of the pox:

> The cause whereof, I see none so great as the licentiousness, and beastly disorder of a great number of rogues, and vagabonds: the filthy life of many lewd and idle persons, both men, and women, about the city of London, and

the great number of lewd alehouses, which are the very nests and harborers of such filthy creatures.

For Puritans the pox was a visible sign of God's retribution which brought a swift, appropriate and painful punishment on those who made use of the prostitutes' 'abominable services'. The numbers of people dying from the pox in the Bills of Mortality were more than likely significantly underestimated. John Graunt stated that 'few of those, who die of the French-Pox, are set down, but coloured under the Consumption'.

Tubercular conditions such as 'The King's Evil', scrofula (which affected the lymphatic glands) and what was then known as 'consumption' and phthisis were all major causes of death. They were spread largely by breathing in air exhaled by someone already suffering from tuberculosis. Bovine tuberculosis was contracted by drinking infected milk. From the twelfth to the eighteenth century English monarchs were thought to possess the ability to cure scrofula by touching the sufferers with their fingers. Queen Mary II (r. 1688–94) died of scrofula at Christmas 1694. It is little wonder that her husband William III (r. 1688–1702) was sceptical about the custom of curing by the 'Royal touch'. The two-year-old Samuel Johnson, who suffered from scrofula, came to London in 1709 to be touched by Queen Anne (r. 1702–14), the last monarch to perform the practice. The first specialist service in London to deal with the disease was the Phthisical Dispensary in Chancery Lane in 1805 and others followed during the nineteenth century. The main form of treatment was fresh air and good nutrition. London unfortunately did not offer much of the former and in the late nineteenth century the Metropolitan Asylums Board established sanatoria outside the city. The virulent nature of the disease is reflected in a famous cartoon in *Punch* from July 1858 where the very bedraggled and polluted-looking 'Father Thames' introduces his offspring 'Diphtheria, Scrofula and Cholera to the fair city of London'.

Ague or 'intermittent fever' was malaria (mal'aria, literally meaning 'bad air'). It was a common condition spread by the mosquitoes in the marshes, especially on the south bank of the Thames in the Southwark and Lambeth areas. The disease caused high levels of mortality in London from the fifteenth to the nineteenth century. People with the disease would experience fever, shivering, pain in the joints, sweating fits, headache, vomiting, convulsions and coma. Ague was mentioned in literature over the centuries. Geoffrey Chaucer (1342–1400) wrote in 'The Nun's Priest's Tale': 'You are so very choleric of complexion./Beware the mounting sun and all dejection,/Nor get yourself with sudden humours hot;/For if you do, I dare well lay a groat/That you shall have the tertian fever's pain,/Or some ague that may well be your bane'. Shakespeare refers to ague in nine plays including *Julius Caesar*. Caesar tells Caius Ligarius, 'Caesar was ne'er so much your enemy as that same ague which hath made you lean' (Act II, Scene II). In Defoe's *Robinson Crusoe*, the stranded Crusoe, on finding a footprint in the sand which was not his own, 'shook with cold, like one in an ague'. Oliver Cromwell (1599–1658) suffered from a recurrent, malarial-type disease, which was believed to have been the principal or sole cause of his final illness. Changes such as the paving of Westminster in the 1760s and the draining of the marshes around the same time contributed towards the decline in deaths from ague. A writer in 1781 observed that 'very few die now of Ague in London.'

Environmental forces affected not only those contracting ague. As deaths from ague diminished, deaths from other diseases resulting from the environment and denser concentrations of people continued or emerged: smallpox, typhus, typhoid, cholera, dysentery, tuberculosis, infantile diarrhoea and a plethora of other afflictions. The debates concerning the causes of disease, bad air (miasma) or polluted water-supplies culminated in the nineteenth century.

In addition to the diseases, which took a particularly high toll of the London population each year, there were also those that appeared each year and only accounted for very small number of deaths. Some of these however created an alarm beyond their actual figures. 'Bitten by mad dog' was a perennial misfortune. There were dangers real and exaggerated from loose dogs. They created fear as potential carriers of disease and rabies as well as contributing to the abundance of excrement in London's streets. Dogs were purged and slaughtered in huge numbers during epidemics. In the early seventeenth century after an outbreak of plague more than 500 were killed in Westminster. Many complaints were made about wild dogs roaming the streets. Joseph Massie in 1754 raged about the problem of 'mad dogs' which had caused many deaths. Pepys recorded in his diary in September 1662 how a child had been torn to pieces by two dogs at Walthamstow. Pleas of insanity were made on the grounds of being bitten by a mad dog. In his defence at the Old Bailey in 1815 for stealing 112 sheep, Joseph Draper claimed that, 'about sixteen years ago, I was bitten by a mad dog ... and I am always insane in the months of July and August.' Few judges would give much credence to such a defence these days.

Deaths described broadly as 'Casualties' or accidents were very common. The *Gentleman's Magazine* for February 1731 reported on the cases of a man dropping dead after an apoplectic fit, a couple of men who suffocated while digging a pit, a man gored by an ox in Cheapside, a man drowned in the Thames and a number of suicides including a silk-weaver who cut his throat and a city butler who did likewise after being fired from his job. Everyday accidents of this sort contribute substantially to the lists of mortality.

Accidents in the night were common and were often reported in the newspapers from the eighteenth century. In November 1725 *Mist's Weekly Journal* reported that 'two poor persons were found dead in the Tower ditch; it's supposed they were in drink, and the rails about the said ditch being much out of repair, these dark nights they fell in and lost their lives.' On a dark night in January 1726 a couple from Bloomsbury were returning home from a public house in Islington when they both slipped into the pond, and were drowned (*Weekly Journal, or The British Gazetteer*).

People of all classes were susceptible to attacks of pain and sickness during sleeping hours and many 'passed away in their sleep'. The hours of sleep find people at their most vulnerable either lying and worrying over matters that seem less important in the light of day or finding that in the early hours, existing pains such as toothache, gout, ulcers and asthma seem to be intensified. The author Thomas Legg expressed this so well when he wrote in 1750 that between the hours of one and two in the morning, sick and lame Londoners were 'meditating and languishing on their several disorders and praying for day-light.' Over a century earlier Thomas Dekker in *The Wonderfull*

Yeare vividly described the screams of pain from plague victims echoing through the streets in 1603. He wrote of how the narrow London streets at night were filled with the appalling groans of the sick and dying. During the Great Plague, night burials were the norm. Samuel Pepys commented on 12 August 1665 that the nights were too short to bury all the dead and that he was particularly conscious of the danger and the unpleasantness which ensued upon meeting corpses being carried out at night.

The watchmen or 'Charlies' attempted to keep an eye on the city and its population as it slept. Their responsibilities had a wide brief which included alerting the authorities when fire broke out, deterring criminal activity by their presence and providing people with information about the weather and the hour by their regular cries. In a particular fracas in 1752, fuelled by alcohol, the watchmen threw twenty-six women into a 'roundhouse' where four died of suffocation.

The multitude of streets, alleys and lanes remained dark or at best badly-illuminated unless it was a good moonlit night. During the early part of the fifteenth century the mayor decreed that there should be lights displayed on houses on the main thoroughfares between October and November. Whilst the eighteenth century saw the use of oil lamps for street lighting in London it was not until the early nineteenth century that a more significant breakthrough occurred. A German immigrant, Frederick Winsor, formed the New Light and Heat Company which provided gas lighting in 1807 on the north side of Pall Mall. Five years later the Gas Light and Coke Company was formed and was given the rights to light the City, Westminster and Southwark. By the mid-nineteenth century nearly 400 lamplighters were employed to light the burners at dusk and turn them off at dawn. Before the nineteenth century, London had relied on a combination of oil lamps, lanterns, candles, moonlight and torches which were carried to light the way through the murky streets and narrow passages. Linkboys, mainly orphans, carried torches or lanterns and hired themselves to anyone seeking guidance through the city at night. Many of these congregated around Lincoln's Inn Fields and Tower Bridge but they also gained a reputation for thieving and other criminal activity.

Drowning appears each year in the Bills of Mortality and newspapers often reported on such incidents. *Mist's Weekly Journal* reported on 17 May 1725:

> A man going down to the Thames side to drown a cat, got into a boat, and threw her into the water, and going to strike her on the head with the boat-hook, over-reach'd himself, fell into the water, and was drown'd.

On 26 March 1726 the same journal also reported that someone had 'drowned in the river of Thames at St. Katherine by the Tower.' Many drowned in places other than the Thames, as the *London Post* for 6–9 March 1702 recorded:

> Yesterday a cooper belonging to Mr. Halsey's brew-house, in Deadmans-Place in Southwark, was repairing some fault in one of the tuns, while the beer was working therein, fell in, and was unfortunately drowned.

Mist's Weekly Journal for 22 May 1725 noted that on Tuesday morning a well-dressed man was found drowned in a pond in St George's Fields.

Foolhardy deeds could have fatal consequences. As the *Grub Street Journal* recorded in May 1730:

> Yesterday a person rashly attempting, for a wager, to lower himself, by the means of a rope, fastened to the gallery of the Monument, to the bottom; before he had descended 12 yards, had the terrible misfortune, by the rope's breaking, to break his neck by the fall.

Death from traffic was not uncommon as the Bills of Mortality for cart accidents show. John Strype commented in 1720 on the dangers of encroaching on the highway and of coaches being driven dangerously along the narrow roads. Many drivers were convicted of manslaughter such as the two men in 1721 found guilty of a hit-and-run incident which killed a mother and her child in Whitechapel. In May 1730 the *Grub Street Journal* reported in a gory style that 'as several young people were gathered about a milk-woman's garland, a cart came by, and in their endeavouring to get away, a boy about six years old was pushed down, and the cart wheel ran over his head, and squeezed out his brains.'

The London Journal from 13 June 1730 recorded that:

> two men, seemingly in liquor, passed the Turnpike by Newington Green, and between Stamford-Hill and Tottenham High Cross, riding furiously, one of them came with such force against a Gentleman that was coming that way, that both the horses were killed on the spot.

In September 1731 a drayman was committed to Newgate for driving his 'dray over a poor man in Rosemary-lane, and breaking his thighbone' of which he died.

Newspapers reported on such deaths as a matter of course. *The Weekly Journal* reported for 13 December 1718:

> Casualties. 1. Burnt to death accidentally at St. Dunstan at Stepney 1. Cut his throat (being lunatick) at St. Andrew in Holborn 1. Drowned accidentally in a ditch at St. Paul at Shadwell 1. Found dead in the street at St. Martin in the Fields 1. Hanged themselves 2, one (being lunatick) at St. Andrew in Holborn, and one at St. Leonard in Shoreditch. Kill'd accidentally by a falling down of two houses at St. Brides 4.

Mist's Weekly Journal for 22 May 1725 noted that: 'A black-shoe boy, kill'd by a carpenter at the new Admiralty Office,' and in the 9 April 1726 edition it noted that, 'A footman belonging to the Prince stabb'd himself in the throat with a penknife. A journeyman shoemaker in an alley in Shoe-Lane, stepping from his own garret window to a neighbour's, fell down and beat his brains out.'

'Planet' was a category of death in the early Bills of Mortality. It was believed that the planets influenced the workings of the human body as much as the rhythms of the seas and the weather. In particular the moon had the greatest influence on a person's physical and especially mental health to the extent that insane people were often described as being 'moon struck'. Between 1583 and 1599 at least twenty-two deaths were attributed to planetary influence in St Botolph's Parish.

Nineteenth-century London witnessed a huge population explosion. This put pressures on the authorities on matters concerning public health and disease. John Graunt recognised the growth in population in the seventeenth century and the consequences this brought:

> That London, the Metropolis of England, is perhaps a Head too big for the Body, and possibly too strong: That this Head grows three times as fast as the Body unto which it belongs ... our Parishes are now grown madly disproportionable.

By the mid-nineteenth century London was struggling to deal with the vast amount of human waste of 2½ million people. Without proper sewerage, cesspools and pits under the privy were the normal means of coping. Not only was the smell emanating from houses and streets indescribably awful but this effluence carried its own dangers. In Woolwich in 1829 a woman and her baby fell through the rotten floor into the mire of filth beneath, drowning both of them.

From the ending of the Great Plague in the late seventeenth century and the cholera outbreaks of the 1830s, London was mainly free from major epidemics. Fevers and smallpox were widespread although they did not make any particular impact on the Bills of Mortality. A belief that prevailed in the medical profession for much of the nineteenth century and into the early twentieth century was that disease was caused by inhaling air which was infected through exposure to corrupting matter. A letter to the *Builder* from Professor H. Booth in July 1844 summed up this view when he commented: 'From inhaling the odour of beef the butcher's wife obtains her obesity.'

The *Globe and Traveller* for 26 May 1852, reporting on the health of London, noted that smallpox was gaining ground on other killer diseases. During one week in May,

> smallpox carried off 38 children and 6 adults. These included a glass painter from Priory Street, Camden Town, aged 22; a labourer from Kensington, aged 24 years; a female servant from Little Camden Street, St. Pancras, aged 31 years; the son of a labourer from Islington, aged 6 years.

Those who had not been vaccinated were clearly more vulnerable. On the death of a four-year-old girl, the registrar, Mr Nason, commented that 'the whole family, consisting of four, have been attacked with small pox. Two have not been vaccinated, and of these one died; the others are going on favourably.' The daughter of a labourer, aged nine years, died of 'smallpox, not vaccinated.' At No. 9 Queen's Place, New Street, Lambeth, a four-year-old boy was also recorded as having died 'without previous vaccination'.

Commenting on the death of a five-year-old girl in 1852, the Registrar stated that 'this is the second death in the family within 8 days. An open drain at the back part of the crescent and adjacent houses has been frequently complained of, but hitherto without effect. There can be no doubt of its being prejudicial to the health of the neighbourhood.' Similarly, on the death of a one-year-old boy at Grafton Place who died of convulsions followed by a coma, it was stated, 'The drains are … very bad.'

Preying on many chronically-ill Londoners were quacks, barber surgeons, apothecaries and charlatans who promised cures for all illnesses. Many of these practitioners worsened the condition of the sick and often contributed to the death of many people who desperately spent a fortune in seeking a cure. As in any age, people worried about their ailments, coughs, colds, bowels and pains. In the Early Modern period they had good cause to be more concerned, given the possibility of death or the type of treatment on offer. The apothecary or physician would attend to illnesses with their gruesome collection of implements and cures. Treatment would involve bleeding, purges and enemas with no guarantee that the condition would be cured. Not surprisingly people made their wills as soon as illness threatened, as the common preamble suggested: 'Being at present sicke and weake in body but of sound and perfect mind.'

Medicines were concocted from a wide, and to today's mind, extremely weird, collection of ingredients including worms and millipedes. The apothecary to William III, James Chase, prescribed 'sixty millipedes bruised in white wine … strained and flavoured with saffron and spirit of maidenhair' for anyone suffering from difficult breathing. Leading herbalist Nicholas Culpeper (1615–54), who was supplied with herbs from Finsbury Fields, Hampstead and Bow, put great faith in the use of millipedes for pains in the ear. The *London Pharmacopoeia*, appearing in 1618, was initially for the use of all London apothecaries and contained 963 compound remedies and 1,190 crude drugs used in remedies. These drugs included roots, leaves and animal parts such as 'horn of a rhinoceros, elephant tusk ... frog spawn, penis of a bull, flesh of vipers ... oil of foxes.'

Physicians had become a cause for contempt as many of them had abandoned Londoners to their fate during the plague of 1665, retreating to safer places in the country. Tom Brown (1662–1704), the English writer and satirist, was scathing about the medical profession. He wrote in his *Amusements Serious and Comical Calculated for the Meridian of London*:

> These [physicians] ... are pensioners to death ... for you must know, notwithstanding distempered humours make a man sick, 'tis the physician has the honour of killing him, and expects to be well paid for the job ... So that when a man is asked how such a man died, he is not to answer, according to custom, that he died of fever or a pleurisy, but that he died of the doctor.

One notorious practitioner was St John Long who set up a practice in 1828 in Harley Street. Despite being a registered doctor some of his methods were those of a charlatan. He became known as the 'King of Quacks' for his many cure-alls and dubious methods. His practice attracted many wealthy women and earned him in excess of £10,000 per year. His good looks and charm were clearly a factor in his success. Long's use of lotions and inhalants, which involved yards of mysterious pink tubing, and his private massage sessions presented a novel alternative to the medicine provided by many of the other practitioners in Harley Street. However his luck ran out when two young women died as a result of his 'unique' treatment.

In 1830 a wealthy women sought out St John Long for the purpose of treating one of her two daughters who was suffering from consumption. His treatment made the girl's condition more severe despite his claims that the girl's health was remarkably well. As the condition of the girl deteriorated the services of an eminent surgeon were called for but the problem had gone beyond any possibility of a cure and the girl died. Long was charged with manslaughter and committed to Newgate to await his sentence. The sentence was lenient: a fine of £250. However at the same time public excitement was further aroused when a further charge of a similar nature was brought against him. This involved the death of forty-eight-year-old Mrs Campbell Lloyd, wife of Captain Edward Lloyd, RN. Her death was alleged to have been a result of the treatment she had experienced under the hands of Long. On this second charge Long was tried at the Old Bailey on 19 February 1831 but the jury returned a verdict of not guilty. Both cases ruined his career and he died at the age of thirty-six from tuberculosis.

The *London Guide* of 1818 warned, especially visitors to London, against the many 'cheats, swindlers and pickpockets'. Included in these were an abundance of 'nostrum-mongers who prepare some panacea, that will cure various and discordant disorders; thus playing with the lives ... health and happiness of those who harken their advice. Whoever has been unfortunate enough to consult a certain loathsome disease, should be upon their guard against pretended doctors.'

The medical system from the sixteenth century moved from lay to medical expertise with many physicians writing books for popular audiences. There were a large number of medical books published in the seventeenth and eighteenth centuries giving advice on how the public could treat serious illnesses. Do-it-yourself manuals were published such as the one by John Archer, *Every Man His Own Doctor* (1672). Cure-alls and treatments were in plentiful supply although their effectiveness might be more uncertain. In the 1690s on Ludgate Hill, next door to the King's Arms Tavern, a shop advertised such panaceas:

> any person may be furnished with a Water for taking away the Freckles, Pimples, Worms and Morphew in the Face, Elixis Salutis, Balsamum Vitae, Tinctura Vitae. Water for the Eyes, Ointments for the Rickets, Burns, Scalds, Wounds.

Advertisements offering cures for venereal disease appeared in most newspapers during the eighteenth century. In January 1702 Mr Nedham, a 'surgeon' of Great Southampton Street, claimed in the *English Post* that for 3 shillings his 'pleasant, gentle medicine' cured the 'clap or running of the reins' (discharges from the kidneys). The Flaming Sword shop in Covent Garden boasted that the famous

'Italian Bolus' (large round pill) at 2 shillings and sixpence never fails 'to root out and carry off the most malignant, virulent, and obstinate kind of the venereal disease' (*Mist's Weekly Journal*, 29 May 1725). Wrights of Bell-Savage Yard on Ludgate Hill left nothing to the imagination in promoting his cleansing tincture:

> urinally discharges all the fæces or putrid relicks of the Lues Alamode [syphilis], and causes its concomitants, the wretched train of that complicated distemper, as a mucous, filthy, sanious matter [puss] lodg'd in the reins [kidneys], or spermatick parts, which either cause a sharpness in the urine, or too frequently provokes it.

The tincture, it was claimed, cleansed 'the urinary passages of all sand, gravel, films, or membraneous pellicles … and all their genital parts, to their original tone and use, though the misfortune and decay be of the longest date, with an equal success in each sex.' This wonder of medicine could be had for 10 shillings a bottle (*Weekly Journal, or The British Gazetteer*, 11 September 1725). If all the above failed then those 'distressed to the last degree with the French disease [and] tired with taking medicines to no purpose, may have a fair, speedy, cheap, and safe cure.' The Golden Ball in Fleet Street offered a medicine that would cure, for 5 shillings, not only 'all symptoms of the French disease,' but also rheumatism and scurvy (*Weekly Journal, or The British Gazetteer*, 5 March 1726). Venereal disease brought with it a terrible scarring as well as a potentially painful drawn-out death.

Other illnesses also brought immense pain and despite their relatively low annual mortality rates they appear each year in the Bills of Mortality. Such illnesses included stranguary (restricted urine flow also associated with 'gravel', a disease characterised by small stones formed in the kidneys); haemorrhoids; scurvy, sores and ulcers. As with all other illnesses and diseases, cures were readily available, albeit at a price. In July 1726 six stones were removed from a man at St Bartholomew's Hospital, 'one as big as a turkey's egg, two as a pigeon's, the others as a nutmeg.' Rider's Lozenges could be bought from John Finder of Bartholomew Close in Smithfield and they could cure, so it was claimed, 'Heart-burn, Hiccough, Belching, Stranguary, and other Distempers.' Haemorrhoids were guaranteed never to return by using 'a pleasant Specifick Electuary' from Jacob's Coffee House in Threadneedle Street. Mr Radford's Toyshop on the Strand provided a pleasant 'Odoriferous Tincture, which after a few drops, would instantly make the most offensive breath smell incomparably fine and charming.' A 'famed elixir' from Mr Spooner's near Whitechapel could relieve wind, belches or hiccups.

Between the sixteenth and eighteenth centuries there was a constant risk of being injured by badly-constructed buildings made from poor quality goods and shoddy workmanship, particularly during bad storms. In June 1553 Henry Machyn recorded that a house fell down in St Clement's Lane whereby 'the good man of the house was killed and the good wife sore hurt and the maid'. Nicholas Hawksmoor, the architect, commented that London was less of a city of houses and streets than a 'Chaos of Dirty Rotten sheds, always Tumbling or taking fire'. The bills of mortality for the week recorded twenty-one deaths in London from the fall of chimneys. The *English Post* reported as 'violent a storm of wind as was ever known in England ... many people were kill'd on their beds, and several wounded.' The *Post* reported on the 'blowing down of trees in St. James's Park, the Inns of Court, Moor-Fields, and divers other places.' In 1725 a 'violent hurricane' hit London and again several chimneys were blown down and much damage was done as well as a number of deaths: 'Four or five drowned persons have been taken up above bridge, some others are not yet found' (*Mist's Weekly Journal*).

Up to at least the nineteenth century people suffered pain because there was little relief in treatment or relief such as anaesthetics, surgery or drugs. The Church attempted to offer some explanation by suggesting that pain was an aspect of God's interaction with humankind rather than it actually being the body that was in distress. With the developments in medicine and surgery there was, by the late nineteenth century, a significant shift in the understanding of pain. This development removed the idea of God's interaction with the body to one whereby pain was a medical challenge.

Between 1870 and 1901 London's mortality rate fell, in line with the national trend, and much of this was a result of improvements in public health and preventative medicine and the decline of particular infectious diseases such as whooping cough and scarlet fever, tuberculosis, typhoid, smallpox, typhus and cholera. London however was by no means purged of the sources of lethal disease and much of the poverty in which such conditions thrived remained to be expunged. The longstanding problem of air pollution or smog – fog that has soot in it – continued to take its toll until effective measures were taken against it in the 1950s and 1960s.

13
Chronicling Death

Many writers, demographers, statisticians and epidemiologists have addressed the issue of death and the causes of death in London over the centuries through poetry, diaries, chronicles, private correspondence, literature, surveys and commentaries. Writing in the aftermath of the Black Death were Geoffrey Chaucer (1340–1400) and the fourteenth-century poet William Langland (1330–87). Langland is believed to have lived for many years in London at Cornhill, with his wife Kitte and his daughter Calote. His poem *Piers the Ploughman* tells the story of Piers, a simple countryman, who, like Langland, was poor. In his poem Langland reflects on death and how 'The grave equates us all.' Langland witnessed the worst effects of the bubonic plague. Consistent with the medieval belief that the plague was a punishment from God, Langland believed that there was a relationship between pestilence and the sins of people. For him, the plague punished a morally corrupt society, a society that had turned towards pride:

> Friars and frauds have faked-up such questions
> For the pleasure of proud men since the pestilence,
> And preached at St Paul's from pure envy of the clergy ...
> Throughout the whole realm, pride has spread so much
> ... prayers are powerless to stop the pestilence.

Geoffrey Chaucer was little more than eight years of age when the plague struck his hometown of London. In the prologue to his *Canterbury Tales* he refers to the conduct of some of the characters during the plague. Where Langland had been critical of the Church, Chaucer praised the clergyman who did not abandon his flock. Chaucer wrote of the pestilence in the 'Pardoner's Tale':

> Ther cam a privee theef men clepeth Deeth,
> That in this contree al the peple sleeth,
> And with his spere he smoot his herte atwo,
> And wente his wey withouten wordes mo.
> He hath a thousand slayn this pestilence.
>
> (There came a sneakthief men call Death,
> Who kills all the people in this country,
> And with his spear he smote his heart in two,
> And went his way without a word
> He has killed a thousand this plague-time).

It is likely that Chaucer lived through at least five outbreaks of the plague and, like Langland, must have heard masses for the dead and the tolling of bells in London. In the 'Pardoner's Tale' drunken revellers, who survive the plague, hear the ringing bells outside the tavern which tells them a corpse is being taken away. However there is also a moral tone in which the Pardoner suggests that money is corrupt and that all humans must be prepared to die. The issues of death, the Apocalypse and the importance of life on earth and life after death were themes taken up by other writers over the centuries following Chaucer.

The diary of the sixteenth-century tailor and furnisher of funeral trappings, Henry Machyn, provides us with a detailed insight into many funerals in London between 1550 and 1563. He wrote his diary during a very turbulent period in England which saw the Reformation followed by the return to Catholicism under Mary. Machyn was born in May 1497 and arrived in London around 1519 to take up an apprenticeship. By 1530 he was admitted to the Company of Merchant Tailors. Machyn was married and had two children,

Jane and John, but his first wife, Joan, died in childbirth in 1548. The Machyn family lived in the City not far from Painter Stainers Hall on Trinity Street. Henry and his brother, Christopher, were both tailors but the latter died in 1550. Machyn was apparently a Catholic and this can be seen in his enthusiasm for the succession of Mary in 1553. His diary documents accounts of funerals which vary from the execution of felons to the procession of eminent citizens.

Machyn records that in May 1552 six felons were executed and two months later James Ellis, described as 'a great cutpurse and thief', was hanged. In December two 'tall' men and a 'lackey' were executed for robbery. In January 1553 two men were killed for the murder of a gentleman and one hanged and quartered for counterfeiting the Queen's signet. Henry Machyn made clear that he attended two and sometimes three executions per day. In the space of one month in 1557 Machyn saw eight felons hanged at Tyburn, three men and two women burnt at Smithfield for heresy and seven pirates hanged at Wapping. Like many Londoners, Machyn witnessed executions as part of the popular calendar ritual.

In July 1551 he recorded an outbreak of the plague which killed 872 people in London. On the tenth day the king, Edward VI (r. 1547–1553), was 'removed from Westminster unto Hampton Court.' The plague clearly took its toll as 'there died in London many merchants and great rich men and women and young men and old.' Two years later in August 1553 young Edward died and 'at his burying was the greatest moan made for him of his death as ever was heard or seen.' In April 1554 Sir Thomas Wyatt and his followers organised a rebellion against the Catholic queen, Mary. Those arrested were executed at different sites in London. Wyatt was taken to the Tower where he was 'quartered on the scaffold and his bowels and his members burnt beside the scaffold there.' Machyn, although less known than many diarists who followed him, left a fascinating chronicle of life and death in mid-sixteenth-century London.

The following century produced famous diarists such as Samuel Pepys and John Evelyn (1620–1706). Both kept accounts of London during the tumultuous decade of the 1660s. Pepys provides an often quoted source for the Great Plague of 1665 in which he reflected that, 'Every day sadder and sadder news of its increase. In the City died this week 7,496; and all of them, 6,102 of the plague'. Evelyn also noted the extent of the plague when on 13 September 1665, he wrote 'There perished this Weeke 5,000' and by 28 August 'The Contagion growing now all about us.' By September he recorded that there were 'perishing now neere ten-thousand poore Creatures weekely'.

Evelyn was also among a long line of writers to bemoan the state of the air and smoke that pervaded London. In 1661, he wrote *Fumifugium, or the Inconvenience of the Aer and the Smoak of London Dissipated*. London had a reputation from the thirteenth century for its smoky atmosphere resulting from the massive concentration of coal burning in stoves and grates, both industrial and domestic. Evelyn complained, 'this horrid Smoake which obscures our Churches, and makes our Palaces look old, which fouls our Clothes, and corrupts the waters, so as the very Rain, and refreshing Dews which fall in the several Seasons, precipitate this impure vapour, which, with its black and tenacious quality, spots and contaminates whatsoever is expos'd to it'. Not surprisingly with the heavy use of seacoal, street names such as Seacole Lane appeared as early as 1228. Evelyn raged that the columns of smoke in London meant that 'inhabitants breathe nothing but an impure and thick mist, accompanied by a fuliginous and filthy vapour ... corrupting the lungs and disordering the entire habit of their bodies, so ... such coughing and snuffling to be heard as in the London churches where the barking and spitting is incessant and importunate'. Evelyn argued that the fumes were unhealthy and the great stinking fogs caused high mortality rates. Unfortunately he could not support his arguments with statistical and scientific evidence – this would have to wait for the work of others.

Evelyn's views about the foul air found expression in other writers who used London's pea-soupers to create a murky and threatening atmosphere. Such scenes found expression in fiction. For example in *Bleak House* (1853) by Charles Dickens (1812–70):

> Fog everywhere. Fog up the river, where it flows among green meadows; fog down the river, where it rolls defiled among the tiers of shipping, and the waterside pollutions of a great (and dirty) city ... Fog in the eyes and throats of ancient Greenwich pensioners, wheezing by the firesides of their wards.

In *Our Mutual Friend* (1865) he comments that the 'whole metropolis was a heap of vapour charged with the muffled sound of wheels and enfolding a gigantic catarrh.' In the *Bruce Partington Plans* (1908), a Sherlock Holmes story by Sir Arthur Conan Doyle, the narrator Watson writes, 'In the third week of November, in the year 1895, a dense yellow fog settled down upon London. From the Monday to the Thursday I doubt whether it was ever possible from our windows in Baker Street to see the loom of the opposite houses.'

John Stow (1525–1605) published his *Survey of London* towards the end of Elizabeth's reign in 1598. Stow was born in the parish of St Michael in Cornhill and became a tailor like his father. He was witness to many great changes in London and these are reflected in his *Survey*. This was the first of its kind to be published and is significant in that it provides an insight into the City as it was before the devastation of the Great Fire more than sixty years later. Prior to his *Survey* he had also written other works including his *Annales or a General Chronicle of England* (1580). Despite his labours, writing did not bring its rewards and he lived in poverty until he died in 1605. He was granted a licence to beg in 1604 but he died shortly after from stone colic and was buried in the church of St Andrew Undershaft.

Although Stow's work draws upon oral tradition and his own observations about the architecture, social conditions, customs, occupations and commerce of London, he offered insights into aspects of death including tombs, epitaphs, monuments, sickness, plague, accidents, catastrophes, executions, leper houses and a special Single Woman's Churchyard for those who did not offer a deathbed repentance. His account of the growth of London comments upon catastrophes such as the fire at the Church of Our Lady of the Canons in 1212, during which great multitudes of people came over London Bridge either to quench the fire or to gaze at it. The wind spread the fire to the south end of the bridge and 'then came many ships and vessels, into which the multitude so unadvisedly rushed that the ships drowned [and] all perished.' Stow tells us that the fire and the shipwreck 'destroyed about three thousand persons, whose bodies were found in part, or half burnt, besides those who were wholly burnt to ashes'. He reminds us of the common nature of fires and the vulnerability of people in houses that were timber framed. Stow writes that in 1484 'a great fire happened upon this Leadenhall, by what casualty I know not, but much housing was there destroyed.' In 1538 in the churchyard of St Margaret's in the Billingsgate Ward 'among the basket-makers, a great and sudden fire ... within the space of three hours consumed more than a dozen houses, and nine persons.' He comments on the regular visitation of plagues, such as that of 1515 which killed twenty-seven people in a nunnery near Aldgate.

Stow recorded the remains of dead bodies found in Spitalfields in 1576 when the digging of a field revealed urns containing ashes, the 'burnt bones of men of the Romans', as well as many burials in churches and churchyards. In St Michael's Church in Crooked Lane (the church was destroyed by the Great Fire and was rebuilt in 1687 by Sir Christopher Wren) Stow notes a number of London citizens buried including John Shrow, a fishmonger who died in 1487. His epitaph read:

> Farewell, my friends, the tide abideth no man,
> I am departed hence, and so shall ye.
> But in this passage the real best song that I can,
> Is requiem aternam, now Jesus grant it me:
> When I have ended all mine advertise,
> Grant me in Paradise to have a mansion,
> That sheddest thy blood for my redemption.

When writing about the topic of chronicling the London dead the person of John Graunt (1620–74) must loom large in any discussion. Despite this, no significant biography has been written about the man who is considered by many historians to have founded the science of demography. The seventeenth-century writer John Aubrey (1629–97) includes Graunt in his collection of short biographical pieces, *Brief Lives*. Graunt was born to Henry and Mary Graunt at Birchin Lane, in the parish of St Michael in Cornhill. He married Mary Scott in 1641 and they had one son and three daughters, one of whom became a nun. Aubrey tells us that Captain (later Major) John Graunt was a 'man generally beloved; a faythfull friend ... He had an excellent working head, and was very facetious and fluent in his conversation'. Samuel Pepys thought Graunt's 'most excellent discourses well worth hearing'. Graunt would rise early in the morning to study. He had a good grasp of Latin and French, was an amateur scientist, wrote in shorthand, had an interest in art and by profession followed his father as a haberdasher of small wares. He served as Captain of the trained bands for several years, but was 'putt out ... for his religion,' a reference to his conversion to Catholicism.

Commenting on the changes in London during the 1660s he noted that 'the use of Coaches, whereunto the narrow streets of the old City are unfit, hath caused the building of those broader streets in Covent Garden, etc.' Showing a similar concern to Evelyn regarding the light and air of London, Graunt reflected on the 'cramming up of the ... spaces, and gardens within the Walls, with houses, to the prejudice of *Light,* and *Air,* have made men Build new ones.'

It was in 1662 that *Natural and Political Observations ... made upon the Bills of Mortality* (1662) was published. The Bills of Mortality were printed details of the numbers of people who died each week, classified according to the apparent cause of death. Graunt had no formal education but despite this he wrote his book which has to become a seminal work in demographic statistics. Commenting on Graunt's book as well as the influence of William Petty, Aubrey wrote, 'I beleeve, and partly know, that he had his hint from his intimate and familiar friend Sir William Petty ... he intended, had he lived, to have writt more of the bills of the mortality; and also intended to have written something of religion'. The latter reference clearly stems from Aubrey's comment that Graunt was, 'bred-up (as the fashion then was) in the Puritan way'. As a young man in his twenties Graunt would have been influenced by Puritan ideas in London during the Civil War and period of Commonwealth. The exact timing of his move to 'Roman Catholique, of which religion he dyed a great zealot' is uncertain but it would have probably been during the first half of the 1660s, a conversion that clearly prejudiced him in some of the positions he held.

In *Observations,* Graunt reflected on the fluctuations in epidemics from one year to the next, particularly the plague, and the extent to which these had contributed to the number of deaths in London. The parish registers, introduced in 1538, recorded baptisms and burials.

Graunt noted that the recording of the London statistics 'first began in the year 1592,' the year of a virulent epidemic. Over a seventy-year period – from 1592 to 1662 – the causes of death became the basis for Graunt's analysis in which he examined the differences between city and rural areas, death rates between the sexes, infant mortality and life expectancy. He was clearly influenced by the work of Sir William Petty (1623–87), the economist, scientist and philosopher. Petty came to prominence under Oliver Cromwell during the Commonwealth whilst working in Ireland where he developed efficient methods for surveying land that was to be confiscated. Petty maintained his reputation after the Restoration and was knighted in 1661.

Graunt questioned, in the first edition of *Observations*, why he bothered to catalogue the patterns of illness and deaths 'having (I know not by what accident) engaged my thoughts.' Nonetheless he acknowledged that the bills contained valuable information and he drew a number of illuminating and important conclusions in which he condensed a great amount of material into 'Tables and Deductions.' Despite deficiencies in his work, such as the omission of some relevant information, he made a vital pioneering contribution to demographic study, drawing attention to details such as the higher mortality rate for males which he stated is evened out by the fact that more males are born than females. He gave a reasonable estimate of London's population at 384,000 and noted the diversity of diseases as well as new trends in disease. He also dispelled some contemporary myths about the spread of plagues, notably that plagues always 'come in with [a new] King's Reigns.' Graunt stressed that the 'plague, a catastrophic illness', was carried by 'fleas that lived as parasites on rats'. Some of his other conclusions were:

> That Autumn, or the Fall is the most unhealthfull season ... That in London there have been twelve burials for eleven Christenings ... That there are about six millions, and a half of people in England, and Wales ... the people in, and about London, are a fifteenth part of the people of all England, and Wales ... That about 6000 per Annum come up to London out of the Country ... That in London about three die yearly out of eleven Families ... Physicians have two Women Patients to one Man, and yet more Men die than Women ... There come yearly to dwell at London about 6000

Strangers out of the Country, which swells the Burials about 200 per Annum ... London not so healthfull now as heretofore.

Many historians have acknowledged Graunt's use and creation of 'life tables' – the ways in which statistics on population and mortality could be presented on a chart – as his most original contribution to demography. This method allowed him to forecast the number of persons who would survive to each successive age and the life expectancy of the groups each successive year. The influence of his work on the Bills of Mortality was immediate and is reflected in the adoption of the registering of births and deaths in France and his membership to the Royal Society.

Many followed the path set down by Graunt in documenting the London dead as well as investigating, naming and analysing the causes of diseases. A pioneer in identifying the causes of mortality was London-born William Heberden (1710–1801). He studied the bills of mortality, tabulating causes of death according to categories, each containing a range of what now seem to us unusual diseases. Held in high regard by George III, Heberden became physician to Queen Charlotte in 1761. Another eminent medical statistician was William Farr (1807–83). Four years after the death of his first wife he remarried and moved to Stoke Newington. His reputation for compiling statistical articles for professional journals led to his being appointed Compiler of Abstracts at the General Register Office (now the Office of Population Censuses and Surveys). In this capacity he shaped the system of national statistics and clarified the naming of diseases on death certificates.

John Snow (1813–58) moved from York to London in 1836 to start his formal medical education. He became a member of the Royal College of Surgeons in 1838, and was admitted to the Royal College of Physicians in 1850. Snow is best remembered for his investigation into the causes of Cholera and is considered to be one of the founders of epidemiology. When the general belief was that cholera was an airborne disease Snow rejected this 'miasma' theory and argued that the disease entered the body through the mouth. He proved his theory in August 1854 following a cholera outbreak in Soho. Snow was also a pioneer in the field of anaesthetics. In April 1853, he was responsible for giving chloroform to Queen Victoria at the birth of her son Leopold.

London provided the material for many social commentators such as Henry Mayhew, *London labour and the London poor* (1851); Charles Booth, *Labour and life of the people* (1889); Blanchard Jarrold and Gustave Dore, *London: A Pilgimage* (1872); John Hollingshead, *Ragged London in 1861*; Andrew Mearns, *The Bitter Cry of Outcast London: An Inquiry into the Condition of the Abject Poor* (1883) and G.R. Sims, *How the poor live* (1889), *Horrible London* (1889). This is but a small sample among many writers who reflected on the social conditions which brought disease and death with them in what would now be described as the deprived parts of London.

Bibliography

Ackroyd, P., *London: The Biography*, London, 2000.
Almond, P.C., *Heaven and Hell in Enlightenment England*, Oxford, 1994.
Anderson, O., *Suicide in Victorian and Edwardian England*, Oxford, 1987.
Anonymous, *The History of the London Burkers*, London, 1832.
Aries, P., *The Hour of our Death*, London, 1981.
Arnold, C., *Necropolis: London and its dead*, London, 2006.
Ashley, P., *London Peculiars: Curiosities in a capital city*, London, 2004.
Aubrey, J., *Brief Lives and Other Selected Writings*, New York, 1949.
Avery, G., & Reynolds, K. (eds), *Representations of Childhood Death*, Basingstoke, 2000.
Bailey, B., *Churchyards in England and Wales*, London, 1987.
Bailey, B., *The Resurrection Men: A history of the trade in corpses*, London, 1991.
Baldick, R., *The Duel: A history of duelling*, London, 1965.
Ball, J.M., *The Sack-'em-up Men: An account of the rise and fall of the modern resurrectionists*, London, 1928.
Barber, P., *Vampires, Burial and Death*, New Haven, 1988.
Barker, F., *Highgate Cemetery: Victorian Valhalla*, London, 1984.
Barker, F. & Hyde, R., *London as it Might Have Been*, London, 1982.
Barton, N., *The Lost Rivers of London*, London, 1992.
Becker, L.M., *Death and the Early Modern Englishwoman*, Aldershot, 2003.

Binski, P., *Medieval Death: Ritual and Representation*, London, 1996.
Blackwood, J., *London's Immortals: The complete outdoor commemorative statues*, London, 1989.
Blatch, M., *A Guide to London's Churches*, London, 1978.
Bondeson, J., *A Cabinet of Medical Curiosities*, London, 1997.
Bondeson, J., *Buried Alive: The terrifying history of our most primal fear*, New York, 2001.
Bowler, P. & Green, J., *What a Way to Go: Some of the strangest deaths on record*, London, 1983.
Bowyer, R.A., 'The Role of the Ghost Story in Medieval Christianity', in H.R. Davidson & W.M. Russell (eds), *The Folklore of Ghosts*, London, 1981.
Brayne, M., *The Great Storm: Britain's night of destruction*, Stroud, 2003.
Brewer, C., *The Death of Kings: A medical history of the kings and queens of England*, London, 2000.
Brimblecombe, P., *The Big Smoke: A history of air pollution in London since medieval times*, London, 1988.
Brooks, C., *Mortal Remains: The history and present state of the Victorian and Edwardian cemetery*, Exeter, 1989.
Burgess, F., *English Churchyard Memorials*, London, 1963.
Burke, T., *The Streets of London*, London, 1949.
Bushell, P., *London's Secret History*, London, 1983.
Chapman, L., *Church Memorial Brasses and Brass Rubbing*, Princes Risborough, 1987.
Child, M., *Discovering Churchyards*, Princes Risborough, 1982.
Clarke, J.M., *London's Necropolis: A guide to Brookwood Cemetery*, Stroud, 2004.
Clayton, A., *Subterranean City: Beneath the streets of London*, London, 2000.
Cobb, G., *London City Churches*, revised edition, London, 1989.
Cole, H., *Things for the Surgeon: A history of the body snatchers*, London, 1964.
Cooper, Q. & Sullivan, P., *Maypoles, Martyrs and Mayhem: 366 days of British myths, customs and eccentricities*, London, 1995.
Curl, J.S., *Death and Architecture*, 3rd edition, Stroud, 2002.
Curl, J.S., *The Victorian Celebration of Death*, Stroud, 2000.
Currie, I., *Frosts, Freezes and Fairs*, Coulsdon, 1996.

Dagnall, H., *Postman's Park & The Watts Memorial of Heroic Deeds*, Compton, Surrey, 2005.

Daniell, C., *Death and Burial in Medieval England, 1066–1550*, London, 1998.

Davey, R., *A History of Mourning*, London, 1889.

Dawes, M.C., *The End of the Line: The story of the railway service to the Great Northern London Cemetery*, Barnet, 2003.

Doebler, B.A., *Rooted Sorrow: Dying in Early Modern England*, London, 1994.

Dollimore, J., *Death, Desire and Loss in Western Europe*, London, 2001.

Dubruck, E. & Gusick, B., *Death and Dying in the Middle Ages*, New York, 1999.

Earle, P., *The Making of the English Middle Class: Business, society and family life in London, 1660–1730*, California, 1989.

Ekirch, A.R., *At Day's Close*, London, 2005.

Enright, D.J., *The Oxford Book of Death*, Oxford, 1983.

Esdaile, K.A., *English Church Monuments, 1510–1840*, London, 1946.

Fido, M., *Bodysnatchers: A history of the resurrectionists*, London, 1988.

Finucane, R.C., *Appearances of the Dead: A cultural history*, New York, 1982.

Frankcom, G. & Musgrave, J.H., *The Irish Giant*, London, 1976.

Friar, S., *A Companion to the English Parish Church*, Stroud, 1996.

Gates, B.T., *Victorian Suicide*, Princeton, New Jersey, 1988.

Gentles, I., 'Political Funerals during the English Revolution', in S. Porter (ed.), *London and the Civil War*, Basingstoke, 1996.

Gillis, J., *Commemorations: The politics of national identity*, Princeton, New Jersey, 1988.

Gittings, C., *Death, Burial and the Individual in Early Modern England*, London, 1988.

Gordon, B. & Marshall, P. (eds), *The Place of the Dead: Death and remembrance in late Medieval and Early Modern Europe*, Cambridge, 2000.

Gorer, W.J., *Death, Grief and Mourning in Contemporary Britain*, London, 1965.

Haining, P., *Sweeney Todd: The demon barber of Fleet Street*, London, 1980.

Halliday, S., *The Great Stink of London: Sir Joseph Bazalgette and the cleansing of the Victorian capital*, Stroud, 1999.

Harding, V., *The Dead and the Living in Paris and London, 1500–1670*, Cambridge, 2002.

Harper, C.G., *Queer Things about London*, London, 1923.

Harrison, M., *London Beneath the Pavement*, London, 1971.

Hay, D. et al, *Albion's Fatal Tree: Crime and society in eighteenth-century England*, Harmondsworth, 1977.

Hibbert, C., *London's Churches*, London, 1988.

Hole, C., *English Folklore*, London, 1940.

Holmes, B., *The London Burial Grounds*, London, 1896.

Home, G., *Old London Bridge*, London, 1931.

Houlbrooke, R., *Death, Ritual and Bereavement*, London, 1989.

Howarth, G. & Jupp, P.C., *The Changing Face of Death: Historical accounts of death and disposal*, Basingstoke, 1997.

Howell, M. & Ford, P., *The Illustrated True History of the Elephant Man*, London, 1983.

Huelin, G., *Vanished Churches of the City of London*, London, 1996.

Inwood, S., *A History of London*, London 1998.

Jackson, P., *London is Stranger than Fiction*, Associated Newspapers, London, 1951.

Jackson, P., *London Bridge: A visual history*, London, 2002.

Jalland, P., *Death in the Victorian Family*, Oxford, 1996.

Jupp, P., *From Dust to Ashes: Cremation and the British way of death*, Basingstoke, 2005.

Jupp, P. & Gittings, C. (eds), *Death in England: An illustrated history*, Manchester, 1999.

Kemp, B., *Church Monuments*, Princes Risborough, 1985.

Landers, J., *Death and the Metropolis: Studies in the demographic history of London, 1670–1830*, Cambridge, 1993.

Lees, H., *English Churchyard Memorials*, Stroud, 2000.

Linebaugh, P., 'The Tyburn Riot against the Surgeons', in D. Hay et al. *Albion's Fatal Tree: Crime and society in eighteenth-century England*, Harmondsworth, 1977.

Linnane, F., *The Encyclopaedia of London Crime and Vice*, Stroud, 2003.

Litten, J., *The English Way of Death: The common funeral since 1450*, London, 1992.

Llewellyn, N., *The Art of Death*, London, 1991.

Llewellyn, N., *Funeral Monuments in Post-Reformation England*, Cambridge, 2000.
Loeb, L., *Consuming Angels: Advertising and the Victorian Women*, Oxford, 1994.
MacDonald, M., 'The Secularization of Suicide in England, 1660–1800', in *Past and Present*, 1986.
MacDonald, M. & Murphy, R.T., *Sleepless Souls: Suicide in Early Modern England*, Oxford, 1995.
Marshall, P., *Beliefs and the Dead in Reformation England*, Oxford, 2002.
Matthias, P., *The Brewing Industry in England, 1700–1830*, Cambridge, 1959.
McLynn, F., *Crime & Punishment in Eighteenth-Century England*, Oxford, 1991.
Meller, H., *London Cemeteries: An illustrated guide and gazetteer*, 3rd edition, Aldershot, 1999.
Milford, A., *London in Flames: The capital's history through its fires*, West Wickham, 1998.
Morley, J., *Death, Heaven and the Victorians*, Studio Vista, 1971.
Murray, A., *Suicide in the Middle Ages*, Vol. 1, Oxford, 1998.
Neal, W., *With Disastrous Consequences: London Disasters, 1830–1917*, Enfield, 1992.
Newton, J. (ed.), *Early Modern Ghosts*, Durham, 2002.
Olsen, D.J., *The Growth of Victorian London*, London, 1976.
Parsons, B., *The London Way of Death*, Stroud, 2001.
Pearson, L.F., *Mausoleums*, Princes Risborough, 2002.
Pierce, P., *Old London Bridge: The story of the longest inhabited bridge in Europe*, 2001.
Porter, S., 'Death and Burial in a London Parish: St Mary Woolnoth, 1653–99', in *London Journal*, Vol. 8, No. 1, pp 76–81.
Porter, R., *London: A social history*, London, 1999.
Puckle, B.S., *Funeral Customs: Their origin and development*, London, 1926.
Richard, T., *The Commodity Culture of Victorian England: Advertising and spectacle, 1851–1914*, Princeton, New Jersey, 1990.
Richardson, J., *Camden Town and Primrose Hill Past*, London, 1991.
Richardson, R., *Death, Dissection and the Destitute*, Pelican edition, Harmondsworth, 1989.
Robinson, T., *The Worst Jobs in History*, London, 2004.

Rose, L., *The Massacre of the Innocents: Infanticide in Britain, 1800–1939*, London, 1986.
Rumbelow, D., *The Triple Tree: Newgate, Tyburn and Old Bailey*, London, 1982.
Schmitt, J., *Ghosts in the Middle Ages: The living and the dead in Medieval society*, Chicago, 1998.
Schor, E., *Bearing the Dead: British culture of mourning from the Enlightenment to Victoria*, Princeton, 1995.
Spencer, H., *An Illustrated History of the Regent's Canal*, London, 1961.
Starck, N., *Life after Death: The Art of the obituary*, Melbourne, 2006.
Taylor, A., *Burial Practice in Early England*, Stroud, 2001.
Thomas, C., *Life and Death in London's East End: 2000 years at Spitalfields*, London, 2004.
Turner, E.S., *Call the Doctor: An intimate history of medical practitioners*, New York, 1958.
Weinreb, B. & Hibbert, C. (eds), *The London Encyclopaedia*, London, 1983.
Wheeler, M., *Heaven, Hell and the Victorians*, Cambridge, 1994.
Whitmore, R., *Mad Lucas*, Hitchin, 1983.
Wilkins, R., *The Fireside Book of Death*, London, 1990.
Winter, J., *Sites of Memory, Sites of Mourning*, Cambridge, 1998.
Wise, S., *The Italian Boy: Murder and grave-robbery in 1830s London*, London, 2004.
Withington, J., *Capital Disasters*, Stroud, 2003.
Wolffe, J., *Great Deaths: Grieving, Religion and Nationhood in Victorian and Edwardian Britain*, Oxford University Press, 2000.
Woodward, J., *The Theatre of Death: The ritual management of royal funerals in Renaissance England, 1570–1625*, Woodbridge, 1997.
Young, E. & W., *London's Churches*, London, 1986.

Websites used

Early Eighteenth-Century Newspaper Reports: a Sourcebook compiled by Rictor Norton <http://www.infopt.demon.co.uk/grub/grub.htm>

Articles and Lectures

Brown, J.W., 'RIP – if you're lucky! A tale of the resurrectionists in Streatham in 1814', in *Local History Magazine*, No.75, Sept–Oct 1999.

Champion, J.A. (ed.), 'Epidemic Disease in London', in *Centre for Metropolitan History Working Papers Series*, No.1, 1993.

Forbes, T.R., 'Life & Death in Shakespeare's London', in *New Scientist*, Vol. 58, No. 5, 1970.

Forbes, T.R., 'By What Disease or Casualty: The changing face of death in London', in *Transcript of lecture to Worshipful Society of Apothecaries of London*, 1975.

Harding, V., 'Location of Burials in Early Modern London', in *London Journal*, No. 14, 1989.

Hardy, A., 'Parish Pump to Private Pipes: London's water supply in the nineteenth century', in *Medical History*, Supplement No. 11, 1991, pp 76–93.

Matossian, M.K., 'Death in London, 1750–1909', in *Journal of Interdisciplinary History*, No. 16, 1985.

Index

Abney Park Cemetery 17, 94
Alderney Road Cemetery 95
Albert, Prince Consort 22, 171, 179, 204
Aldgate Churchyard 96
All Saints, Fulham 190
Anatomy Act, 1832 45
Anne, Queen 219
Arandora Star 193
Aubrey, John 20

Baby farming 48–50
Bacon, Francis 73–4
Barber-Surgeons, Company of 29–30
Barratt, Michael 142
Bartlett, Edwin 63–4
Bateson, George 131
Bazalgette, Sir Joseph 157, 181
Beckford, William 196
Beeton, Samuel 23
Bemtham, Jeremy 200–1
Bermondsey Abbey 11
Bethlehem Hospital aka 'Bedlam' 204

Bethnal Green 152
Bills of Mortality for London 51–2, 212, 223, 224, 229, 230, 239
Bitten by mad dogs 220–1
Blackfriars 11
Black Death 95, 105
Blake, William 114
Boer War 183
Boyce, William 12
Brady Street Cemetery 95
Bramah, Joseph 153
Britton, Thomas 65
Broadsheets 54
Brompton Cemetery 17, 93, 94
Brookwood Cemetery, Woking 93, 98–100
Brown, Tom 227
Brunel, Isambard Kingdom 181
Bunhill Fields Cemetery 94–5, 187
Burial Boards 93–4
Burials, medieval 10, 83–4
Burial (plague) pits 95–6, 123
Burton, Sir Richard 98

Butchell, Martin Van 70
Byrne, Charles (The Irish Giant) 71–3
Byron, Alfred, Lord 56–7

Cade's Rebellion 136
Canning, George 68
Canute, King 11
Caroline, Queen 139–40, 171
Carpue, Joseph 38
Cassells Household Guide 25
Castlereagh, Viscount 56–7, 68
Catacombs 101
Cavell, Edith 181
Cawthorne, Lawrence 129
Chadwick, Edwin 13–15, 90–3, 152–3
Chapman, Israel 40
Charles I, King 77–8, 169, 179, 204
Charles II, King 29, 170, 179
Charnel houses or 'boneholes' 11, 86
Chaucer, Geoffrey 220, 234
Chelsea Old Church 12
Cheselden, William 30
Cholera 154–5, 157
Christ's Hospital, Newgate Street 84
Christchurch Greyfriars, Newgate 124
Chrysom babies 190–1, 213
Church rulings on burials 28
City of London Cemetery 95
Clerkenwell House of Detention 142
Cloudesley, Richard 120
Cock Lane Ghost 124
Collins, Wilkie 218
Commercial Road 66–7
Conan Doyle, Sir Arthur 127, 162, 203, 236
Cooper, Sir Astley 36–8
Cornwell, Jack 176–7, 184
Crachami, Caroline (The Sicilian Fairy) 73
Cremation 59–61
Cremorne Pleasure Gardens 69
Crisp, Sir Nicholas 196

Crocker's Folly pub 201
Cromwell, Oliver 28, 134, 172, 180
Crouch, Ben 39, 40
Culpeper, Nicholas 226
'Cut-Throat Lane', Kensington 118

Davenant Road Burial Ground, Whitechapel 90
Death practices, medieval 10
Deathbed scenes in painting 108–9
Deaths from dangerous driving 223–4
De Groof, Vincent 69–70
Devereux, Robert, Earl of Essex 172
Dickens, Charles 35, 58, 85, 89, 159, 162, 181, 202, 236
Dirty Dick's pub 202
Donne, John 198–9
Doppelganger 125
Dore, Gustave 113, 163
Duelling 67–9

East Smithfield 11
Edward I, King 11, 169
Edward III, King 22, 76
Edward VI, King 179
Effigies 106–8, 198–200
Elizabeth I, Queen 169, 171, 179
Embalming 11
Enon Chapel, Clement's Lane 16, 88
Euston Railway Station 185
Evelyn, John 86, 161, 235, 236

Farquhar, John 196–7
Farr, William 241
Fatal diseases 213–4, 215, 216–7
Fenians 142
Ferrari, Carlo, 'The Italian Boy' 44
Fitzherbert, Mrs, died from surfeit of laughter 65–6
Fleet River 149
Flushing water closets 153–4
Franklin, Benjamin 168

Frederick, Prince of Wales 79–80
'Frost Fairs' 134
Fry, Elizabeth 180
Funerals 168–75
Funerary feasts 18–21

George I, King 207
George II, King 78–9, 169, 170
George III, King 171
George IV, King 140, 170, 207–8
Ghost Club 126
Gilray, James 111–2
Gordon Riots 138
Gout 217–8
Gower, John 109
Graunt, John 217, 225, 238–41
Great Conduit 148
Great Plague 95–6, 128–9, 213, 222, 235–6
'Great Stink' of London 157
'Great Storm' 1703 133–4
Great Western Railway 185
Grey, Lady Jane 192
Guy's Hospital 30
Guy, Thomas 179, 208

'Half-hanged Smith' 32
Haggerty & Holloway, highwaymen 139
Hammersmith Ghost 1803 126
Hampton Court Palace 120
Hardy, Thomas 188–9
Hatchments 199
Haunted pubs 125
Haunted theatres 125
Heberden, William 241
Henry III, King 168
Henry V, King 169
Henry VIII, King 22, 29, 78, 144, 169, 171
Highgate Cemetery 17, 46, 94
Hogarth, William 20, 33, 111, 112
Hood, Thomas 40–1, 53

Human anatomy, study of 29–31
Hunter, John 31
Hunter, William 31
Hunterian Museum 71–2, 172
Hyde Park 67, 68, 101

Infanticide 47–50, 160
Infant mortality 159–60, 212–3
Infant Protection Act 1897 50
Irving, Sir Henry 181
Isabella, Queen 124

Jackson, Peter 187
James I, King 22, 169
James II, King 179, 206
Johnson, Samuel 122, 123, 124, 219
Jonson, Ben 187, 188

Kennedy, Geoffrey Anketell Studdert 195
Kensal Green Cemetery 17, 65, 89–90, 97, 170
King's Cross 208
Kipling, Rudyard 185
Kirke, Anne 136–7

Langland, William 233
Langlie, Charles 21
Leicester Square 207
Levellers 172
Liverpool Street Station 184–5
Livery Companies of City of London 173
Lollards 144
Long, John St John 227–8
London Bridge 135–7
London Cemetery 89
London Cenotaph 183–4
London Foundling Hospital 47
London Hospital 30
London Necropolis Railway 16, 93, 99–100

London Society for the Prevention of Premature Burial 131–2
London & South Western Railway 186
Loudon, John Claudius 94
Lucas, 'Mad' James 195–6
Lutyens, Sir Edwin 183
Lydgate, John 105, 106

Machyn, Henry 234–5
Macklin, Charles 190, 194
Malaria 219–20
Manners for Women 22, 24
Marochetti, Baron 207
Martin, John 114
Mary I, Queen 76–7
Mary II, Queen 169, 219
Mausoleums 97
Mazarine, Duchess of 122
McCrae, John 184
Merrick, Joseph (The Elephant Man) 71
Metropolitan Board of Works 157
Metropolitan Burials Act 1852 93
Metropolitan Interments Act 1850 93
Meux's Brewery Explosion 138–9
Miasmas 151
Milborne, Sir John 21
Mile End Road Jewish Cemeteries 95
Milton, John 181
Monument, The London 53–4, 56, 179
Monuments 178–82, 204–5
Monumental brasses 104–5, 200
Mortlake Roman Catholic Cemetery, Mortlake 98–9
Mourning dress 15, 21–4
Mourning 'industry' and undertakers 10, 13–4, 17–8, 21, 24–5
Mrs Beeton's Book of Household Management 23, 25
Mumford, Lewis 203
Mural paintings in medieval churches 105–6
'Murder Act' 1752 31–2

Museum of London Archaeological Service 11

Naples, Josh 40
National Maritime Museum, Greenwich 111
Naysmith, Robert 66
Nelson, Horatio 111, 174, 205–6
Neoclassical funerary art 111
Newgate Prison 44, 139, 142, 158
New River 148
New Southgate Cemetery 95
New Southgate Necropolis Railway 100
Newton, Sir Isaac 181
Noorthouck, John 216
Norwood Cemetery 94
Nunhead Cemetery 17, 94

Obituaries 167–8
Old Bailey 139, 158
Old St Paul's Cathedral 106
Overbury, Sir Thomas 74–6

Pankhurst, Emmeline 208–9
Parish funerals 15–6
Parr, Thomas 189–90
Paxton, Joseph 181
Peasants' Revolt 138, 144
Penn, Sybil 120
Pepys, Samuel 136, 151, 188, 236
Perceval, Spencer 197
Pere Lachaise Cemetery, Paris 86
Peter Robinson's 24
Poe, Edgar Allen 127
Pollution in London 149–50, 160–5, 216, 231, 236
'Postman's Park' 210–1
Price, Ann 47
Price, Dr William 61
Primrose Hill 87
Proposed burial places for the great 96–7

Index

Public Health Act, 1848 92, 153
Purgatory 119–20, 121

'Quack' doctors 226–9, 230

Raikes, Robert 181
'Rakers' 150–1
Regent's Canal Explosion 70–1
Regent's Park Lake Disaster 137
Remembrance Day 177, 184
Remembrance poppies 184
Reynolds, Azariah 12
Reynolds, Thomas 32–3
Richard I, King 207
Richard II, King 178
Richard III, King 28
Rogers, John 144
Romantic Movement 114
Rossetti, Dante Gabriel 46
Rowlandson, Thomas 106
Royal College of Surgeons 30
Royal Hospital Chelsea Burial Ground 100–1, 190
Royal Society 168
Russell, William 12

St Alphege, Greenwich 86
St Andrew Undershaft 104, 191
St Austin Papey, Priory of 84
St Bartholomew's Hospital 30
St Bartholomew the Great 84, 145, 191
St Benet Sherehog 12
St Botolph, Aldgate 193
St Botolph in Aldersgate 81
St Botolph-without-Bishopsgate 184
St Brides Cemetery, Farringdon 12
St Catherine Cree, Leadenhall Street 84
St Dunstan in the West 193, 200
St Edmund the King 194
St George's, Bloomsbury 179
St Giles, Cripplegate 21, 130

St Giles Rookery 215
St Helen's, Bishopsgate 83, 84, 104, 192, 200
St James, Garlick Hythe 126
St John at Hackney 195
St John the Baptist, Cloak Lane 194
St Lawrence Jewry 11
St Leonard's, Shoreditch 21, 195
St Luke's, Charlton Village 197
St Martin Outwich, Camomile Street 84
St Martins-in-the-Fields 101, 104, 173
St Mary Aldermary 200
St Mary Graces, Abbey of 11, 211
St Mary Magdalene, Bermondsey 84
St Mary Merton Priory of 12, 211
St Mary Spital, Priory & Hospital 11, 119
St Marylebone Cemetery 94
St Mary's, Rotherhithe 197
St Nicholas, Deptford 84
St Olave, Hart Street 84, 85
St Pancras and Islington Cemetery 93
St Paul's Cathedral 205
St Peter ad Vincula 195
St Peter's Italian Church, Clerkenwell 193
St Peter le Poer, Broad Street 86
St Peter upon Cornhill 192
St Thomas' Hospital, Southwark 30
Savoy Chapel 190
Savoy Palace 137–8
Seacoal 160–1
Self-medication 228
Shakespeare, William 181, 220
Sheppard, Jack 172–3
Sherlock Holmes pub 203
Shillibeer, George 24
Siddons, Sarah 181
Sin-eating 20
Smallpox 216–7, 225–6
Smithfield 63, 44–5, 235
Smollett, Tobias 214

Snow, Dr John 155–6, 241–2
Southey, Robert 45–6
Southwark Cathedral 104, 109
Spenser, Edmund 113
Spiritualism in Britain 127
Stone, Nicholas 109
Stow, John 192, 214, 237–8
Street Lighting 222
Suicide 50–8, 137
Suicide in Literature 58–9
Surgery & surgeons 30–2, 34, 38–41, 43–4
Sutton, Thomas 19
Swift, Jonathan 150
Symbols on headstones and tombs 110
Syphilis 218–9

Tayler, William 14
Taylor, Henry 65
Taylor, John 189
Temple Church, Fleet Street 107
Tennyson, Alfred Lord 175
Thomas, Sir Henry 60, 61
Todd, Sweeney 142–4
Tombs and memorials 109–11
Tooley Street Fire 140–2
Tooting Broadway Tube Station 179
Tower Hamlets Cemetery 17, 94
Tower of London 125, 194
Tuberculosis 159, 219
Turner, J.M.W. 114
Tyburn 32, 122, 128, 172, 235
Typhoid Fever 156–7
Typhus 158

UK National Inventory of War Memorials 183
Undertakers 13–4, 17–18, 24

Valois, Catherine of 187
Vesalius, Andreas 29

Victoria, Queen 22, 176, 179, 205
Victorian attitudes to death as seen in art 115
Villiers, George, Duke of Buckingham 171

Wakes 18
Walker, Dr George 87–9
Wall paintings in medieval churches 112–3
Wallace, William 144
Walpole, Horace 170
War Memorials 183–6
Waterborne diseases in London 154, 156, 157
Watchmen 222
Water sellers 148
Water supplies to London 148–9, 150, 151
Watts Memorial of Heroic Deeds 209–10
Wax images in Westminster Abbey 108
Weever, John 109
Wellington, Duke of 68, 130, 174–5, 205–6
Westminster Abbey 108, 110, 182, 187, 188–9
Westminster Cemetery 94
West Norwood Cemetery 17
Whitehead, Sarah 123
Widow's Son, The, pub 203
Wild, Jonathan 172
Wilkes, John 68
Wilkinson, Nicholas 21
William I, King 11
William III, King 78
Wilson, Field Marshal Sir Henry 185
Winslow, Jacques-Benigne 128
Winsor, Frederick 222
World War I 183
Wycliffe, John 28